COUNSELLING SKILLS AND STUDIES

FIONA BALLANTINE DYKES ● TRACI POSTINGS ● BARRY KOPP

WITH AN INTRODUCTION BY DR ANTHONY CROUCH

2ND EDITION

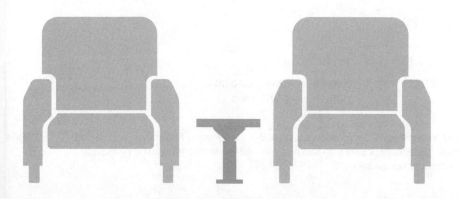

⑤SAGE

Los Angeles | London | New Delhi
Singapore | Washington DC | Melbourne

Los Angeles | London | New Delhi
Singapore | Washington DC | Melbourne

SAGE Publications Ltd
1 Oliver's Yard
55 City Road
London EC1Y 1SP

SAGE Publications Inc.
2455 Teller Road
Thousand Oaks, California 91320

SAGE Publications India Pvt Ltd
B 1/I 1 Mohan Cooperative Industrial Area
Mathura Road
New Delhi 110 044

SAGE Publications Asia-Pacific Pte Ltd
3 Church Street
#10-04 Samsung Hub
Singapore 049483

Editor: Amy Jarrold
Editorial assistant: Charlotte Meredith
Production editor: Rachel Burrows
Marketing manager: Camille Richmond
Cover design: Shaun Mercier
Typeset by: C&M Digitals (P) Ltd, Chennai, India
Printed by: CPI Group (UK) Ltd, Croydon, CR0 4YY

© Fiona Ballantine Dykes, Traci Postings and
Barry Kopp 2017
Introduction © Anthony Crouch 2017

First edition published 2014. Reprinted 2014, 2015 (3 times),
2016 (twice)
This second edition published 2017

Apart from any fair dealing for the purposes of research or
private study, or criticism or review, as permitted under the
Copyright, Designs and Patents Act, 1988, this publication
may be reproduced, stored or transmitted in any form, or by
any means, only with the prior permission in writing of the
publishers, or in the case of reprographic reproduction, in
accordance with the terms of licences issued by the Copyright
Licensing Agency. Enquiries concerning reproduction outside
those terms should be sent to the publishers.

Library of Congress Control Number: 2016954241

British Library Cataloguing in Publication data

A catalogue record for this book is available from
the British Library

ISBN 978-1-4739-8099-0 (pbk)
ISBN 978-1-4739-8098-3

At SAGE we take sustainability seriously. Most of our products are printed in the UK using FSC papers and boards.
When we print overseas we ensure sustainable papers are used as measured by the PREPS grading system.
We undertake an annual audit to monitor our sustainability.

This book is dedicated to our students and our clients . . .

Contents

List of Figures and Tables

FIGURES

TABLES

About the Authors

FIONA BALLANTINE DYKES

Fiona is an experienced counsellor, supervisor and trainer and was Head of Qualifications at CPCAB for 13 years before moving to BACP as Head of Professional Standards in 2016. She has always championed vocational training as an important route into the counselling profession and has a background in delivering counselling programmes in Further Education. Fiona is a contributory author to *Understanding Counselling and Psychotherapy* (SAGE, 2010).

ANTHONY CROUCH

Anthony is a counselling psychologist and the founder and CEO of CPCAB and the Counselling Channel. His passionate belief in high-quality counselling training led to the development of the CPCAB model in the early 1990s, which has been reviewed regularly over the past two decades to incorporate the latest research on effective counselling. Anthony is also the author of *Inside Counselling* (SAGE, 1997).

BARRY KOPP

Barry is an experienced therapist within the person-centred family of psychotherapy and counselling and is currently a Senior Verifier and Head of Tailor-Made Qualifications at CPCAB. He has extensive experience delivering counselling courses, and he is also trained in a range of complementary therapies.

TRACI POSTINGS

Traci is an experienced counsellor and supervisor and has taught extensively in adult education. She is a training consultant in the homelessness sector, and has also compiled a training manual which highlights the value of counselling skills in health and social care. Traci has a special interest in substance misuse and addiction and is currently Qualification Leader for Levels 2 and 3 at CPCAB.

Introduction

WHO IS THIS BOOK FOR?

This is a very practical book for people wanting to learn about using counselling skills in helping work and for people starting training in counselling. Helping and counselling is all about a special kind of conversation and the book aims to reflect this by being written in a similar conversational style throughout. It is structured as follows:

Part I – **Counselling skills** for helping work
(organised into seven helping work processes)

Part II – **Counselling studies** for counsellors
(organised into seven counselling processes)

Part III – **Study skills.**

The questioning style is intended to reflect the natural curiosity of a new learner in friendly and accessible language, supported by lots of practical help and examples based on the writers' many years of experience both as counselling practitioners and as counselling tutors.

The terminology used in the book has been chosen to clearly articulate the distinction between those who use counselling skills to enhance existing helping roles and those who are preparing to work as counsellors in a formally contracted counselling relationship. Consequently, throughout Part 1 we have used the terms *helper*, *helpee* and *helping work* – terms which are commonly used to identify those who use counselling skills but are not counsellors – whereas in Part 2 we have used the terms *counsellor* and *client* to signal the shift to formally contracted counselling. Much of Part 1, however, is both relevant and necessary for people who are beginning to train as counsellors. Part 2 takes learners further and deeper – as they begin their journey towards providing formally contracted counselling work.

The seven processes which are reflected in the structure of the first two parts of the book are based on a research-informed model developed by Anthony Crouch at the Counselling and Psychotherapy Central Awarding Body[1]. The contents of this book are, however, applicable to anyone wanting to learn counselling skills or embarking on the first stage of their training to be a counsellor.

A brief description of this model is offered below for those interested in understanding more about these seven processes, together with other aspects of the CPCAB model of helping and counselling. A more in-depth explanation, together with more detailed examples, can be found on the above CPCAB website link.

THE UNDERPINNING MODEL[2]

The CPCAB model – on which the structure of this book is based – emerged from a research project in the early 1990s which identified the core elements of counsellor competence and their development in counselling training. Since then the model has been updated to reflect the latest research findings on, for example, the various factors that contribute to therapeutic change.

Background

For many years, researchers tried to understand what made counselling effective by comparing different 'treatments' specific to the various counselling and psychotherapy approaches. In other words, there was an unquestioned assumption, based on the medical model, that it was the treatment that was the sole 'active ingredient' that 'caused' clients to change. This research assumption was always problematic for counselling because counselling itself is a huge challenge to the medical model. Carl Rogers founded counselling in the 1940s by turning the medical model on its head – making the client, not the treatment, the active ingredient and questioning the whole idea of there being a treatment at all (Rogers, 1942, 1951, 1961). In other words, clients, rather than experts-with-their-treatments, were suddenly placed at the centre of things. Rogers changed the profession with this revolutionary approach and, since then, researchers have struggled to catch up with this new paradigm.

Contemporary research has, however, confirmed that it is not so much the specific treatment but certain shared elements – common to all the approaches – that make the primary contribution to effective counselling. These shared elements are known as the 'common factors' and they consist of:

---

[1]www.cpcab.co.uk/public_docs/cpcab_model
[2]The description of the CPCAB model is reproduced by kind permission of CPCAB.

- **relationship** factors – the quality and effectiveness of the therapeutic relationship
- **client** factors – divided into those that can be *observed* (the difference and diversity of each client) and those that can only be *inferred* (the client's own individual characteristics and preferences, e.g. motivation, hope.)
- **therapist/counsellor** factors – the qualities and effectiveness of the particular counsellor, together with their ability to use self-awareness in the therapeutic process.

Evidence for the importance of these common factors comes, for example, from an American Psychological Association Research Task Force (Norcross, 2011), which encompassed 100,000 clients across more than 400 quantitative research studies and concluded that the common factors make the greatest contribution to client change, with the client factors being the most important of all.

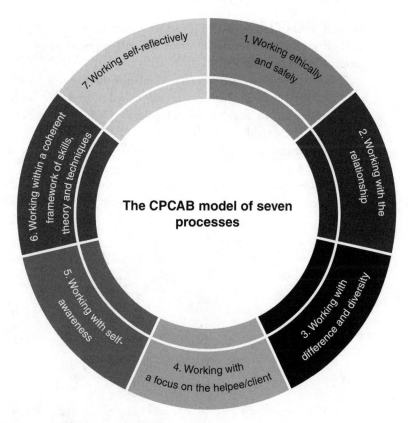

FIGURE 0.1   The seven processes

The seven processes

The seven processes, which represent the first part of the model on which this book is based, are derived from combining both the **common** and the **treatment** factors. These factors are then sandwiched between two other key elements of helping and counselling practice – working ethically and safely and developing the skills of reflective practice (professional factors). This is where the CPCAB model of seven helping and counselling processes comes from:

1. Working ethically and safely (professional factors)
2. Working with the relationship (relationship factors)
3. Working with difference and diversity (observed client factors)
4. Working with a focus on the helpee/client (inferred client factors)
5. Working with self-awareness (counsellor factors)
6. Working within a coherent framework of skills, theory and techniques (treatment factors)
7. Working self-reflectively (professional factors).

At each level of training, the seven processes reflect the depth and focus of that level of training and articulate the associated increase in the learner's skills, competence and autonomy.

These seven processes do not exist in isolation from each other but rather interact with one another. They are, therefore, a little bit like seven 'balls' which the helper or counsellor 'juggles' when supporting helpees and clients to make changes in their lives and in themselves.

The seven chapters in Part 1 of this book explore these seven processes in relation to the use of counselling skills in helping work. Helpers can work with these seven processes to enable a person to reflect on themselves and their life, get clearer about their problems and identify better ways of coping. Additionally, when a

FIGURE 0.2   The juggler

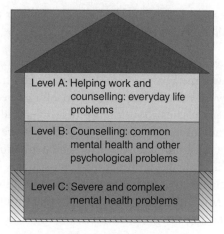

FIGURE 0.3 The three service levels of client change

helper uses these seven processes to help someone explore their problems, they are working in a way that is supported by the latest research on what's actually effective. The seven chapters in Part 2 of this book explore these same seven processes in terms of preparation for counselling work.

There are two other key elements of the CPCAB model, both of which concern working as a counsellor rather than a helper:

* three different *levels* of client change/problems which require different levels of counsellor competence
* three *dimensions* of client problems and associated therapeutic change.

Three levels of client change/problems

All clients come to counselling because they want to change something. Recent research has demonstrated that counselling works when the client instigates change supported by a particular kind of therapeutic environment in which the counsellor utilises not just their theoretical understandings and skills, but also themselves and the counselling relationship, together with an ethical and reflective approach to their work. The first part of the CPCAB model integrates these research conclusions within the seven processes. The second part of the model proposes that the counsellor can provide these seven processes in relation to three different *levels* of client change/problems:

1. **Service level A** – change in the way clients cope with their everyday life problems
2. **Service level B** – change in clients themselves (both explicit and implicit) who are struggling with common mental health problems and other psychological problems
3. **Service level C** – change in the foundations of clients themselves who are struggling with severe and complex mental health problems.

Service level A: Supporting clients to change their ways of coping with everyday life problems

We all have good times and bad times in life. Sometimes, in the bad times, we can get overwhelmed by our problems and need help to cope with them. Informal helping work provides support by enabling a person to reflect on themselves and their life, get clearer about their problems and identify better ways of coping. This is important and useful but where problems are more acute a person might seek to change things for the better by seeing a counsellor.

The CPCAB model proposes that – at this level of work – a counsellor can support clients to cope better through a more in-depth exploration of the client's life problems. The model also proposes that problems of living can often be understood as having three 'dimensions': (1) the individual person, (2) in their relationships, (3) at a particular life stage. At this level of work, the counsellor/helper can draw, therefore, on their understanding of persons, relationships and the life course when supporting clients to cope better with their life problems.

Service level B: Supporting clients to change when they are struggling with common mental health problems

Sometimes, however, the problem is not 'out there' in life but within ourselves. The medical model labels these types of problems as mental health disorders which are normally divided into common mental health problems (MHPs), such as anxiety and depression, and severe and complex MHPs, such as bipolar disorder and schizophrenia. But rather than focusing on disorders and their treatment, the CPCAB model focuses on the kind of change that is required – that is, change within the self. It proposes that changing the self can be at both an 'explicit' level (service level B1) and an 'implicit' level (service level B2). Importantly, at the explicit level it may be possible to work in a goal-directed way towards change but at the implicit level the client may need to change aspects of themselves that have been deeply hidden. This kind of change is often incremental rather than linear; it takes more time and requires a deeper level of trust.

Service level C: Supporting clients to change when they are struggling with severe and complex mental health problems

The CPCAB model takes account of the distinction between common mental health problems (service level B) and severe mental health problems (service level C). Clients categorised as having severe mental health problems often haven't had the opportunity to develop solid foundations within themselves and may require the counsellor to emotionally hold and support the client for a sufficient length of time for them to 'internalise' the experience. This is the kind of change needed at this level. It is also important, however, to recognise that many clients with severe mental health problems are not suitable for counselling and may need to be referred to secondary mental health services.

This service-level model is far from perfect and sometimes difficult to apply in the real world of clients, but it offers a useful framework for thinking about different levels of client need and associated therapeutic change. It is also helpful for trainee counsellors to reflect on the different service levels in relation to their limits of ability.

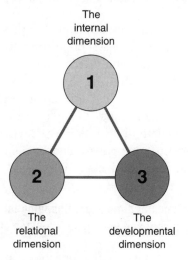

FIGURE 0.4   The three dimensions of change

Three dimensions of client change/problems

This third element of the CPCAB model proposes that, as part of the process of changing themselves (service level B), it is helpful for clients to explore three dimensions of the 'self', and that counsellors can support clients to change:

1. the way they relate within themselves – internal dimension (the self)
2. the way they relate to others – relational dimension (patterns of relating)
3. the way they relate with their past and manage life-stage challenges – developmental dimension (personal history).

1. The internal dimension: Changing the way we relate within ourselves

Clients cannot change who they are, but they can often change things for the better by changing the ways that they relate within themselves. Different theories offer different ways of understanding this internal dimension of the self. The Freudian model of id, ego and super-ego is one theory of the way that we relate within ourselves, but there are many other theories. In Transactional Analysis, for example, the counsellor might help the client to uncover a conflict between an angry internal 'parent' and an anxious internal 'child' and then work to change this relationship for the better. As clients learn to relate differently within themselves, they develop a more resilient sense of self – enabling them to cope more effectively with their problems of living.

2. The relational dimension: Changing the way we relate to others

Clients cannot change other people but they can often change things for the better by changing their ways of relating to others – their habitual patterns of perceiving, communicating and behaving with their partner, parents, children, friends or colleagues. Initially, these changes often need to take place within the safety of the counselling relationship, where the client can test out new ways of relating. By changing their unhelpful patterns of relating, clients develop better ways of coping with difficulties in their relationships and are consequently able to develop more open, supportive and resilient relationships that directly contribute to their health and well-being.

3. The developmental dimension: Changing the way we relate with our personal history and managing life-stage challenges

Clients cannot change the past but they can often change things for the better by changing the ways that they relate with their past. They can, for example, change the stories that they tell themselves about their personal history or change their emotional response to past traumatic events. As clients change the ways that they relate with their personal history, they become more resilient within themselves, through, for instance, letting go of blaming themselves or feeling less overwhelmed in the present by painful memories of the past. They can also be supported to manage their life-stage challenges including, for example, starting at college, becoming a new parent or giving up work.

Throughout this book, you will see the elements of this underpinning CPCAB model in the organisational structure, in the language used and in the way in which topics are explored. Over the last two decades, over 150,000 students have trained within the framework of the CPCAB model and many have come to value it simply because, when they used it, it worked well for them. This does not mean, however, that this book is only relevant to learners on CPCAB courses. The strength of the model is that it draws on contemporary research and reflects best practice in both counselling skills and counselling training. The CPCAB model is a living model that is regularly revised to reflect the latest research findings on what makes counselling and helping work effective. Updated versions of the model are published on the CPCAB website.

1
Using Counselling Skills Ethically and Safely

This first chapter is concerned with safety: working in a way that is safe both for the person using counselling skills (the helper) and the person being helped (the helpee). It is ethically important to work safely.

But what do we mean by 'safe' and what do we mean by 'ethically' in this context?

ETHICS AND SAFETY

Let's start with safety. In the dictionary, the definition of 'safe' is:

> Protected from or not exposed to danger or risk; not likely to be harmed or lost. (*Oxford English Dictionary*)

A safe is also where we put valuables; a place that affords protection.

REFLECTION

- Who do you feel safe with?
- What skills and qualities does that person have that help you feel safe?
- Where do you feel safe?
- Make a list of what you would need in order to create a 'safe space' to talk to someone about something personal.

There is a strong link between working ethically and working safely, although they are not the same. One definition of 'ethics' is:

> Moral principles that govern a person's behaviour or the conducting of an activity. (*Oxford English Dictionary*)

 It sounds simple. But how do I know what the right thing to do is?

 Professional bodies such as the British Association for Counselling and Psychotherapy (BACP) place great importance on working ethically and safely because part of their role is to protect the public. This is particularly important in the field of counselling because people seeking help are often in a vulnerable state. The BACP has developed the Ethical Framework for the Counselling Professions (2016) which helps practitioners think about what the right thing to do is.

The BACP Ethical Framework doesn't tell you what to do because no two situations are ever exactly the same, but it helps practitioners think about the right thing to do by offering some *ethical principles* for counselling and psychotherapy. These principles are:

- **being trustworthy** – honouring the trust placed in you (also called fidelity)
- **autonomy** – respecting a person's right to make their own choices
- **beneficence** – acting in the best interests of the person
- **non-maleficence** – not doing any harm
- **justice** – being fair and impartial
- **self-respect** – having integrity, self-knowledge and taking care of yourself.

 Some big words … but I think I get it.

 So, although the document is for counsellors and psychotherapists, it is also really helpful for people who use counselling skills when thinking about doing what is right – what is ethical and safe. We will look more closely at the Ethical Framework as we go along …

 Stop! What exactly is the difference between a counsellor and someone who uses counselling skills?

 This is a good question which gets to the heart of working ethically and safely.

KNOWING YOUR LIMITS

A *counsellor* is someone who is fully trained to work therapeutically with clients within a coherent framework of underpinning knowledge, theory and skills which informs the way they work. The counsellor and the client agree a formal contract to work together for the explicit purpose of helping the client. It takes at least four years to train to be a counsellor and there are a number of different theoretical approaches and counselling models which inform the nature and content of the training. Some examples of counsellors are:

- a counsellor in a GP practice
- a Relate counsellor
- a school counsellor
- a counsellor in private practice.

A person *using counselling skills* is not a fully trained counsellor but someone who has learned some general counselling skills (mainly listening and supporting skills) which they use to enhance or complement another professional or voluntary role. People also learn counselling skills as the first step in training towards becoming a counsellor. Some examples of people who use counselling skills in other roles are:

- nurses
- teachers
- parents
- teaching assistants
- pastoral assistants
- line managers
- dieticians
- healthcare workers
- support workers.

Counselling is just one role in a wide array of supportive relationships. Most people who suffer emotional or psychological distress never get to see a trained counsellor but many will be helped by people who use counselling skills as part of another role. Counselling skills are sometimes called 'helping skills' because they are used in lots of formal and informal helping roles and in many different settings. Helpers who use counselling skills provide meaningful and lasting psychological support and contribute significantly to the well-being and mental health of the public.

EXAMPLES OF PEOPLE USING COUNSELLING SKILLS

Laura works in the Human Resources (HR) department of a large company. An employee comes in to ask for unpaid leave. He breaks down as he explains that his wife has left him and he is trying to manage the crisis both personally and in terms of child care.

(Continued)

(Continued)

Laura uses counselling skills to listen to him and support him as part of her HR role but recommends that he sees a counsellor through the Employee Assistance Programme.

Steve is a youth worker. A 15-year-old boy at the youth centre is reluctant to go home at the end of the evening. Steve uses counselling skills to help him talk about what's going on at home. From what the boy says, there is no immediate risk of him being harmed so Steve agrees to talk with him each week within his role as youth worker. He lets him know that there is further help and support available if needed.

Mel meets a friend after work. Her friend is frantic, having got drunk and kissed a colleague at work. She is confused about her feelings and what this means for her marriage. Mel uses counselling skills to help her explore these issues. At the end of their meeting, her friend is feeling relieved and ready to face things.

One way we can make the difference clearer between counsellors and those who use counselling skills is in the language that we use in training:

- A person using counselling skills is often called the 'helper' and the person they are 'helping' is the 'helpee'.
- A fully trained person is called a 'counsellor' who enters into a contract for counselling with the 'client'.

What does all this have to do with working ethically and safely?

It's important that you understand the difference between counselling and helping work because you need to recognise the limits of your ability and not mislead others about your level of training. In other words, although you might have all sorts of other skills you must make it clear to others that as far as counselling goes you have learned counselling skills but are not a trained counsellor. Table 1.1 lists the differences between a helper and a counsellor.

TABLE 1.1   Differences between helper and counsellor

What is a helper?	What is a counsellor?
A helper uses counselling skills in a listening capacity within different roles to enable an individual to start to express what is going on for them and explore different avenues of professional support as required.	A counsellor is a qualified professional trained to work at depth with individual issues.
A helper may have other relationships with the client, e.g. co-worker, line manager.	A counsellor is most likely to only have a professional role as counsellor with the individual client.
The helping role is on a more informal basis where boundaries are agreed.	A counsellor will have a formal, legal, contractual agreement with the client.

tip

When a helper works with a helpee, it is usually called a 'helping session', a 'helping interaction' or a 'helping conversation'. The word 'session' can be confusing as it is used for both helping work and counselling work. However, a 'helping session' might be a 'one-off' short meeting of about 10–15 minutes which is agreed at the time of the session, whereas counselling sessions are usually part of a prearranged series of meetings which are at a set time and typically 50–60 minutes in length.

> A useful … conversation can take place within about eight to ten minutes. This length of time represents a typical window of opportunity that a teacher, doctor or manager may have to allow someone to talk through something that is troubling them … there are many situations in which longer periods of time may be available … but it is nevertheless important to recognise that a 10-minute talk can make a difference. (McLeod and McLeod, 2011: 2)

- It's important for your well-being to ensure you are not out of your depth or overwhelmed or put at risk as this would be unethical and unsafe for you.
- It's important for the person you are helping that they do not have unrealistic expectations or a false impression of who you are and what you can offer. This would make it unsafe and unethical for them.

Look back at the list of ethical principles and think about which ones would be broken if you did not make the limits of your ability clear to a person seeking help.

REFLECTION

Go to a gym or sports centre. Try to pick up the heaviest weights there. Unless you are very fit you will not be able to do this.

Reflect on what stops you picking up the heaviest weight straight away. What would you need to do to be able to pick up the heaviest weight?

This activity is a good analogy for the limits of your ability. You cannot pick up the heaviest weight because you haven't practised and started on lighter weights and worked towards lifting heavier ones. With more experience and practice, you would be able to pick up heavier weights. Also, by trying to lift weights too heavy for you, you could hurt yourself or cause an accident that hurts someone else.

Similarly, when you first begin learning and practising counselling skills, you do not have the knowledge and experience to work with in-depth emotional and psychological distress and might cause harm to yourself or the person you are working with. However, as you learn and gain understanding and knowledge, the limits of your ability will change and you will be able to continue to work safely and appropriately according to your level of training and experience.

Now that you have investigated the ethical principles in the BACP Ethical Framework, have a look at the 'personal moral qualities' needed for working in this field. How many of these overlap with your list of what qualities you would look for in a person who makes you feel safe? Why do you think 'courage' might be an important quality for a counsellor?

ACTIVITY

Reflect on each of the personal moral qualities shown in Figure 1.1.

FIGURE 1.1   BACP Ethical Framework – personal moral qualities

- How would you honestly score yourself out of ten against this list of moral qualities?
- Are any of the scores you have given yourself less than six?
- How might this affect your suitability to work as a counsellor or as someone in a helping role?

You might want to write down your scores so you can look at them later in your training. It may be interesting to see how they change as time goes by and what factors contribute to this change.

I notice that there seems to be an overlap between the moral qualities and the ethical principles. For example, if I act with 'integrity' I suppose I must also be 'trustworthy' because if I was not trustworthy I could not act with integrity. Or could I?

Or another example: if I work with 'care', I will also do no harm (non-maleficence). But how do I know if I am working with 'care' or 'diligence'? Does it also mean that if someone needs help and support that I am not trained to offer, I have to say I can't help them and send them somewhere else in case I do them harm? This demonstrates my commitment to 'care' for the helpee and 'diligence' about not working beyond my own skills and knowledge to ensure a good outcome.

OTHER SOURCES OF SUPPORT

 I like the way you are thinking and questioning what you are learning. You are applying your critical thinking skills. But to actually answer your last question … one way of showing 'care' and 'diligence' is about being clear what you can or can't offer and then also working with the person to decide what other kinds of help they might need and where to look for it. Sometimes it's about helping someone decide what their next step is or what their options are. It's really about recognising your personal limits and making sure you can signpost people to other kinds of help if they need it. Even experienced practitioners have limits to what they can offer and need to recognise if a client needs specialist help or another kind of help.

ACTIVITY

Research what other support services are available in your area. Some areas you could explore include:

- counselling services
- Health professionals
- Legal services
- Citizens Advice Bureau
- Debt agencies
- Social services
- Occupational health
- Housing advice
- Self-help groups.

SUMMARY

In order to work ethically and safely using counselling skills, you need to:

- Have a framework for looking at what appropriate behaviour and attitudes are.
- Recognise the limits of your ability and monitor your own values.
- Convey the limits of what you can offer to the person you are helping.
- Enable the person you are helping to find other support where appropriate.

2
Establishing a Helping Relationship

This chapter looks at how to establish and sustain the boundaries of the helping session and the helping relationship. It explores the role and importance of boundaries and how to manage the beginning and ending of a helping session.

BOUNDARIES

 What do we mean by boundaries and why are they important?

Let's begin in our usual way by looking at what the word 'boundary' actually means:

1. *noun* – a line determining the limits of an area
2. *noun* – the line or plane indicating the limit or extent of something.

To help us understand how that relates to helping work, let's think of parenting. We often hear the word 'boundary' applied to what a child is, or is not, allowed to do. This may be in relation to bedtime, behaviour, eating sweets, and so on. If the parenting is 'good enough', the boundaries ensure the child's safety and well-being. In the same way, boundaries in helping work are about safety and well-being. They are there for both the helper and the helpee.

 So actually boundaries are just rules.

 'Rules' has quite a harsh, punitive feel to it but in a sense you are right. Boundaries clarify the helping relationship so that both the helper and helpee know what to expect from the relationship. Boundaries outline what is acceptable in the relationship.

Clear boundaries also let the helpee know exactly what they can expect from the helper and from the session. For example, boundaries include being clear about the time and length of the session, the limits of confidentiality and the frequency of meetings. Boundaries can also include things which are less immediately obvious and which may relate to events outside the session. For example, a helper and helpee might discuss and agree on what would happen if the helper and helpee met in the street or in a social situation. If all these issues are made clear before entering into the helping relationship, the helpee can make an informed choice about whether or not to enter into the relationship and how much to disclose in the session itself.

Boundaries also create a secure framework for the helping work which makes it possible for the helper to build a close, even intimate, relationship with the helpee which is based on trust and respect without the constraints associated with friendship.

 It reminds me of a preview for a film. I like to read a bit about the plot and who is in it before I go to see it. Maybe boundaries are a bit like that. By understanding how a helping session works, I know what to expect both from the helper and the session itself. In that way I won't feel let down or cheated if I find out half-way through that it's not what I was expecting. Or maybe boundaries are like the ingredients in a recipe. Each recipe has a list of ingredients and instructions on how to use them to get the desired outcome. Mmm … interesting ways of thinking about the subject!

 Before we move on to looking at some boundaries in more detail, we need to be aware that boundaries can be split into two kinds: professional and personal.

> **Professional boundaries** create and support the framework for the helping session itself.

> **Personal boundaries** are our own personal limits. You can think of them almost as the rules which we live by in relation to other people and the world in general. They exist to keep us safe and protected. They inform people what is acceptable to us and what is not. For some of us, maintaining our personal boundaries is very difficult. For example, we might find ourselves agreeing to things we really don't want to do or accepting behaviour from others that is unacceptable. Personal boundaries generally grow from experience and what we have learnt about behaviour from family and friends. Another way of understanding personal boundaries is to think that they draw a line which defines where we stop and where the other person begins. When our personal boundaries are challenged or compromised, we can often feel very uncomfortable. What we do with that discomfort is a very individual response. Therefore, we can see that personal boundaries are those that help us, as helpers, manage ourselves within the helping session.

Let's look at what boundaries we need to ensure the session is safe for all concerned.

CONFIDENTIALITY

 I can see why confidentiality is top of the list. I wouldn't be able to speak freely and openly if I was worried that other people might find out what I had been discussing.

 Yes, confidentiality is important. All of us have things we want to keep private and some things we feel ashamed of or frightened of; things we may not want others to know about for fear of being judged or hurt. Also, we may not want to talk about certain things in case we hurt those we care for. In a helping relationship, confidentiality helps to build trust, which is essential for an honest and respectful relationship. A helpee needs to be able to talk openly and reflect on what they are saying in order to better understand themselves and their situation, and then hopefully to begin to explore and discover different ways of coping and managing their lives. Having a confidential space takes away a lot of the constraints which are there in everyday conversations and exchanges with friends and relatives.

 So it's a bit like a priest and a confessional. A priest will not divulge anything that is said to him, no matter what.

 Actually no, that's not quite correct. In helping and counselling relationships, even confidentiality must have its limits. Without limits to confidentiality, the safety of the session may be compromised and the very boundary which has been put in place to create safety may end up actually jeopardising that safety.

 So is it confidential or isn't it? This feels really confusing.

 Yes, a helping session must be confidential. However, if the helpee talks about something that could be very harmful to themselves or to someone else, then the confidentiality boundary may have to be breached. The important thing is that the helpee needs to know exactly what the confidentiality boundary is and what limits there are before the helping session begins. This must happen first before they begin to talk about their problems or issues.

> **REFLECTION**
>
> When considering the limits of confidentiality, it is useful to reflect on what we mean by 'harm' and why the risk of harm might make it necessary to breach confidentiality. Use these questions to reflect on the examples that follow:
>
> - Who is at risk of harm?
> - What is the nature of the risk or harm?
> - What action would you need to take and why?

1. The helpee is in a very violent or volatile relationship where a child is being hurt.
2. The helpee is feeling very depressed and says that life is so awful they don't want to carry on living.
3. The helpee who has a history of violence arrives in an angry and aggressive mood.

If confidentiality has to be broken, it is always better if the helper is able to involve the helpee in the process rather than going behind their back, although this is not always possible. In an ideal situation, the helper would gently remind the helpee of what was said at the beginning about having to breach confidentiality if someone was at risk of harm and then explain why they think it is necessary at this point.

Answers

1. The child is at risk. Under child protection legislation, the relevant authorities must be informed.
2. The helpee is at risk. A helper should not be working with this level of difficulty and should support the helpee to go to their GP for help.
3. The helper is at risk. The helper should explain that they cannot work with the helpee if there is an immediate risk of violence.

What are your personal thoughts and feelings about being in such a situation?

It can be very challenging to be in a helping session where confidentiality may need to be breached.

It was mentioned earlier that there may also be certain situations where you personally would find it difficult to maintain confidentiality. You may be faced with issues that go against your personal values and beliefs. You may be faced with issues that remind you of your own current or past hurts or problems. These are issues that we need to find a way of working through and dealing with without breaching confidentiality.

REFLECTION

Take a moment to think about what your thoughts and feelings might be in the following scenarios:

- You realise the person you are listening to is talking about a close friend of yours.
- The person you are listening to tells you they are racist and have very strong political views on mixed-race relationships and immigration.

(Continued)

(Continued)

- You realise the person you are speaking to is having an affair with your sister's husband.
- The person you are listening to tells you they are HIV-positive and practising unsafe sex.
- The person you are listening to tells you that they have been stealing money from work.
- The person you are listening to tells you some really scandalous gossip.

We can now begin to see how there can be links between professional and personal boundaries and that sometimes it may be challenging to maintain professional boundaries because of our personal thoughts and feelings. Let's explore this further.

CRITICAL THINKING

The boundaries of the helping relationship and the helping session are in many ways more difficult to manage than the boundaries of counselling work where boundaries are much more clearly defined:

- The helping role is often very context-specific.
- There may be dual roles/relationships between helper and helpee.
- An appropriate place and time for the session can be difficult to create and protect in helping work.

EXAMPLE

Laura and Mel are colleagues in a financial services company. Mel seems to be struggling at work so Laura offers him a helping session during the lunch hour because she has done some training in counselling skills. During the session, Mel discloses that he has been struggling with depression and has got himself into serious debt; sometimes he feels unable to cope. At the end of the session, he asks if she could lend him £50 to tide him over until next week.

- What are the different roles of Laura and Mel?
- Does Laura have an obligation to breach confidentiality and, if so, to whom?

TIME BOUNDARIES

Stating a clear time boundary/limit for the session communicates to the helpee how much time belongs to them. This allows them to make choices around how they will use the session and what and how much to discuss and disclose. Time is therefore very valuable in this context. It is gifted to the helpee by the helper. This value is demonstrated by the helper ensuring sessions don't overrun but also that they are not cut short. A time boundary thus ensures that the session is contained and offers consistency and reliability. It can be very disruptive and potentially harmful if a time boundary is broken.

- If the helper is not there when the helpee arrives for a session at the agreed time, this can threaten the trust and safety of the helping session because the helper could be seen as unreliable.
- If the helper does not set a time boundary at the beginning of the session and then suddenly announces that it has ended, the helpee can be left feeling cut off and abandoned or overwhelmed by their feelings.
- If a helper allows the session to overrun the agreed time boundary, the helpee can be left feeling confused and ungrounded or come to expect that all sessions will be longer than agreed.

ACTIVITY

It is helpful to think about what can affect us in setting and maintaining time boundaries. What are our vulnerabilities? What's our Achilles heel in relationships? Do we want to be liked? Does this cause us to 'people-please' or to offer more time than we can spare? Are we worried about hurting people's feelings? Does this cause us to go over the time agreed, even when we have stated a time boundary? Do we feel anxious or frightened when with certain people or when talking about particular issues or topics which might tempt us to end the session early? Do we place unrealistic expectations on ourselves? Do we offer more time than we can actually manage and find ourselves overwhelmed, anxious or unable to listen properly?

What do you find difficult about setting time boundaries? Consider what you would do in each of the following situations:

- If a helpee began crying at the end of a session when the agreed time boundary had elapsed.
- If a helpee arrived late but still asked for the same amount of time they usually had.

(Continued)

(Continued)

- If a helpee said they were leaving before the end of the time stated.
- If a helpee continued talking after you had said the session had ended.
- If the helpee disclosed something very distressing and/or shocking very near the end of the session.

I can understand why time boundaries are important; I like to know where I stand. It is hard to keep to time boundaries sometimes though, even in everyday life. I often end up doing more for people than I intend to. I wonder if this is also something to do with boundaries.

ACTIVITY

Practise setting time boundaries with friends, relatives and acquaintances. Be mindful of how it feels to do this.

When you answer the telephone to friends or colleagues, let them know how long you have to talk and then ensure you end the conversation at the time you stated.

- Why do you find it easier to set a time boundary with some people rather than others?
- What is it about you and them that makes setting boundaries difficult or challenging?
- What gets in the way of setting clear time boundaries?
- Is your ability to set clear boundaries affected by how you are feeling, e.g. sad, angry, tired?
- What helps you to set and maintain boundaries?

SETTING

Another element to consider in helping work is the setting (or place) where the helping work takes place. Strictly speaking, the setting is not in itself a boundary but having an appropriate setting can enable appropriate boundaries to be established and maintained. For example, a session that can be overheard by others can impinge on the confidentiality boundary, making the session unsafe. If a helping session takes place in a room that is too small, personal boundaries around space and closeness could be challenged, thus making the session uncomfortable and therefore unsafe.

I'd like a really cosy room, with bean bags and candles and maybe a plant.

That sounds really nice but it's important to consider what other people might need. Someone with a disability might find bean bags difficult to negotiate.

ACTIVITY

Sketch, describe or imagine a setting that you feel would be appropriate for a helping session.

Consider the following elements: privacy, interruptions, seating, proximity, furniture, décor, space, entrance/exit, lighting, contents of room, time of day.

- What do you think needs to be in the setting?
- What would help you personally to feel comfortable and able to talk about your problems or issues?

It is important, when thinking of the setting, to reflect on what is an appropriate space between the helpee and helper. It is also important not to sit too close as this can feel uncomfortable, overwhelming and engulfing. By the same token, if there is too much space, it can prevent a connection taking place and the helpee may struggle to be heard.

To find out what feels comfortable to you, practise sitting talking to someone. Slowly move your chair closer and be mindful of how you are feeling. This will allow you to find out where is comfortable for you.

 There's a lot to think about. I can see how important boundaries are though. Basically, they just set the scene and keep both the helpee and helper safe. I can see why it's important to make the boundaries clear right at the beginning of the helping session, so that everyone knows where they stand and what to expect from the session. I also see how it can be quite challenging to maintain boundaries through the session itself and how my personal boundaries can affect my professional boundaries.

That just leaves ending the session. I know I need to keep within the time boundary but how does the session end? Do I just say goodbye?

 Endings are a very important and sensitive part of helping work and therefore it is vital that the end of a session is managed with care and understanding. Endings can be difficult and painful. It is important to ensure the helpee is safe and able to go back into the world after a helping session ends. If a session is not ended well, the helpee could be left feeling vulnerable or it could trigger painful feelings of loss and abandonment from their past.

HOW TO END A SESSION

- Give the helpee a few minutes' warning before the time runs out.
- Use the skills of summarising (see Chapter 6) to draw together the threads of the session and to show that you have heard and understood.
- Try not to introduce a new topic or ask a searching question that is likely to require an in-depth answer near the end of a session.
- Check that the helpee is OK before they leave the room.

I see the importance of ending on time but wouldn't know what to do if the helpee starts disclosing something really important when the session is almost at an end. I would feel awful just ignoring them and ending the session anyway.

Yes, this can be quite a tricky one! It is, of course, not in the spirit of helping work to just ignore the helpee but it is very important to keep within the boundaries agreed and that includes ending on time. What can be helpful is to acknowledge that what the helpee has said is very important and that it took a lot of courage to say it. You can also acknowledge that there could be difficult and painful feelings present but you can then suggest arranging another helping session where it can be given the time and respect it deserves. This way you are acknowledging and valuing the helpee's experience but also maintaining the boundaries of the session.

REFLECTION

Build your awareness around endings by becoming mindful of endings in your personal relationships:

- How do interactions with friends, relatives and acquaintances end?
- Who usually brings the interactions to a close – you or the other person?
- How do you find ending interactions? What feelings are present?
- Do you like abrupt and neat endings or prefer them to be drawn out?
- How do you feel about endings? What comes to mind when you think about endings?

OUT-OF-SESSION BOUNDARIES

As a helper, there are a number of boundary issues to consider outside the helping session. It is better to have thought these things through before starting the session rather than being caught on the hop. For example:

1. Can a helpee contact you personally to arrange a session?
2. Can a helpee contact you other than when you have a session arranged?
3. If so, what form of communication would you be willing to respond to (telephone, text, email, messaging, face-to-face)?
4. If face-to-face, where?
5. When are you available and for how long?
6. If you say 'contact me anytime', do you really mean at 'any' time?
7. If a helpee needs your help at a time or in a setting that is not appropriate, can you say 'no'?
8. Are you able to offer a more appropriate time or setting?
9. If you see the helpee in everyday life between sessions, do you acknowledge them or ignore them? How did you arrive at this decision?
10. Have you researched appropriate referral routes to other sources of support in case the helpee needs a different kind of help?

SUMMARY

- Boundaries are essential to keep both helper and helpee safe.
- There are personal and professional boundaries, and personal boundaries can impact on professional boundaries.
- Boundaries may have limits and these need to be communicated at the start of the helping session.
- A helping session needs to have an appropriate ending.
- Boundaries provide a framework for helping work so they must be:
  - clear
  - appropriate and context-specific
  - firm but caring
  - not controlling or manipulative
  - not hurtful or harmful
  - not invasive or dominating
  - respectful.

3
Working Empathically as a Helper

This chapter is concerned with the meaning and purpose of empathy in the helping role and is also about how personal issues, fears and prejudices impact on the ability to empathise with others.

EMPATHY

What do we mean by empathy and what is its role in a helping relationship?

Let's begin in the usual way by looking at what the word 'empathy' actually means. In its simplest form, empathy means to understand something from another person's point of view. When working in a helping or counselling role, it means to gain an insight and appreciation of someone's situation, thoughts and feelings.

It is often said that empathy is 'seeing the world through someone else's eyes, feeling it through their heart'. To truly empathise is to actually work hard to understand the helpee and then communicate to them that you do understand.

So empathy is a bit like sympathy.

No, but that's a very common misunderstanding. Empathy is actually very different from sympathy. Sympathy is something that is done *to* someone. Empathy is something that is done *with* someone. Sympathy suggests feeling sorry for someone and that in turn suggests some sort of power imbalance, i.e. the person sympathising is in a greater position of power. Empathy is about being on an equal footing, by entering into the helpee's world to try to understand and also communicating with each other to clarify and confirm that understanding. So, the helper needs to enter the helpee's *frame of reference* to be able to imagine how they are feeling. 'Frame of reference' is a common counselling term and simply means seeing things from the helpee's point of view. The helper can then communicate their understanding to the helpee and they in turn can confirm that understanding.

Perhaps another way of explaining it is that sympathy is really about recognising someone's feelings and feeling FOR them, while empathy is actually sharing someone's feelings and feeling WITH them, if only briefly. So empathy is a deeper emotional experience.

CRITICAL THINKING

This raises an interesting question. Is it possible to empathise with someone who you don't feel sympathy for?

Consider this example: if you heard that someone had stolen a large sum of money from their elderly relatives and had then gone on to squander all the money, ending up alone and homeless, would you find it possible to empathise with them and understand the choices and reasons that drove their actions?

Would you be able to sympathise with someone who had, to all intents and purposes, brought about their own downfall?

 I guess both sympathy and empathy have a role to play in relationships but, in a helping relationship, empathy is very important in terms of the helpee being able to understand where the helpee is coming from.

 Yes, that's very true. However, the most important thing is not about the helper understanding the helpee; it is about the helpee feeling understood. This is a vital difference – the emphasis here needs to be on the helpee, not the helper.

ACTIVITY

As you reflect on the meaning of empathy in a helping relationship, you can begin to see why it is so beneficial. Your focus can shift to the importance of understanding and feeling understood.

Complete Table 3.1, which asks you to focus on a time when you felt understood by someone and a time when you did not feel understood. Try to really clarify for yourself what the other person did or said that helped you to feel understood:

- What did you need to feel understood?
- How did it feel when those needs were met?
- How did it feel when those needs were not met?

(Continued)

(Continued)

TABLE 3.1   Feeling understood

Event	Time I felt understood	Time I didn't feel understood
What happened?		
Who was involved?		
What was said to you?		
What was the person's attitude towards you?		
How did you feel?		
How did the experience affect you?		

I can certainly see the importance of understanding and being understood. If I feel understood, I feel able to be honest and open about who I am and how I am feeling. If I don't feel understood, I feel judged and can begin to feel uncomfortable and even ashamed or angry. I certainly wouldn't want to talk about my problems and difficulties with someone I felt didn't understand me. I'm a bit worried that I'm not empathic enough. How can I develop the skill of empathy?

It is important to acknowledge and accept that empathy is always a work in progress. Empathy is not a skill that is just learnt and then done with. Empathy is a quality that develops over time as a relationship develops and as you work on your own self-awareness and insights. In order to develop the quality of empathy, there is a need to be honest about personal prejudices and stereotypes. Bring them into the light of day so that their origins can be explored and new ways of understanding and challenging them can be found. You need to understand the fears and hurts in your own heart that may cause you to sit in judgement of others. Then work can be done towards self-acceptance and tolerance of personal shortcomings. If you can afford empathy and understanding for yourself, you are more likely to be able to extend that acceptance to others. Empathy is on the list of personal moral qualities in the BACP Ethical Framework for the Counselling Professions (2016). This definition includes the importance of not just understanding another person but being able to communicate that understanding:

> Empathy: the ability to share someone else's feelings or experiences by imagining what it would be like to be in that person's situation. (dictionary.cambridge.org)

There's a lot to it but I can already see how important it is for me to build my self-awareness. I have noticed that I am more judgemental when I am not feeling good about myself. That may not be true for everyone but it is certainly true for me.

Some days I wake up and when I look in the mirror I quite like what I see – not perfect by any means but good enough. On those days, I look around my home and feel safe and comfortable when I see all my belongings around me. When I leave my house, I wave to my neighbours and go off to work quite happily. At work, I hear my colleagues laughing and join in with the joking; I love working here.

Other days I wake up and look in the mirror and all I see are lines and wrinkles and how big my nose is. I feel my heart sinking when I see the grey hairs and bags under my eyes. I look around the room at the mess and dust gathering; everything looks cluttered and gets on my nerves. I get ready for work and as I leave I see my neighbour looking over at me. I think, 'What does that so-and-so think he's looking at? He can get lost.' I arrive at work and as I walk into the room everyone's laughing. I hate them all; they all turn to look at me and the laughter stops. I think they've been talking about me and I feel like just running out and never coming back. I hate working here.

On both of these days, my face hasn't changed, my house hasn't changed, my neighbour and work colleagues haven't changed. What has changed is my perception. I sit in judgement on everything because of my perception and how I feel about myself. It's like wearing the opposite of rose-tinted glasses. I have learnt, though, that when I feel that way, I can't always trust my judgements.

That's a good example. It also highlights the need for a helper to practise self-care in order to be able to be present and attentive to the helpee's needs. However, there will still be issues or situations that you find difficult to understand and empathise with. It is important to know your personal blocks to empathy so that you can explore and resolve them. It is simply not possible to offer empathy to someone you are judging.

Actually, I don't really sit in judgement. I know that we are all the same really and therefore I will try to treat everyone accordingly.

WORKING WITH DIFFERENCE

It's very interesting that you say that. Do you really believe that everyone is the same? That statement makes an assumption and once we make assumptions we stop really listening to someone because we assume we already know what they are like and how they are feeling. In truth, we are not all the same; we are all very different. We can learn so much about each other by learning about our differences and how they impact on our relationships and life in general. Let's imagine someone who was in a wheelchair wanted to meet and talk with you; if you assume that everyone is the same, you will not be able to acknowledge that the person in the wheelchair has different needs from a person who is able to walk. In the same way, if you assume that we are all the same, you will assume that we all have the same needs and this is simply not true. It can be very dangerous to make assumptions. In a helping relationship, we work hard to truly listen to and understand someone. We value their uniqueness and individuality. We take time to consider what it might be like for them in their situation, and to do that we need to understand what blocks us from empathising. It can actually take a lot of courage to acknowledge difference and diversity and also to look at our own reactions to it. It is hard sometimes to admit we have prejudices and that we hold various stereotypes. It can also be difficult to air our fears and reflect on where they have come from.

STEREOTYPING

Let's begin by exploring what we mean by a stereotype:

> A widely held but fixed and oversimplified image or idea of a particular type of person or thing. (*Oxford English Dictionary*)

For example, 'All teenagers are rebels' or 'All French people are romantic'. When we stereotype, we assume that an individual has exactly the same characteristics, abilities and behaviours of a whole group, race, culture, etc.

Stereotyping can seem to help us simplify social situations because in a way we are calling on our past experience, beliefs and what we have been told to make a rapid appraisal of a person or situation. Unfortunately, when we stereotype we stop seeing someone as an individual and assume we know all about them, without taking the time to get to know them. We ignore differences between individuals from the same group, race and culture, and so on. We actually believe things about someone that simply aren't true, and when we do that we judge them; and once we judge, we are unable to empathise. In addition, most stereotypes are negative and assume characteristics that are unpleasant or horrible.

It is not always a bad thing to hold stereotypes. Most of us hold stereotypes and actually sometimes we need them to make snap judgements to keep ourselves safe. For example, if I were walking towards my car late at night and saw a group of hooded youths coming towards me making a lot of noise, I would almost definitely hurry to get into my car and lock the door. My stereotype would probably be: all youth wearing hoodies are troublemakers. I would most likely assume that they intended to harm me and my fear would urge me to make myself safe. Once I had time to reflect, I could challenge my stereotype. There is no way I could know for sure that this particular group of youths meant me harm and certainly not all young people are troublemakers, but in that moment of fear my stereotype made a judgement and I acted on that.

Our stereotypes come from many places. Some are based very loosely on the truth of other people's experiences. We may have been told things about groups of people as we grew up. We may have been hurt or frightened by someone from a particular group and then made the assumption that all people from that group are the same. We will have picked stereotypes up from a wide range of places, people and experiences.

What we need to do is be able to see past our stereotypes, explore where they came from and then challenge how accurate they are. When we meet someone and make a judgement based on their characteristics, we are almost certainly making that judgement from a stereotype. Once we are able to acknowledge that and challenge it, we are then free to see the person as an individual.

ACTIVITY

Complete the following with the first things you think of. You could write one or several words.

Americans are …

Germans are …

French people are …

Italians are …

Scottish people are …

English people are …

Welsh people are …

Irish people are …

Young people are …

Old people are …

People with red hair are …

Women with blonde hair are …

Single parents are …

Black people are …

People on benefits are …

Immigrants are …

Mentally ill people are …

Fat people are …

Rich people are …

Women are …

(Continued)

(Continued)

- When writing the words you associated with each group, were you able to be honest or did you censor your responses, fearing you would be judged if you were brutally honest?
- Do you have specific personal experiences that inform the words you wrote for each group?
- If you have no personal experience, what led you to write the words you did?
- Were the words you wrote mostly positive or negative?
- Did it make a difference if you belonged to one of the groups listed?
- Have you ever been judged based on a stereotype?
- How did this feel, and what did you do in response to the judgement?
- What do you think influenced your answers – friends, TV, newspapers, parents, etc.?
- Do you believe the words you wrote are true?
- What are the possible negative effects of stereotyping?
- If we judge based on the actions of a few, how can we explore, understand and move past our judgements?
- Can you judge a person on only a few characteristics?
- Does it make a difference to your attitude if you know someone personally?
- How will the above activities support your helping work?

 It's difficult to be honest when writing about stereotypes. I feel ashamed about some of the things I think and want to keep them to myself.

 Yes, once stereotypes are opened up and explored, it can be quite shocking to confront the thoughts and judgements we hold about groups of people. To help us move past our fear and shame around the stereotypes we hold, and in order to challenge and understand them, we can think of them as being like mushrooms. If mushrooms are put in the dark and have large amounts of dirt shovelled over them, they grow very large. If the dirt is removed and the room flooded with light, the mushrooms cannot flourish and eventually wither and die. Stereotypes are like that – they cannot stand up to the light of enquiry and only flourish in the darkness of secrecy and fear.

PREJUDICE AND DISCRIMINATION

Let's now look at 'prejudice':

> Prejudice: preconceived opinion that is not based on reason or actual experience. (*Oxford English Dictionary*)

For example, a person may hold prejudiced views towards a certain race or gender.

If we break the word down, we get 'pre-judge', which is making a judgement without having all the relevant information, or making a judgement based on a stereotype. The judgement is usually negative. It is important to look at what our prejudices are and to explore all parts of ourselves in relation to the prejudice and how it impacts on society and individuals. We can begin by identifying our thoughts and beliefs towards a specific group; then we identify the feelings we have in relation to that group; and finally we look at how we behave towards the members of the group. The beliefs and thoughts we hold form the stereotype. The feeling part is whether we like or dislike, whether we feel warmth or hostility towards, the group. The behavioural aspect is how we discriminate against certain groups. It is vital that we identify and explore our prejudicial behaviour and how we discriminate in order to fully understand and work with difference and diversity in helping work.

> Discrimination: the unjust or prejudicial treatment of different categories of people, especially on the grounds of race, age, or sex. (*Oxford English Dictionary*)

 If I'm really honest, I have harboured some prejudices towards certain groups of people whose background is different from my own but I don't think I hurt anyone by having them. I certainly don't attack anyone or enter into a conflict just because someone is different from me.

 Discrimination can be very subtle. There are many ways we can act out our prejudices. Jokes can be very funny but when they make groups of people the butt of the joke they are a form of discrimination. We may gossip or talk about certain types of people or exclude them from our group of friends. This is not always conscious and often happens out of awkwardness and fear rather than direct maliciousness. Also, we can avoid certain groups because of our discomfort and uneasiness around difference and diversity – and this is discrimination. Further up the scale, people can be excluded from various areas of society, including employment and welfare. In extreme cases, certain groups are physically and verbally attacked and when we look at the worst extreme, genocide can take place.

So it is very clear that we need to identify our prejudices and understand them in order to be able to empathise and understand someone without the shadow of prejudice making this impossible.

I don't know whether or not that's possible. I think there will always be certain people, places and things that trigger prejudice in me but I guess it's what I do with it that's important.

Absolutely; the quality and practice of empathy is always 'a work in progress'. It is important to keep in mind that the goal is progress rather than perfection.

There is another element of this that needs to be taken into consideration. That element is willingness. Sometimes we might not want to understand something; we may find it abhorrent or so against what we believe in or value that we simply don't want to understand and empathise. It is important to be honest with ourselves about the things we are not willing to understand.

COMMUNICATING EMPATHY

ACTIVITY

Imagine you are listening to the following statements. As you read them, consider how you are feeling in relation to the person or the situation. Reflect on how judgemental or accepting you feel. Does the situation/person remind you of anything from your own personal experience? How does this affect how you think or feel about the person/situation?

At the end of each section, there are a number of responses. Identify the one you feel is the most empathic response.

1. I'm really worried that I'm pregnant. I'm too scared to take a test in case I am. I know that sounds awful but I just don't know what I'd do. I've wanted a baby for so long; actually *we've* wanted a baby for so long. I'm married, you see. We've even considered IVF, we wanted a family so much, and it didn't seem to be happening. The problem is I had a fling with a work colleague – only the once, but it only takes once, doesn't it? What will I do if I am pregnant? I'd have to tell my husband but that could mean the end of my marriage. Oh God, what a mess.

    (a) You need to find out straight away; that's the only way to set your mind at rest.
    (b) You are in such a difficult situation and are so frightened and unsure of what to do.
    (c) You are feeling guilty and ashamed for doing such a terrible thing to a loving husband.
    (d) I had an unwanted pregnancy once. It was so awful, I know exactly what you're going through.
    (e) You don't know whether to lie or tell the truth.
    (f) You don't have to tell your husband. Do you think you could keep the secret to yourself?

---

2. Oh no! I've just seen my rota for next week and I've got three long shifts and an overnight. It had to be this week, didn't it? I don't know what to do. John's dad is in hospital and I have to drive him there three times a week and I've promised the girls I'd do their hair and nails on Wednesday – not to mention everything else that needs doing. The house is a pigsty and all I want to do is crawl into bed and sleep for a week. I'm so stressed. I really am at the end of my tether.

   (a) You sound absolutely exhausted and overwhelmed by all the demands on your time.
   (b) You are really angry that your family don't appreciate you and treat you so badly.
   (c) Can you ring work and ask to change your shifts?
   (d) Oh you poor thing, what a horrendous week; can I do anything to help?
   (e) Don't get so stressed out, just leave the housework. The dust will still be there tomorrow.
   (f) How about enrolling on an assertiveness course? Learn to say no!

3. I've just had an argument with my best friend and think the friendship might be over, and it's all my fault. She told me something in confidence and I told my neighbour. I feel so guilty. She found out what I'd done and accused me of betraying her and she's right. She's so angry with me and I don't blame her. I don't even know why I did it. I was jealous, I think, because her boyfriend bought her a new car. What a horrible friend I am. I felt guilty even before she found out. I hate myself.

   (a) What did she say exactly? Did she tell you she didn't want to be your friend?
   (b) What on earth made you say that? Your poor friend will never be able to trust you again.
   (c) How sad. You've lost your best friend and all over a car.
   (d) You are really hurting. You feel so bad about what's happened and are giving yourself a really hard time for it.
   (e) Phone her up. I'm sure she'll forgive you. Do you want me to have a word with her for you?
   (f) My best friend saw me out one evening when I'd told her I was babysitting. That caused a big fight too.

Answers: 1 (b), 2 (a), 3 (d)

So, communicating empathy is about understanding the importance of acknowledging and working with difference and diversity both in ourselves and in others, and working together to try to understand. It takes practice.

ACTIVITY

In everyday life, practise communicating empathy with family and friends. Try not to give advice or offer solutions.

1. Try to find a private space with no distractions and no risk of interruption.
2. Listen without interruption; let the person just talk.
3. Listen to the words but also how the words are communicated, such as the tone of voice and posture.
4. Be attentive; stay focused on what the person is saying. If your mind wanders, bring it back to what they are saying.
5. Concentrate on your breathing and allow yourself to relax.
6. Use facial expressions to let the person know you are paying attention.
7. Pause and imagine how the person might be feeling.
8. Reflect back to the person what you have heard.
9. Let the person know you understand.
10. Check with the person that your understanding is accurate.
11. Be respectful.

SUMMARY

In order to develop empathy as a helper, you need to:

- Understand the difference between empathy and sympathy.
- Work to understand difference and uniqueness in others.
- Challenge your own prejudices and stereotypes.
- Practise being able to communicate empathy.

4
Focusing on the Helpee's Needs and Concerns

This chapter is about focusing on what the helpee needs and wants from the helping session.

 This sounds like a very straightforward and simple thing to do but actually it can be quite tricky. When two people are in any kind of relationship, there are at least two sets of needs and wants, two sets of thoughts and feelings, and two sets of hopes, fears and expectations. In fact, of course, there are two sets of everything. In a helping relationship, the helper needs to find a way to bracket off their own feelings, desires and wants in order to be fully present for the helpee. It can be easy to confuse the helpee's wants, feelings and agenda with our own, and part of this chapter looks at how we can differentiate between the helpee's agenda and our own. We will also be exploring how to work with the helpee to meet their objectives once we understand what their needs are.

Let's begin in the usual way by looking at what the words in the title of this chapter mean:

* focus
* need
* concern.

FOCUS

Definition:

The centre of interest or activity;

The act of concentrating interest or activity on something.

Isn't focus also about being able to see clearly? For example, we need to focus if a page of writing is blurred, or if we are looking at something indistinct in the distance or perhaps looking at something very small and detailed.

That's actually a very clever way of thinking about focusing in a helping session. We do want to see and hear the helpee clearly and, in order to do so, we focus on them and block out everything else, including our own opinions and feelings, in order to get a very detailed and concise understanding of the helpee: this is a picture not blurred by outside influences.

Now let's think about need.

NEED

Definition:

Require (something) because it is essential or very important;

Circumstances in which something is necessary or requires some course of action.

Is a 'need' the same as a 'want'? I would have thought helping work was about the helpee being able to get what they want.

That's a very interesting observation. It could be said that a need is something that is essential to life, that we can't live without. If this were the case, the only needs we would have would be for air and sustenance when actually, as sentient beings, we have a wide range of needs, from the most basic need to survive to higher needs around self-esteem and achievement. Therefore, we have a wide range of needs and some of them could be considered 'wants'. A skilled helper can work with the helpee to identify what their needs really are and how they can get those needs met.

So, generally, a need is something *essential* and a want is something *desired* but there can be a cross-over between needs and wants.

Yes, I can see there are various levels of need and that some of the less basic needs could be seen as wants and, of course, it depends on the nature of the need. For example, I have a big car. This could be seen as a want because I have legs and therefore don't need a car as I could walk or catch public transport, but actually by having a car I am able to better manage my home and work–life balance. I could catch a bus to work but this might mean a very long journey which would be stressful and difficult. So actually, although my car is not essential to life, I need it to maintain my well-being and to manage my stress and responsibilities.

In 1943 Abraham Maslow first developed the idea of a 'hierarchy of needs', a concept that succinctly illustrates our various needs. His hierarchy can be shown in a triangle with the essential/fundamental needs at the bottom, followed by other types of needs. His central claim was that we need to meet our needs at each level before we can progress onto the one above. Only when all our needs are met, can we 'self-actualise' and be all that we can be and reach our full potential.

Maslow stated that although only the very bottom layer of needs was necessary to sustain life, the other needs were very important as until they are met a person will feel a degree of stress and worry. The more needs are met, the more a person will be motivated towards success and achievement. Maslow made clear distinctions between the various needs, as illustrated in Figure 4.1.

> **Physiological needs**: These are essential to survive. They consist of breathing, eating, drinking and basic physiological requirements like emptying your bladder! These are, of course, the most important, as without them we cannot survive. Therefore, these needs have to be met before any others.

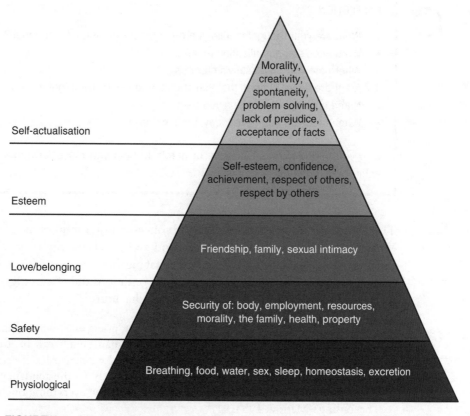

FIGURE 4.1 Maslow's hierarchy of needs

Safety needs: Once the physiological needs have been met, safety becomes a priority. These needs can include, for example, physical and emotional safety. It's no good talking to a refugee in a war zone about their lack of self-esteem when their primary need is safety.

Love and belonging: After physiological and safety needs are fulfilled, the third level of need focuses on love and belonging. It is very important to feel esteemed and wanted and to feel part of a group, culture or family.

Esteem: Once all these other needs have been met, we then need to feel respected and to respect ourselves, thus cultivating a sense of self-esteem and confidence. This can only be achieved when we feel safe and valued.

Self-actualisation: Once all the above needs are met, we are able to meet our potential and be all we are capable of being. Self-actualisation is different for each of us.

REFLECTION

- What are your thoughts/feelings around Maslow's hierarchy of needs?
- What does self-actualisation mean to you?
- Where are you on Maslow's hierarchy?
- Are there areas of need that you should address? How might you do this?
- Name a dream or ambition you have.
- What needs do you have today, both met and unmet?

Can you use Maslow's hierarchy of needs to help you move forward in order to achieve your dreams or ambitions?

There are some notable stories from the concentration camps of the Second World War where some prisoners gave their food away, even though they were starving themselves, and supported others while staying hopeful – some might even say 'happy' – despite the awful life-threatening conditions they faced every day. Given Maslow's theory, how can you explain this behaviour?

> Musicians must make music, artists must paint, poets must write if they are to be ultimately at peace with themselves. What human beings can be, they must be. They must be true to their own nature. This need we may call self-actualization... It refers to man's desire for self-fulfillment, namely to the tendency for him to become actually in what he is potentially: to become everything one is capable of becoming. (Maslow, 1954: 91)

Finally, let's look at what we mean by a concern.

CONCERN

Definition:

- a worry or problem
- an anxiety
- a matter of interest or importance to someone.

It is often someone's concerns which will lead them to seek help. A helpee will certainly have worries and/or problems that they need help in understanding and resolving. In some cases, their concerns can hinder them from meeting their needs. Therefore, it is important to explore the helpee's concerns and to understand how those concerns are impacting on the helpee's life and whether there is a link to any unmet needs.

PUTTING ASIDE OWN NEEDS

 So, to support the helpee I need to be able to almost step outside of my life and focus on the helpee's needs and concerns?

 Absolutely, and that can be quite tricky. Our day-to-day relationships and communications, especially in friendships, are a two-way street. We share our situation and feelings and hear how our friends are doing. Often, our feelings can be present and affect how we communicate without us even being aware of them! We need to become particularly aware of ourselves in order to ensure we do not act out our feelings while mistakenly believing that what we are doing is for the benefit of the helpee.

 If I'm not aware of how I'm feeling, how do I know if I am doing the wrong thing? This is getting really confusing now. I'm not sure I understand this at all. Maybe this type of work isn't for me.

 Interestingly, I can take what you just said and my initial response to it in order to learn a lot about my patterns of relating and how that might impact on our relationship. When I heard that you were confused and didn't understand, I felt responsible for your feelings and wanted to make you feel better. At this point, it is important for me to stop and think about whose feelings I am really trying to ease. Do I actually want to ease your feelings of confusion? Or do I want to make myself feel better because I feel incompetent and frightened that I am not communicating clearly? If I am very honest with myself, I can see that it is, in fact, my own feelings that I am looking after, which means the focus is on me rather than on you.

Let's look now at a couple of similar situations in helping work. I am the helper as part of my role in an HR department. A woman is very upset after being told she is on the short list for redundancy. She becomes very distraught and cries as she tells me she is a single parent with money problems and can't bear to lose her job. As a helper, my role is to listen to her concerns and work to empathise and understand her feelings; to walk alongside her in her hurt and fear. We all have different responses to others' grief. I might feel inadequate and not good enough and feel that listening and understanding are simply not enough. I might feel guilty that I have a job and hers is in jeopardy. I am likely to feel very uncomfortable and her pain may even put me in touch with my own pain and grief. If I am not aware of my feelings, there is a risk I could overstep the role of helper and engage in unhelpful patterns of relating.

I might, for example, try to make the helpee feel better. This is known as 'res-cuing' or 'fixing'. I could say things like, 'Don't cry. I'm sure your job will be OK.' This is very unhelpful on two counts. First, I am communicating to the helpee that crying is not OK; that I am unable to cope with her tears and grief; and that in some ways I am saying she shouldn't be crying. Second, I have no idea whether or not she will be made redundant. Helping work is about being with the helpee's feelings, whatever they might be. To share someone's pain has a powerful healing quality, but so often we think we have to change the feelings and make someone feel better, when actually our feelings are clear indicators of who and how we are.

So, if I look carefully at interaction, I can see that actually I am looking after my own feelings rather than the helpee's feelings. I can't bear my own feelings of discomfort, guilt and inadequacy, and it is those feelings that I am trying to soothe. I might also give advice to try to solve the situation and make myself feel better. Helping work is about facilitating a space where the helpee can find their own solutions – helpers don't need to solve other people's problems. As such, I don't need to make the helpee feel better. There is nothing wrong with their feelings exactly as they are. I don't need to change the subject when I feel out of control or uncomfortable.

tip

TOP TIPS

- You don't need to tell people what to do or talk about yourself and your experiences.
- You don't have to ask hundreds of questions to fill the silence.
- Sometimes you simply need to listen and understand, and accept that doing this is enough.

ACTIVITY

Sitting with other people's feelings invokes our own feelings. Part of the journey to becoming a helper is to learn to identify our own feelings and 'bracket' them off in order to focus fully on the helpee. Complete Table 4.1 by identifying how you feel in relation to someone else's feelings, what you think and what you do in relation to those feelings.

TABLE 4.1 Responses to helpee's feelings

Helpee's feeling	Your (helper's) feelings in response	Your (helper's) thoughts	Your (helper's) actions	Comments
Anger (example)	Fear, shock, resentment	I don't like this and don't know what to do. Be quiet and stop scaring me.	To rescue, offer platitudes, end session early, collude.	I felt frightened when the helpee started getting very angry about his wife leaving. It reminded me of my father's anger and how I hated it when he shouted and banged the table. I felt very small and frightened and just wanted him not to be angry.
Fear				
Sadness				
Resentment				
Guilt				
Joy				

(Continued)

(Continued)

Some spaces have been left for you to identify feelings you find difficult to be with and to listen to.

Once we are more aware, we are better equipped to stay focused on the helpee. We will become aware of the things that may lead us to lose focus and get side-tracked. Once we are able to focus on the helpee, we can work together to achieve the helpee's objectives.

Are objectives the same as needs and concerns?

OBJECTIVES AND GOALS

Objectives are what the helpee wants to achieve from the session. The helper needs to take the helpee's needs and concerns into consideration. If the helpee's concern is having no job and needing an income to pay outstanding debts, one of the helpee's objectives might be to find a job.

It can be useful for a helper to know some goal-setting techniques but it is very important to remember that it is not the helper's role to set goals for the helpee. The helper's role is to support the helpee to meet their goals by using active listening and a range of responding skills conducive, rather than coercive, to change. Sometimes a helping session is simply about being present with the helpee's feelings, and understanding and acknowledging where they are on their life's journey. Sometimes a helping session can be about providing a space for the helpee to come to terms with a situation or explore and reflect on pertinent issues in their life. Sometimes a helper is simply there to listen to the helpee get things off their chest.

The setting for the helping work can often influence the work itself. If the helper is in some kind of mentoring role, this can involve working with the helpee to set and achieve goals. The same could be said for people using helping skills in the workplace around performance and achievement. In settings such as health and social care where people may be a little more vulnerable and facing life-course difficulties, the helper's role is more likely to be around listening and offering a time and space for the helpee just to be.

Is it enough just to help the helpee identify their goals? Often, I know exactly what I want to do but for various reasons I just don't get around to it or can't seem to manage it. Let me give you a specific example: I have been trying to lose weight for my holiday. My goal is to lose a stone. I decided I wanted to lose a stone over a month ago and so far I've put on two pounds. I really do want to lose the weight, so I am very clear what my goal is but I am failing miserably and I don't know why.

 So how did you plan to meet your goal? It really helps to break the goal down into small bites (if you'll excuse the pun). If we set a huge goal, we often set up to fail, and this knocks our confidence and self-esteem.

SMART GOALS

One way of setting goals is to use the SMART method, as illustrated below:

S – Specific

M – Measurable

A – Attainable

R – Relevant

T – Time-bound

Specific

It is important to clearly state what the goal is. To get fit is very vague, whereas to walk for 20 minutes at a brisk pace three times a week is a clearly defined goal.

The SMART model asks us to consider three questions around the goal we are setting:

- WHAT are you going to do?
- WHY is this important to do at this time?
- HOW are you going to do it?

Measurable

If you can't measure it, you can't manage it. If the goal is not measurable, it can be difficult to know when it has been achieved. To get fit is not measurable, as fitness has many variables and levels. To be able to run 3 km without stopping is a measurable goal and also a goal that can be fitted in with a larger goal around lifestyle, fitness and well-being. By measuring progress, you maintain motivation and experience a sense of achievement that will encourage further achievements and accomplishments.

Attainable

Goals you set which are too far out of your reach set you up to fail. Although you may start with the best of intentions, the goal is doomed to failure from the outset. A goal needs to stretch you slightly so you feel you can do it but it will still need a real commitment from you. For instance, if you aim to lose 20 pounds in weight in one week, we all know that isn't achievable. If you set a goal to lose one pound and when you've achieved that, aim to lose a further pound, it will remain attainable.

Relevant

The goal needs to be relevant for you and your life as it is today. It needs to take into account your lifestyle, family and occupation. If you are a breast-feeding mother, for example, it is simply unrealistic and foolhardy to set yourself a diet regime. It is also unrealistic to set a strict lunch-time exercise regime if you are at home with toddlers all day. The goal needs to take these things into consideration to be effective and achievable.

Time-bound

Set a time limit for the goal: for next week or in three months, for example. Setting an end point gives you a clear target to work towards. If you don't set a time, the goal can tend to be put off and become the 'I'll start tomorrow' syndrome. It tends not to happen because you feel you can start at any time. Without a time limit, there's no urgency to start taking action.

THE GROW MODEL

Another useful goal-setting technique is the GROW model:

G – Goal

R – Reality

O – Options and obstacles

W – Will

Goal

The helper works with the helpee to identify and agree the goal. The SMART method outlined above can be used to identify an appropriate goal. Some helpful things to reflect on and explore together might be:

- What does the helpee want to achieve?
- How will the helpee know that they have achieved their goal, and what will the helpee's life look like when the goal has been achieved?
- Why does the helpee want to achieve the goal?

Reality

It is important for the helpee to be able to describe where they are right now and what their current reality is. The starting point is crucial to inform the journey ahead. The helpee can often gain clarity about what they need to do just by talking about and exploring their current life and situation.

The helpee might reflect on what is happening in their life right now:

- Who is in the helpee's life?
- What has the helpee done so far to achieve the goal?
- What is happening now for the helpee?

Options and obstacles

At this stage, the helper works with the helpee to identify and explore all the options they have and all the obstacles. The helper and helpee can work together to explore ways of overcoming the obstacles and explore what is possible – meaning all the many possible options for achieving the goal. It is important that the helpee is able to identify these things for themselves rather than the ideas coming from the helper.

Will

By examining current reality and exploring the options and obstacles, the way towards achieving the goal will become clearer. In order to meet any goal, motivation and commitment are important, and the helper can use active listening and responding skills to support the helpee in committing to the steps necessary to meet their objectives.

Goals can also be broken down into short-term, medium-term and long-term goals. A career goal might look like this:

- **Five-year goal**: Become manager of a department store.
- **One-year goal**: Volunteer for projects that the current manager is leading on.
- **Six-month goal**: Go to college to complete a business diploma.

- **One-month goal**: Apply for a permanent junior position.
- **One-week goal**: Identify the skills and qualities needed by the company.

The future looks more manageable when it is broken down into chunks.

ACTIVITY

Identify a goal for yourself. Is your goal:

Specific?

Measurable?

Attainable?

Relevant?

Time-bound?

- What is your current situation in relation to your goal?
- What is in the way of you meeting your goal?
- What are your options/obstacles?
- What do you need to achieve your goal?
- Whose help do you need?
- What motivates you to achieve your goal?
- How will you maintain your motivation?
- What will your life look like once your goal is achieved?

 OK, beach holiday here I come!

DON'T QUIT

When things go wrong, as they sometimes will,
When the road you're trudging seems all uphill,
When the funds are low and the debts are high,
And you want to smile, but you have to sigh,
When care is pressing you down a bit,
Rest, if you must, but don't you quit.
Life is queer with its twists and turns,
As every one of us sometimes learns,
And many a failure turns about,
When he might have won had he stuck it out;

Don't give up though the pace seems slow–
You may succeed with another blow.
Often the goal is nearer than,
It seems to a faint and faltering man,
Often the struggler has given up,
When he might have captured the victor's cup,
And he learned too late when the night slipped down,
How close he was to the golden crown.
Success is failure turned inside out–
The silver tint of the clouds of doubt,
And you never can tell how close you are,
It may be near when it seems so far,
So stick to the fight when you're hardest hit–
It's when things seem worst that you must not quit.
(Author unknown)

 It is useful for a helper to have some knowledge of goal-setting techniques but this is by no means a replacement for the relationship the helper forms with the helpee. A relationship built on trust, respect, understanding and acceptance is actually the greatest catalyst for change.

Less is often more in helping work. We need to learn to give the helpee space to explore and reflect and to allow a silence we would previously have filled with unnecessary words.

Personal development and self-awareness are an ongoing process which we will explore further in the next chapter. The more aware we become, the more we are able to focus on the helpee and their needs and concerns.

SUMMARY

In order to work with the helpee's needs and concerns, you need to:

- Be able to listen for what the helpee needs and wants.
- Resist the temptation to 'rescue' or make things better.
- Put aside your own thoughts, feelings and wants.
- Use techniques to assist the helpee to identify SMART goals.

5
Using Self-awareness in Helping Work

In the preceding chapters, we looked at establishing a safe, empathic helping relationship that meets the helpee's needs. Throughout these chapters, we have referred to the helper's feelings, thoughts and behaviours. We have looked at the importance of the helper recognising and responding appropriately to prejudices and stereotypes based on their own beliefs and value systems. As such, we are beginning to get a very clear picture that although the helping work is focused on the helpee's problems, issues and agenda, the helper also needs to be self-aware in order to be able to provide this safe empathic relationship.

> Your visions will become clear only when you can look into your own heart. Who looks outside, dreams; who looks inside, awakes. (Jung, 1973: 574)

ROLE OF SELF-AWARENESS

So what is meant by the term 'self-awareness'?

> Conscious knowledge of one's own character, feelings, motives, and desires. (*Oxford English Dictionary*)

So, self-awareness simply means knowing and understanding yourself. This sounds very simple but actually we often talk and behave in ways that we are not really conscious of much of the time. We do what we do without pausing to consider or reflect on why we do the things we do!

Are you saying that I don't really know what I'm doing? That's a bit worrying, really.

Not at all. Everyone has unknown parts of themselves. Freud's conception of the human psyche took the form of an iceberg. Only a small part of an iceberg can be seen above the water, which could be seen as the conscious mind. Much of the iceberg is below the water and could be seen as the unconscious mind. Raising self-awareness is a bit like working towards making more of the unconscious, conscious.

 Ah, that makes sense. When I think of icebergs, I think of the *Titanic* and how it sank because it hit an iceberg that couldn't be seen because it was underwater.

 Absolutely, and to learn from the *Titanic* we need to be careful of not banging into things we cannot see. Therefore, the more aware of ourselves we are, the less likely we are to capsize!

Another way of thinking about this is to imagine yourself as a house with many different rooms. It may be that we only live in a couple of the rooms and only go in the others very occasionally. Some of the rooms might not be used at all. If we imagine that the rooms are in various states of tidiness or repair, we can see self-awareness work as an exploration – a clean-up of all the rooms and parts of the house. Some rooms may need refurbishing – they might have been furnished by our ancestors. We can think of these rooms as being like the values and beliefs that have been handed down from previous genera-tions. They may not suit us any longer and we may need to clear out the old to make way for the new.

Some rooms may be very dimly lit. These may be the parts of our self that we know little about or are unable to see clearly. We may need to turn the light on and shine it into gloomy corners to learn more about these parts of ourselves. Only when we see clearly can we see if any repairs are needed or if things need to be rearranged.

Some rooms may be locked tightly or boarded shut. There may even be rooms in the house that we don't know about – a cellar, a hidden loft or roof space, a secret passage. These could be the hurt, wounded parts of ourselves that might contain a lot of painful and difficult feelings. We may not want to revisit these feelings but deep inside we know that there is a great freedom in facing our fears and hurts, and part of self-awareness and personal development work is opening these rooms and allowing them to see the light of day and be tenderly cared for. By doing so, we are instigating and allowing our own healing.

The windows in the house may be dirty. Perhaps we are not looking at things too clearly and our perception may be clouded. By cleaning the windows in the house of our psyche, we are removing old blocks and shadows from our view of the world. We can look at all parts of the house as parts of ourselves and can explore the house and make the changes we desire to support ourselves in feeling 'right at home' within our self.

Helping and counselling can be hugely beneficial when we think of the psyche in these terms. It can be frightening exploring a house that we don't know very well – a house that might feel scary and intimidating. We may be frightened of opening some doors and worried about what we will find behind them. A helper or counsellor can help us explore the house of ourselves in a safe, intimate relationship. We don't have to do the work all alone.

BECOMING MORE SELF-AWARE

So, how can I become more self-aware? I like to think that as a helper, and one day as a counsellor, I could form the type of relationship that would help someone else to explore their 'house of the self', as you put it, in 'a safe, intimate relationship'.

So, what do you think of when you reflect on the term 'safe, intimate relationship'?

I think of a close relationship, with trust, respect and understanding.

'Intimacy' is an interesting word and one that can really capture the nature of a helping/counselling relationship. The word actually comes from the Latin verb *intimare* (which means 'make known or announce') and the linked word *intimus* (which means 'inmost'). But here is another way of breaking this word down:

INTIMACY = 'INTO ME SEE'

Therefore, intimacy is about facilitating a space that is safe enough for someone to allow us to see who they really are. Part of being able to do this is about forming an intimate relationship with ourselves. We have to be willing to look within and learn about all the different parts and aspects of ourselves: the good, the bad and the downright ugly! Try the following activity to encourage your own self-awareness.

ACTIVITY

Reflect on the following statements in relation to yourself. Rather than just answer 'yes' or 'no', take some time to really reflect on the answer you give and what that means to you. As you respond, ask yourself 'why' you respond that way. Are you comfortable with your responses or would you rather respond differently in some situations? If you would rather respond differently, why don't you? Be aware of your

---

sensations and feelings as you ponder and explore these statements. It might also be useful to ask other people to consider the statements in relation to you. Do the responses match? Do other people view you as you view yourself?

There is no right or wrong way of responding to the statements. They are there simply to encourage you to take a look at who you are and how you react and respond to yourself and the world around you.

I question myself and why I do, say or think the things I do.

If someone is angry, I try to placate them.

When someone tells me a joke, I laugh even when I don't think it's funny.

I don't always say and do what I really want to for fear of upsetting other people.

I work hard to gain other people's approval.

I can generally identify and articulate what I am feeling.

I put other people's needs before my own.

I worry about what other people think of me.

I listen and attend to how I feel inside.

I enjoy looking at my reflection in a mirror.

I feel uncomfortable in new situations.

I know what I need to feel safe and peaceful.

Before dressing, I wonder if people will like what I am wearing.

I can tell others how I am feeling.

I know what I need to feel safe.

I can meet my own needs.

I know what I like and dislike.

I am critical of myself.

I have firm beliefs and opinions.

I can take an instant dislike to some people.

I go along with what others want to do.

I prefer email and text to phone calls and face-to-face meetings.

I copy how others behave.

I often feel lonely.

I am an angry person.

I don't get angry.

(Continued)

(Continued)

Take your time over this activity. Give yourself space to really consider each statement. Once you have finished, consider how you would feel sharing your reflections and responses with other people. If you feel you could not do this honestly, what stops you? What, if anything, would you most like to change about yourself?

 Some of those questions are really thought-provoking. I don't think I've ever really questioned why I do certain things. I know I find it hard to say 'no' to people but I had never stopped to think why I find that so hard.

 You are beginning to see that simply reflecting on your own personality increases your self-awareness.

JEANIE

Jeanie wrote the following entry in her reflective journal after completing the self-awareness exercise at college:

It feels a bit like a light switch has turned on. I am thinking about things differently and wondering why I do and say the things I do to certain people and in some situations. Like I said, I knew that I found it difficult to say 'no' but I never really questioned it. I just knew I often said 'yes' to things I didn't want to and then felt resentful. I think this goes a long way back for me. I grew up in quite an angry family and for most of my childhood I was never really given a choice. I just had to do what I was told, or else. I remember when I was about 8 my mum asked me to take the rubbish out and I said I didn't want to. She got really really angry with me and shouted and threatened to hit me. This didn't really bother me as I was used to her shouting and bawling. When she'd finished shouting though, she sat in the chair and cried and cried and said she couldn't cope anymore and wished she could just leave and not have to look after me all the time. I remember how awful I felt and also how frightened but most of all I felt guilty for being a burden and a nuisance. I am beginning to think that might have something to do with why I find it so hard to say 'no' now, because whenever I try and say 'no', I feel awful, just like back then – awful, frightened and guilty.

 You can see that Jeanie made a very important link between her past and present by reflecting on her personal history and this in turn increased her self-awareness. She stated that she felt she had to say 'yes' to people when really she wanted to say 'no', but her feelings prevented her from being true to herself at that moment. She then realised that this made her feel 'resentful'. 'Resentment' is an interesting word.

It can be said that resentment is like drinking poison and waiting for the other person to die. Let's look at the origins of this word, which comes from the French *ressentiment* (16th century), which in turn comes from *ressentir* (to re-send). Once again, when we break it down we find this meaning:

RESENTMENT = 'RE-SENT'

If something is 're-sent', it suggests it has been sent before. If we apply that to everyday life, perhaps we can understand resentment as something which reminds us of something difficult and challenging from the past that we were unable to resolve. It has been re-sent.

This is quite challenging ground for me. I am beginning to think there is a lot more to being a good helper than I imagined. I did not realise that so much of it would be about looking at myself – I thought it was about helping others to feel better.

I wonder if you are also saying that there is a lot more to you than you had imagined. Also, you are challenging your old beliefs around what you thought helping and counselling was about. It might be useful to stop and reflect on why you are actually interested in being a helper, on what has drawn you to this line of work.

REFLECTION

Take a little while to reflect on what has brought you here now and think about the following questions:

What decisions have you made that steered your ambition in this direction?

Why are you interested in helping others?

What role do you generally take in your personal relationships?

Why do you want to become a helper/counsellor?

What skills and qualities do you bring to the role?

What part of the work might you find challenging and/or difficult?

How do you feel about seeing a counsellor?

Where do you go for help and support?

It can be quite common for people in the helping/counselling field to put other people before themselves. Actually, to be a good counsellor it is essential to be able to look after yourself and meet your own needs. It is impossible to give from an empty vessel. An integral part of the work is around self-care. How do you care for yourself?

PAULA

Paula reflects in her journal on why she is drawn to this kind of work:

I have realised I have many reasons for wanting to help others. Initially, it was just because I thought that helping someone else was a good thing to do. Also, other people had said I give good advice, but actually I have now learnt that this work is not about giving advice. I do still want to help others but if I'm really honest there are other reasons too. There is a pay-off for me. When I help others, I feel good about myself. I feel a bit ashamed writing this but it's the truth, and also it feels good to be needed and appreciated. By discovering those things about me and other things about my patterns of relating, I have realised I need to do work on myself too and actually I feel quite excited by that. It reminds me of that saying in the *Star Trek* programme: 'To boldly go where no man [or woman] has gone before'. Oh, I just remembered another reason that supports my ambition to do this type of work: I'm a good listener and can listen for hours if someone has a problem.

BLOCKS TO LISTENING

Listening is without a doubt the most important skill in helping and counselling work, and self-awareness has an important role in our ability to listen effectively. To truly listen to someone else, we need to put our own thoughts and feelings to one side and this is very difficult. Also, we all have different blocks to our listening ability. Once we are aware of what our listening blocks are, we can work hard to overcome them.

ACTIVITY

Table 5.1 below is partially completed, listing a range of listening blocks. The list is split into two groups – 'internal' blocks and 'external' blocks, i.e. things inside us that get in the way of listening, and things outside of us that get in the way of listening.

Try to add something to each list and then tick the ones that most apply to you. Also, reflect on how you might address these blocks and overcome them.

TABLE 5.1 Blocks to listening

Internal blocks to listening	External blocks to listening
Personal feelings	Noise
Personal thoughts	Interruptions
You feel attracted to the person	Lack of privacy

Internal blocks to listening	External blocks to listening
Trying to think what to say next	The person looks different or unusual
Thinking of what advice you can give	The person reminds you of someone
Being judgemental	A threatening or unsafe environment
Feeling hungry or thirsty	The person has a heavy accent
Feeling too hot or too cold	The person speaks very quietly or loudly
Needing to go to the toilet	Something interesting is happening elsewhere
Not liking the person you are listening to	Nowhere to sit
Time pressures	Distractions
Should be somewhere else	Décor
Mind wandering	Insects
Mind reading	
The conversation triggers your personal memories	
The need to be right	
Rescuing and caretaking	

I think my biggest blocks are my own thoughts and feelings. Also, I am often thinking about what to say next to the person, trying to think up something interesting, amusing or clever to say or something to make them feel better. I'm not sure what some of the blocks are. For example, what do 'rescuing' and 'caretaking' mean?

It means to do something for someone that they need to do for themselves. It means being overly responsible or taking responsibility for other people inappropriately. It means trying to make someone feel better when actually they have a right to feel exactly how they feel, no matter how sad or painful that might be. It means being unable to sit with someone's feelings and rushing to try to 'fix' the situation to ease your own discomfort. It means feeling inadequate just being with someone and not knowing, and so trying to force a solution or outcome.

There is a big difference between caretaking and care-giving. As helpers and counsellors, our aim is to be care-givers – NOT caretakers and rescuers.

Is there something wrong in trying to make someone feel better?

It's not really about that. It's more about exploring why we respond the way we do. For example, let's imagine someone is feeling devastated after a bereavement, betrayal or separation. How could we make that person feel better? We simply do not have the power to reverse the abandonment, bereavement or betrayal. We do not have the power to make things right. What we can do is be with someone and be by their side as they walk through their pain and grief and confusion. We can walk at their pace, neither rushing ahead nor holding back. So, why do we try to make someone feel better? Often, when we listen to someone who is in great distress, we feel uncomfortable; we may be reminded of and in touch with our own hurts, or our own feelings of fear and inadequacy might be triggered, and we react by 'rescuing' the person we're listening to.

Oh, so really we are being quite selfish doing that and really we are trying to make ourselves feel better.

ACTIVITY

This is what Carla wrote when reflecting on her feelings when her sister's marriage ended:

I remember my sister being heartbroken when her marriage ended. She would just sit and sob and, to be honest, I couldn't bear it. I hated feeling so powerless and useless. I was frightened she would do something silly. I felt useless and also a bit embarrassed, if I'm honest, and I also felt guilty in a way because I was in a happy marriage and she wasn't. I said all sorts of things to try and make her feel better: 'you're worth more than him', 'he will regret this', 'what goes around comes around', 'don't cry', 'your future will be better and brighter', 'you're better off without him', 'he is a fool', 'he's mad', 'you will be OK', 'he's not worth crying over', 'good riddance', 'he'll be back'. My goodness, I came out with them all!

Look at the statements she made and give them a reality check:

- How do you measure worth? How did Carla arrive at the fact that her sister's worth is greater than her husband's?
- How does she know her husband will regret his decision?
- Is she sure that what goes around comes around?
- What's wrong with her sister crying?

- Does she have a crystal ball? Is that how she knows her sister's future will be better and brighter?
- Is her sister really better off without him? Her distress suggests differently.
- Is her husband a mad fool? How do you know and by what authority can you make this judgement?
- Is she sure her sister will be OK?
- Her husband is obviously worth crying over, because her sister is crying.
- Are you sure her husband will be back? Is he 'the Terminator'?

 So you can see that it is very easy to make a whole number of statements that actually mean very little. They may fix the situation for a second but that is all. Sometimes grieving and hurting are like big gaping wounds. By 'rescuing', we are slapping plasters over the wounds, plasters of false promises and hope, plasters of platitudes, plasters of unasked-for advice, plasters of cups of tea, cake and alcohol, plasters of all sorts of things. The plasters cover up the wound but unless it is allowed to breathe and heal, it becomes infected and throbs and hurts beneath all the plasters and so we pile more and more plasters on and the infection spreads. Helping and counselling work is not about covering up the wound and pretending it is not there. It is about protecting the wound and very slowly and carefully removing the plasters, some of which could be years and years old. Once the plasters are removed, the wound is very gently cleaned and the hurts and fears are processed and understood and released. The wound is exposed and this is very frightening, but once it is cleaned it will heal naturally. There may always be a scar and this scar is a reminder to be careful around that area – but the gaping, open wound is gone.

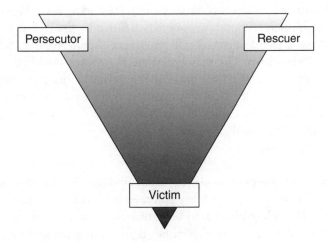

FIGURE 5.1   Karpman's drama triangle

I like that analogy. I also understand that when I 'rescue' or try to 'fix' a situation I am actually attending to my own feelings ahead of the other person's. This is fine, I think, and a natural part of everyday friendships and relationships, but helping and counselling work is about focusing on the other person's feelings first.

So you can see how self-awareness informs our helping work on many levels. There is a very useful model (in Figure 5.1) which links in with three roles we often adopt in our relationships and interactions with each other. It is commonly known as the *drama triangle* and was described by Stephen Karpman in 1968.

DEFINITIONS OF THE ROLES IN THE DRAMA TRIANGLE

Rescuer: The message of the Rescuer could be 'I'm good'. Rescuers tend to do more than their fair share of the work and often offer help without being asked. They do what they think is needed, rather than asking what someone needs. The Rescuer can end up feeling hard done by and resentful. They may feel their help is not appreciated. The Rescuer is actually taking responsibility for others rather than themselves. A Rescuer may feel they are not worthy of being loved and so try to make themselves indispensable and therefore needed. As the Rescuer feels more and more resentful and hard done by, they can end up slipping into the Victim or Persecutor roles. The Rescuer will always end up feeling the Victim, but sometimes may be perceived by others, who are on the outside looking in, as being the Persecutor.

Victim: The message of the victim could be 'I am blameless and helpless'. The Victim feels unable to take responsibility for themselves and feels powerless and inadequate. They feel unable to cope or manage their life and look to apportion blame for their situation to others. They look for a Rescuer to help them. They might then feel let down or overwhelmed by the Rescuer and could move into the Persecutor role, but will still experience themselves internally as being the Victim.

Persecutor: The message of the Persecutor could be 'I am right' and this gives them a sense of power over others. Although the Persecutor can appear powerful, they are actually unaware of and unable to use their own personal power. Either way, the power used is negative and often destructive. They try to get their needs met by force and coercion.

To remedy this:

- The **Rescuer** needs to take responsibility for themselves, and acknowledge their own vulnerability and their own difficult and challenging feelings.
- The **Victim** needs to recognise their own power and ability and take responsibility for themselves rather than waiting for someone else to do it for them.
- The **Persecutor** needs to believe they can meet their needs without force and be able to own their power without abusing it.

DRAMA TRIANGLE

- Identify a relationship where you find yourself slipping into the role of Victim, Rescuer or Persecutor.
- Describe the situation and who was involved.
- How could you manage this differently?
- What role do you tend to take on in your relationships?

 I definitely take on the Rescuer role and then slip into others. I had a friend who used to ring me just about every day to talk about her problems. I listened and gave advice and was always available. I offered to look after her children and go along to appointments with her. I never said 'no' and then I started to feel resentful that she never asked about me. I didn't want to rescue her any more but I just couldn't say 'no'. I can see now that I had slipped into the Victim role. I really didn't like this person and would ask my partner to answer the phone and say I wasn't available. I actually felt persecuted by the person I started off trying to help.

 It's interesting that you portrayed yourself differently to the friend you mentioned, to your partner and to yourself. We can learn a great deal about ourselves and the masks we wear by talking to others about how they perceive us. The activity below is helpful in doing this.

ACTIVITY

	Known to self	Not known to self
Known to others	Open	Blind
Not known to others	Hidden	Unknown

FIGURE 5.2   The Johari window

(Continued)

(Continued)

The Johari window is a model created by Joseph Luft (Jo) and Harrington Ingham (Hari) in 1955 for mapping the known and unknown parts of ourselves. It is useful for looking at how others see us and whether that matches what we think about ourselves. As such, it is a valuable personal development tool. There are four areas to the Johari window:

The OPEN area is known to both self and others.

The BLIND area is known to others but not to self.

The HIDDEN area is known to self but not to others.

The UNKNOWN area is not known to self or others.

To participate in this activity, look at the list of 56 adjectives listed below and pick five or six that you feel describe your personality. Ask people you know from different areas of your life, such as friends, family and colleagues, to pick out words that describe you.

TABLE 5.2   Characteristics of self

able	extroverted	mature	self-assertive
accepting	friendly	modest	self-conscious
adaptable	giving	nervous	sensible
bold	happy	observant	sentimental
brave	helpful	organised	shy
calm	idealistic	patient	silly
caring	independent	powerful	smart
cheerful	ingenious	proud	spontaneous
clever	intelligent	quiet	sympathetic
complex	introverted	reflective	tense
confident	kind	relaxed	trustworthy
dependable	knowledgeable	religious	warm
dignified	logical	responsible	wise
energetic	loving	searching	witty

You then map these adjectives onto the Johari window:

Place the adjectives chosen by you and others in the open area.

Place the ones that only you picked in the hidden area.

Place the ones picked by others but not by you in the blind area.

All the other adjectives are placed in the unknown area. These represent our potential.

Reflect on the following questions:

Do the views of other people match your own?

Do you behave differently (wear a mask) with different groups of people such as friends, family and colleagues?

If you do act differently, why do you think this is?

Who can you be most yourself with?

What stops you being yourself?

 Well, we have looked at how reflecting on our own personality, our relationships and our patterns of relating increase our self-awareness. We have also acknowledged how important self-awareness is in helping work. Self-awareness is an ongoing process. It is a journey and there are always unchartered places to find and explore. With self-awareness, the emphasis should be on the journey rather than the destination.

CRITICAL THINKING

Consider the following quotations:

Once a thing is known it can never be unknown. (Brookner, 1983: 5)

Ignorance is bliss. (Gray, 1771: 12)

Only by much searching and mining are gold and diamonds obtained, and man can find every truth connected with his being if he will dig deep into the mine of his soul. (Allen, 2013: 7)

- Is it always a good thing to know more about yourself?
- What might be the risks of self-awareness?

SUMMARY

- Self-awareness is essential in helping work.
- Lack of self-awareness blocks the ability to listen or put others' needs first.
- Specific tools like the Johari window can prompt greater self-awareness.
- Without self-awareness, there is danger of unconsciously acting out unhelpful patterns of behaviour.

6
Using Counselling Skills

This chapter is about the nuts and bolts of helping work. Here, we will look at the counselling skills necessary to be a helper and facilitate the helping interaction. These counselling skills provide the tools for working with helpees, as well as providing a solid platform for counselling work.

 To further understand the role of these skills, let's explore what the word *facilitate* means. To facilitate simply means to make something happen; to assist the smooth progress of something.

   This is exactly what a helper does: by using a range of appropriate listening and responding skills a helper enables the helpee to reflect on themselves and their life, get clearer about their problems and identify better ways of coping.

LISTENING AND RESPONDING SKILLS

Paying attention to someone is such an important act. It conveys respect and positive regard. To pay full attention to someone communicates a sense of valuing and being interested in who they are and what they have to say. In order to pay attention to someone, we need to listen. Listening is without doubt the most important skill. At first, it may seem that listening is very easy – it's something we do every day – but actually to truly listen to someone else is very challenging. As we learnt earlier in the book, many things can block the ability to listen and be attentive to another person.

LISTEN

When I ask you to listen to me

And you start giving me advice,

You have not done what I asked.

When I ask you to listen to me
And you begin to tell me 'why' I shouldn't feel that way,
You are trampling on my feelings.
When I ask you to listen to me
And you feel you have to do something to
solve my problems,
You have failed me, strange as that may seem.
Listen! All I ask is that you listen;
Not talk, nor do – just hear me.
And I can do for myself – I'm not helpless
Maybe discouraged and faltering, but not helpless.
When you do something for me, that I can
and need to do for myself,
You contribute to my fear and weakness.
But when you accept as a simple fact that I do feel what I feel,
No matter how irrational
Then I quit trying to convince you
And can get about the business of understanding
What's behind this irrational feeling?
When that's clear,
The answers are obvious and I don't need advice.
Irrational feelings make sense when we
Understand what's behind them.
Perhaps that's why prayer works sometimes for
some people;
because God is mute, and doesn't give
advice to try to 'fix' things,
. . . just listens, and lets you work it out
for yourself.
So please listen, and just hear me, and if you
want to talk,
Wait a minute for your turn,
And I'll listen to you.
(Anonymous)

This poem was written by a mental health patient who was institutionalised over a number of years in Queensland, Australia. He wishes to remain anonymous.

His words acknowledge that simply listening is sometimes enough. No clever interventions or suggestions or useful pieces of advice can take the place of simply and truly listening to someone and accepting what they have to say without opinion or judgement.

ACTIVITY

Tick the responses in Table 6.1 that best apply to you.

TABLE 6.1   Myself as a listener

QUESTIONS	RESPONSES			
	Nearly always	Often	Occasionally	Almost never
1. Do you get bored listening to something that doesn't interest you?				
2. Do you only pretend you are listening to someone speaking when, in fact, your mind is far away?				
3. Do you pretend to listen and make appropriate noises and gestures when you aren't really listening?				
4. Do you concentrate on what the person looks like rather than what is said?				
5. Do you want people to hurry up so that you can say something?				
6. Do you continue doing other things while listening – writing, typing, reading, etc.?				
7. Is your attention easily distracted, e.g. by phone ringing, external noise?				
8. Do you take notes while listening?				
9. Can you easily remember what someone has said to you hours later?				
10. Do you think some people have nothing interesting or useful to say?				
11. Do you talk over people?				
12. Do you look at the person who's talking?				
13. Do you interrupt others?				
14. If your emotions are affected by the conversation, does this affect your ability to listen?				

QUESTIONS	RESPONSES			
	Nearly always	Often	Occasionally	Almost never
15. Do you find it easier to listen to people you like?				
16. Do you find it difficult to listen to people who appear not to like you?				
17. Do people have to remind you of things they have asked you to do?				
18. Do you forget traffic directions?				
19. Do you change the subject of conversation when someone is talking?				
20. Do you forget names easily?				
21. Do you find it difficult to sit or stand in one spot for more than two minutes?				
22. Do your thoughts race?				
23. Do you have to ask people to repeat themselves often?				
24. Do you have a very busy life?				

This activity will raise your awareness of yourself as a listener and identify areas of growth.

 I understand that being able to truly listen is very difficult and there are lots of things that can get in the way of doing so, but I don't understand why listening is seen as a skill and why it's so important. I listen every day. It's not really a new skill.

 Perhaps attentive and active listening is a new skill. To focus on another as much as possible is a constant area of growth even for the most experienced counsellors, helpers and therapists. It's interesting that you wonder why it's important. What might be the reasons why listening is so important? Imagine someone is listening to you, really listening, and is interested in what you are saying. How does that feel?

 I think I would feel valued, important.

 Exactly; you would be aware of a sense of worth. Being listened to also helps us to listen to ourselves; it can afford a sense of clarity. Sometimes just talking things through brings a greater understanding of a problem or situation. Listening carefully lays the foundations of a respectful, trusting relationship. Listening can allow the helpee to talk through, understand and release challenging emotions, thereby reducing tension. It can also encourage more information to surface and support problem solving.

I hadn't thought of listening as being important at all. I also think I would feel more focused if I felt listened to. If I'm talking and think I'm not being listened to, I tend to repeat myself over and over and rush what I'm saying. I guess I'm trying to fit everything in before the person listening loses interest completely.

I think what you are saying is that being truly listened to is a rare thing and also that if you feel heard and valued, you feel held and contained. Perhaps a useful image here is of a mother soothing a baby, holding the baby close. But actually listening – and communicating to the other person that you are listening – are not the same thing. Communicating that you are listening requires additional skills.

This can be done verbally or non-verbally. Actually, non-verbal communication is the majority of all communication. Therefore, listening and feeling listened to consist of much non-verbal communication. We do this through our body posture and movements, our facial expressions and small gestures and movements.

ACTIVITY

If you were talking to someone, which of the statements below would make you feel you were being listened to?

TABLE 6.2 Non-verbal communication

1. Fidgets	16. Looks alert
2. Has a calm manner	17. Smiles
3. Leans far back	18. Sits higher than you
4. Has head very close to yours	19. Shuts eyes
5. Takes notes	20. Has a high-pitched voice
6. Looks towards you	21. Leans slightly towards you
7. Sits on same level as you	22. Looks clean
8. Picks nose	23. Has a comfortable speech pace
9. Waves arms	24. Has a low-pitched voice
10. Nods	25. Has body posture open to you
11. Stares at you	26. Shuffles about
12. Looks out of window	27. Has vacant look
13. Has relaxed seating position	28. Has warm voice
14. Slouches	29. Whispers
15. Raises eyebrow	30. Looks anxious

> Pay careful attention. Some seem very straightforward but are actually quite tricky. For example, 'smiling' seems a very positive way of conveying attentive listening but if you were talking about something very sad, someone's smiling would actually convey that they weren't listening.

Messages can be communicated through movement and touch, body language or posture, physical distance, facial expression and the nature or degree of eye contact. These are all types of non-verbal communication. The way you speak also contains important information which you convey by your tone of voice, pitch, volume and accent, as well as how you stress certain words more than others.

In helping work, some non-verbal communication can take the form of *minimal encouragers*. This literally means to do as it says – to use minimal/little gestures (or encouragers) to let the helpee know they are being listened to and to encourage them to continue talking without actually interrupting them.

Would this consist of things like nodding, smiling, head tilting, saying 'hmm'?

Exactly; they are little ways that acknowledge listening, understanding and interest. There is a very simple acronym that a helper can keep in mind to enable them to remember to focus, attend and listen carefully to the helper. A useful acronym for remembering different aspects of non-verbal communication is SOLERB.

SOLERB

Suggestions for when seated:

Sit	**S**traight towards the other person
	Open body posture (arms unfolded, feet flat on the floor)
	Lean forwards occasionally
Offer	**E**ye contact (appropriately)
Be	**R**elaxed, don't fidget (check shoulders are not tense or hunched)
	Breathe (check you aren't holding your breath)

By using SOLERB, you will convey to the helpee a warm, non-intrusive interest in what they are saying. It will also communicate an interest in hearing more.

LISTENING PRACTICE

Hone your listening skills by using and reflecting on this activity as regularly as possible. You can practise on friends, family, colleagues and acquaintances. Make a note of any comments you receive.

For five minutes, commit to just listening to someone. Use only minimal encouragers and non-verbal communication. Use SOLERB.

When there is a silence or the person pauses and seems stuck for what to do or say next, what do you want to do? Do you feel a need to fill the space? How do you feel about silence? Are you comfortable doing and saying nothing? Once you have done this a few times, allow yourself to reply/respond but keep to the following rules:

During the listening activity, you can say absolutely anything – except you cannot:

- give advice
- try to make someone feel better by offering platitudes
- rescue or try to fix the situation
- ask any questions
- talk about yourself.

Acknowledge and reflect on how it felt to do these activities and how challenging it was for you.

How did you get on with that activity?

Hmm, I think I am beginning to realise how hard it is to really listen and how I very rarely listen. I seem to get myself involved in conversation even when I'm trying not to. I realise how much time is spent on my own agenda.

SILENCE

How did you feel when the helpee stopped talking and there was a silence?

I really wanted to ask a question or say something, anything to fill the space. I felt very awkward and uncomfortable and also inadequate because I felt the helpee was waiting for me to say or do something. I did notice that the helpee went on to talk further 'though' and this seemed to open up the conversation and move it in some ways to a deeper level.

EXAMPLE

When Sonny was little, he played a game with his brother called 'Blindfold'. The two boys were blindfolded and had a sort of race to see who could go the furthest before stopping. This was so nerve-wracking that after a few steps Sonny would almost wince as he moved forward, waiting to encounter some block or hindrance. He would feel scared and his heart would beat fast. When he was asked to try out the listening activity, in a strange way he felt it was a bit like the blindfold game. Both he and the helpee sat in silence and he really wanted to speak because he found it so uncomfortable, but he stayed with the silence and actually doing so supported the helpee to open up and get in touch with their feelings and begin to explore and process what was happening for them, their feelings, thoughts and situation.

The spaces between words are highly significant in any counselling conversation. In these spaces a client may be engaged in a process of experiencing an unfolding of feelings or memories, they may be reflecting on the meaning or implications of something that has just been said or felt, or they may be desperately struggling to find some way to avoid talking about something that is in their awareness but which is too hard to put into words at that precise moment. (McLeod and McLeod, 2011: 62)

Silence may also be a way of helping a client or helpee to 'focus' when their thoughts and feelings are scattered. (Mearns, 1997: 114)

 So, it is just as important for the helpee to listen to the silence as well as the words. Silence has other benefits too. It can slow down the pace. Often, minds are full of thoughts, worries, ideas and a myriad of other random things, all whizzing and whirling around. Silence can sometimes simply slow all that down, allowing space for reflection and clear thinking. Silence allows us to feel, which in turn broadens our understanding and awareness. At other times, it is simply a space to be with each other. After all, we are human 'beings', rather than human 'doings'.

 I will remember that and just keep my mouth shut and pause every time I want to say something.

CRITICAL THINKING

Being able to deal with silence is generally regarded as a useful counselling skill but an individual's personal history will often determine their reaction to silence. Consider the following scenarios and imagine what silence might mean to each of the following individuals:

(Continued)

(Continued)

- Carl grew up in a small house with seven siblings and never had his own room.
- Sarah's parents argued and shouted at each other throughout her childhood.
- Dawn's parents never argued, but when they were not getting on whole days would pass without either parent speaking directly to the other.
- Clem was diagnosed with dyslexia at school and dreaded the moment when the teacher would ask him a question in front of the whole class.
- Pete was an only child and happy with his own company. When he got into trouble, his dad would shut the door of his study and deliver the inevitable tirade, ending with the question 'What have you got to say for yourself?'

Research shows that young people are often more uncomfortable with silence than adults. Why might this be the case? Some useful questions to consider are:

- Who initiates conversations with children and when does this change?
- How do young adults make the transition to adult-to-adult communication?
- What is the balance of power at each stage of a young person's development?
- Is the power balance ever equal between a parent and their adult child?
- How is this relevant to future relationships between individuals and authority figures?

PRACTISING SILENCE

Find a place and a space in the day where you can sit undisturbed for 15 minutes with no distractions or interruptions. Just sit quietly for 15 minutes. Ensure the TV etc. is turned off and do nothing at all. Simply sit in the silence. Be mindful of your thoughts and feelings and bodily sensations.

Once the 15 minutes have elapsed, reflect on what you found in the silence. Try to capture your experience via a creative medium:

- Paint or draw your silence.
- Make a mind map of your silence.
- Make a collage or sculpture of your silence.

What was in the silence for you? Work on your relationship with silence. Who or what is silence for you? How do you feel towards it? What could improve or deepen your relationship with silence?

So far, we've looked at all the things not to ask or say in a helping session. Let's now look at the skills we *can* use in a helping session.

REFLECTION

The skills of reflection can be divided into the helper reflecting 'meaning' and reflecting 'feeling'. Let us look at reflecting feeling first.

Sometimes it's important to pick up on those of the helpee's feelings which have not actually been put into words. The helpee might say how they are feeling but they might communicate it through body language, facial expression or in the content of what they are saying.

Reflection is when the helper communicates how they think the helpee is feeling back to them. Reflection recognises emotions in others. For example, the helpee rushes in, laughing, saying, 'I've had the greatest day', and sits down smiling broadly.

Reflection: You seem so excited and happy!

This response shows that you have paid attention to the helpee's behaviour and included it in your response. The helpee knows that you are paying close attention to them.

ACTIVITY

In the following examples, choose the response from (a) to (c) which is a 'reflection'.

1. The helpee comes into the room and sits down. They do not look at you but stare down at their knees, frowning.

    (a) You look troubled.
    (b) Hi, are you OK?
    (c) I am ready to hear what you want to say.

2. You work in a nursery school and a colleague, Patti, comes to offload in your office after a very busy day. It is 5pm and most of the children have been picked up. Patti looks exhausted.

    (a) How are you feeling?
    (b) You look like you could do with a rest.
    (c) You need to take good care of yourself tonight.

(Continued)

(Continued)

3. Your daughter Sara comes home from school looking very disappointed and low. She has to re-write an assignment she thought she had done well.

   (a) Tell me what the teacher said.
   (b) You're upset and feel all your work is for nothing.
   (c) Do you want to talk about it?

Answers: 1 (a), 2 (b), 3 (b)

Keep in mind that your response doesn't have to be perfect. If you guess wrongly about the helpee's feelings, they will tell you. The important thing is to listen closely and reflect back what you pick up, keeping the focus on the person's emotions and demeanour.

Reflection also takes place when the helper communicates their understanding of the helpee's meaning behind what they have been saying. In this case, the helper is recognising what they have heard.

 So, sort of clarifying what I have understood?

 Yes. For example, the helpee tells you that they are having difficulty claiming on their household insurance after damp appeared in the kitchen.

Reflection: Your kitchen has got damp and you are having difficulty claiming on your insurance.

Not all counselling skills books define reflection in the same way. Some books will consider the skills of reflection as just reflecting 'feeling'. In any case, reflection always means sensitively and carefully reflecting back to the helpee in a few words the key message of what they are communicating, either verbally or in their body language. Sometimes a reflection is about using the exact word(s) the helpee has just used. This is also sometimes called 're-stating'.

Helpee: I am just so angry about it.
Reflection: You're just so angry. (reflecting feeling)
Helpee: Whatever the ins and outs, it was not my fault.
Reflection: You believe it's not your fault. (reflecting meaning)

 Doesn't this make me sound a bit like a parrot?

Well, you're right, it can do! This is why it is a skill that must be used very sparingly and sensitively. At its best, it shows the helpee you have heard them; it avoids the risk of any kind of misinterpretation; it does not interrupt their flow; and it offers an opportunity for the helpee to expand on what they have said without getting side-tracked. Try it for yourself!

PARAPHRASING

Paraphrasing, in its simplest form, means taking the content of what the helpee has said and feeding it back to them using your own words. The challenging part of this is being able to do so without changing what the helpee has said by bringing your own thoughts and feelings into it.

 Sounds easy … but it also seems a bit pointless. What's the point of just rewording what someone has said? I would just get annoyed if someone only kept telling me what I have just told them.

 So, it seems a bit of a waste of time just saying the same things back, something you would find irritating?

 That's exactly it, so what is the point … hmm, but was your response an example of paraphrasing?

 Yes, it was. Does it still seem completely pointless or can you think of any possible benefits?

 I think I'd have to have been listening very carefully to feed back accurately what the helpee had said.

 Yes, indeed. Therefore, paraphrasing would help the person feel listened to and valued. It also shows why it's important to capture the spirit of what has been said but use your own words to say it back. Can you think of any other benefits?

 I think paraphrasing would help me clarify a situation; help me get things straight in my mind. It might also be like hearing myself speak and that would help me understand a situation better. I guess I'd feel understood and that would strengthen the helpee–helper relationship.

 Yes. Another benefit is that the helpee could correct the helper if they had mis-understood or misheard.

ACTIVITY

From the following examples, select the best 'paraphrase'. The object is not to select the most effective response (which may be empathic or a good question) but simply to decide on the most accurate paraphrase.

1. I wish I didn't find it so difficult to concentrate on my homework but my mum has to go to hospital today for tests and I can't help worrying about her all the time.

    (a) You don't want to do homework when you're feeling so worried about her.
    (b) We can't afford to have people at school who aren't prepared to work.
    (c) You'd like some time off while your mother's ill.
    (d) You're terrified that your mother might be seriously ill.
    (e) Try concentrating and then you can forget about her while you're here. Worry doesn't do her any good.
    (f) You feel pulled between your loyalty to school and your loyalty to her.
    (g) I know what it's like – I felt the same when my child was in hospital.
    (h) Worrying about your mother makes it difficult to give your mind to the work.

2. I have to give a talk to a big crowd tonight and I'm terrified of messing it up and making an idiot of myself. I really want to phone and say there's been an emergency but I know I will hate myself and get in trouble if I do.

    (a) You're angry you've been put on the spot to do this talk.
    (b) You can do this, I know you can. Have some rescue remedy beforehand and then just go for it.
    (c) I think you are worrying too much. It is only a talk. You can do this.
    (d) You're feeling very nervous about this evening's talk. You're tempted to cancel it but there would be negative consequences if you did.
    (e) Do you want me to phone up your boss and make an excuse for you?
    (f) I felt just the same when I had to speak in church; it was awful, I really understand.
    (g) This makes it difficult for you to believe that you can get through this. It's very very challenging for you.

3. My best friend tells me that my boyfriend back home is going out with another girl, but he denies it. He says he's longing for me to be home.

    (a) It's very difficult for you to know who to believe.
    (b) You just can't trust men, can you?
    (c) You feel hurt and confused by the different stories you are hearing.
    (d) Your boyfriend is a liar.
    (e) What do you expect if you live so far from home?
    (f) You are frightened that you are being betrayed by someone you care for.
    (g) Your friend and boyfriend are telling you conflicting things.

4. I hate my best friend's husband. He's really creepy. He keeps trying to kiss me and making suggestive comments. I don't know whether to tell her or not. I'm scared I'll lose her friendship if I tell her but I'd want to know if it were me. He's the same with other friends. Maybe ignorance is bliss because she has no idea he's like that, but should I be the one to burst her bubble? It's an awful situation.

   (a) I would talk to him first if I were you. Tell him you will tell her if he doesn't stop.
   (b) You find this man repugnant and disgusting and hate him for what he's put your friend through.
   (c) You are frightened and unhappy.
   (d) Are you doing something to make him think you find him attractive?
   (e) It's so unfair that you are in this dreadful situation.
   (f) It's a dreadful situation to be in, isn't it?
   (g) You're trying to weigh up the advantages and disadvantages of telling your friend about her husband's inappropriate behaviour.
   (h) It sounds like there have been a lot of problems for you lately.

Answers: 1 (h), 2 (d), 3 (g), 4 (g)

As you can see, paraphrasing is about accurately capturing the content of what the helpee has said, without the helper's opinion, agenda or interpretations coming into play.

SUMMARISING

Summarising is collecting all the main points of a conversation and putting them together in a brief summary which also reflects the balance of what's been said. This is often done at the end of a helping session to bring the session to a close. It covers the main points of the session and has the same value and benefits as paraphrasing. In some ways, a summary is a 'daddy' paraphrase. As with all responding skills, it is important to check out what you have said with the helpee to ensure you have got it right.

Summarising can be used periodically throughout a helping session if a number of different topics have been mentioned. It can be used to help bring things together, to simplify them and make them manageable.

Summarising is also useful in assisting the helpee decide what's important for them to talk about in the helping session. A good summary can focus the helpee, as they may begin the helping session by talking about a lot of different things.

> **EXAMPLE**
>
> Helpee: I've had a really awful day. When I got up the dog had been sick on the floor and then the children wouldn't get up and I ended up shouting my head off. I was feeling so cross I reversed the car into the gate post. My dad will go crazy, as I still owe him money for the car. My relationship with my dad's hard enough as it is. I hate being on my own bringing up children. It wouldn't be so bad if their dad would help pay for things but he's busy having fun. I've got no money to pay for the school trips coming up and I hate my job but can't leave because I need the money.
>
> Helper: There's a lot going on. You've mentioned the challenges in some of your relationships, your children, their father and your father. You spoke about how your anger and stress affect your life. You also talked about money worries and your job. Which one of those would you like to talk about today?
>
> This response acknowledges all that has been said and gives the helpee the choice to talk about what's important to them. It's important that the helper does not choose the topic to focus on.

But in that example I would have thought that the children's father would be the most important thing to talk about. If he pulled his weight, a lot of the other problems would disappear.

That's how you see it and maybe that touches on your personal history but it is not for us to decide what's important; only the helpee can do that. In the example above, after making a brief summary, the helper asked a question.

You said earlier not to ask any questions in a helping session.

That was for that particular activity. Questions can be a very valuable skill but they need to be used wisely. They also need to be asked for the helpee's benefit and not for the helper's. Sometimes a helper could ask questions out of curiosity or because they just don't know what else to do. Sometimes questions are used as a way of managing silence or uncomfortable pauses. There are many different types of questions but we will focus on two types: closed questions and open questions.

CLOSED QUESTIONS

Closed questions are those that can be answered with one word or phrase or a platitude. They are a conversation stopper. They are very useful for fact and information gathering. Doctors, interviewers and police are groups of people likely to use a lot of closed questions. Closed questions are mainly about what the person asking the question wants or needs to know. Therefore, they would generally come from the helper's agenda. Some closed questions can be useful in a helping session for clarifying a situation or clarifying understanding. Use closed questions to finish a conversation or part of a conversation.

1. Are you alright?
2. What's your name?
3. Is this the right way to do this?
4. Are you interested in films, or do you prefer sport?
5. Where do you live?
6. When did the problem first start?

OPEN QUESTIONS

Open questions are those that cannot be answered by a single word or phrase, and invite the other person to talk and volunteer new information. Open questions are more about the helpee and what they want to talk about. With open questions, the helpee decides where the session goes and what they talk about. Use open questions to get the other person to speak more fully.

1. How, exactly, do you do this?
2. What is your favourite sport and why?
3. What is your relationship with your boss like?
4. How do you see your future?
5. What can you tell me about the children in this photograph?
6. What brings you here?

Of course, the helpee can respond to a closed question with a long speech, or to an open question with a single word or phrase, but open questions generally open things up and closed questions generally close things down.

QUESTIONS

Complete Table 6.3 by identifying a closed question and then identifying its open counterpart. There are some examples to get you started.

OK, now that we have all the parts of the jigsaw puzzle, it's time to put it all together.

TABLE 6.3 Open and closed questions

Closed	Open
Do you like swimming?	What sort of sports do you like?
Are you angry?	What are you feeling at the moment?

ACTIVITY

To bring together the listening and reflecting skills learnt so far, practise beginning a helping session by:

- welcoming the helpee
- explaining your limits of ability
- outlining the boundaries for the session.

Be mindful of the following:

- SOLERB
- minimal encouragers
- non-verbal communication
- silent listening
- questioning
- paraphrasing (reflecting content and meaning)
- reflecting feelings
- focusing
- summarising
- difference and diversity
- communicating empathic understanding
- blocks to listening.

As the relationship deepens, there are other skills that can be learnt and applied in helping work. These skills need to be used carefully and the helper needs to have self-awareness and judgement to decide whether or not they are appropriate for the helpee at any given moment. One size does not fit all and the helper's real skill is in choosing what skill to use and when to use it. The skills used should always be in the helpee's best interest and meet the helpee's needs, not the helper's.

It might be useful to think of counselling skills as tools in a toolbox. Some 'jobs' can probably be done using only one tool while another job might need almost everything in the toolbox. The more tools in the box, the more options the helper has but also the more skilled the user needs to be. Expertise comes from being able to use the right tool for the right job. You also need to keep the tools in good condition: a blunt saw rips rather than cuts and a rusty nail might break or bend. As a helper, it is necessary to keep the tools in good condition by using them regularly and handling them carefully.

Here are some more tools for the toolbox:

CHALLENGING

This is a skill to be used with great care. Used carefully and sensitively, this skill can support the helpee to move forward and make changes. It can also support a helpee to get in touch with difficult and painful feelings in order to gain clarity and understanding about a situation they have been reluctant to face.

Sometimes 'challenging' can be used simply to gently query a discrepancy in the helpee's story.

> **EXAMPLE**
>
> Helper: Last week you talked about how happy you are in your marriage and this week you have talked about feeling lonely and ignored in your marriage. It seems that something has changed or you are seeing things in a different way. I would be interested to hear more about how you feel.

This is a very gentle challenge and gives the helpee the opportunity to further explore what is happening in their marriage and their feelings of loneliness.

Sometimes what the helpee says seems to be at odds with how they look or behave and this can create a space for the helper to make a gently enquiring challenge. There is a game show on UK television called *Catchphrase*. In this game show, contestants have to guess the hidden meaning in pictures and symbols. The game show host invites them to 'say what you see'. In the same way, it can be useful for the helper to literally 'say what they see' in order to challenge the helpee.

EXAMPLE 1

Helper: You are talking about how your son doesn't want you to visit at the moment and that you haven't seen your granddaughter for several weeks and yet you are laughing and making a joke about it. Is that how you really feel?

Helpee: No, of course not. It really hurts; I hate the situation.

Helper: And yet you were laughing and smiling when you talked about it. I wonder what that was about.

Helpee: I'm not sure. I do it quite a lot. I make a joke about lots of things and I tend to make fun of myself too. I hadn't really thought of it before. I think I do it so that I don't feel uncomfortable.

Helper: It's a way of managing difficult feelings.

Helpee: When I'm talking about sad things, I start to feel sort of panicky and awkward and so I make a joke just to break the silence.

Helper: (stays silent)

Helpee: (laughs a little) I want to make a joke now.

Helper: What would happen if you did things a little differently and didn't use humour to manage your feelings?

Helpee: (after a few moments starts to weep) I miss my son and granddaughter so much. What have I done wrong?

By the helper just 'saying what they saw', the helper identified that the helpee was being *incongruent* – in other words, the feelings she was expressing did not match how she was behaving. In this example, the helpee was able to acknowledge how hurt she was and also learnt about how she uses humour to manage challenging emotions. The helper's challenge helped the helpee's self-awareness as it made her aware of previously unacknowledged information.

However, if the helper challenges in a confrontational, harsh or clumsy manner, the helpee is likely to become more defensive and the helping relationship could be harmed.

EXAMPLE 2

Helper: Why are you laughing?

Helpee: I wasn't laughing.

Helper: Yes, you were. You were laughing about your son not wanting you to visit.

Helpee: Why would I laugh about that?

Helper: That's what I would like to know.

Helpee: I'm sorry, I don't know, but I will make sure it doesn't happen again.

These last two examples of the helper's challenge result in very different outcomes. It is important to remember that an essential ingredient of the helping relationship is trust and acceptance. Therefore, challenging should only be used when the helping relationship is formed and trust has been established. It should generally only be offered tentatively as an enquiry, rather than as a criticism or directive. The thing being challenged can then become something for the helper and helpee to explore together.

Challenging should always be for the helpee's benefit and to meet their needs. Sometimes a helper may feel frustrated and impatient because the helpee seems a little slow in moving forward. The helper may think they know what the helpee needs to do or know. In this situation, the helper could use challenging inappropriately to manipulate the helpee into arriving at what the helper believes to be the solution.

In Example 1, the helper allowed the helpee to see how she used humour. The helper may well have thought that was the case long before the helpee realised it. The helper may have wanted to impose her beliefs on the helpee. This could be because the helper wanted to appear 'clever' and insightful or to move the session on out of frustration and impatience, consequently using challenge inappropriately.

EXAMPLE 3

Helper: When you laugh like that, I think it's to avoid the fact that you feel so bad about the situation with your son.

Helpee: You are probably right.

And yes, the helper is probably right but by using challenge in this way it closed the session down and prevented the helpee being able to reflect on and wonder about her own experience.

Let's look at the definition of 'challenge':

1.   A call to someone to participate in a competitive situation or fight to decide who is superior in terms of ability or strength.
2.   A call to prove or justify something.
3.   To dispute the truth or validity of something.
4.   To invite someone to engage in a contest. (*Oxford English Dictionary*)

 Yes, I can see that; the helper gently asks the helpee to *prove or justify* something. The helper, by challenging, *is disputing the truth or validity of something*, but, because the helping relationship has been built into a safe, trusting one, the helpee can hear that the challenge comes from a place of care and respect.

ACTIVITY

Reflect back to times in your life when someone has challenged you. Try to think of a time when the challenge helped you and another time when the challenge hurt or harmed you.

- Identify what was different about the two challenges.
- What relationship did you have with the people who offered you the challenges?
- Did the relationship affect how you received the challenge?
- What impact did the challenges have on you?
- Did the challenges have any influence on what you did next?
- How can these insights inform your helping work?

 That's an interesting activity. I had a teacher once who challenged me all the time. She was very straightforward and to the point, with no pretty words or phrases. She would hold up my excuses, rationalisations, negativity and my games for me to see them for what they were. She would let me know that she saw me – if that makes sense. What I most remember though is that I never ever felt judged; part of me just knew that it came from a caring place. Now I realise that she must have cared quite a lot to even bother challenging me. It would have been so much easier for her to look the other way and not take the time to try to help me. I had other teachers who challenged me but they did it very differently and I felt criticised and punished and judged, and even less likely to change my behaviour. When I look back, all I can say is I could tell when the challenge came from a good place; it felt different. I was able to hear it and learn from it.

 Absolutely; the challenge must come from a caring place and be for the helpee's benefit and growth. Only then will challenge be an effective counselling skill.

ACTIVITY

- How do you feel about challenging?
- What do you imagine the consequences of your challenge might be?
- Are you worried about how the helpee might react?

Reflect on the following scenarios and decide whether it would be appropriate to challenge the helpee. If you decide it would be appropriate, think about how you would challenge the helpee in each one. What skills would you use? What qualities would you need? Also think about why you would challenge and what you hope the challenge would achieve.

---

1. I get on fine with my children because they know who is boss when I'm at home. I don't believe in hitting children for no reason but sometimes it's important to keep discipline. It never did me any harm. Most of the problems in society are due to youngsters having their own way too much. I've said to my children that it's my house and if they don't like the way I run it they can go and live elsewhere. That's not unreasonable, is it?

2. I'm so fed up with my weight. I've joined the gym but I haven't lost a pound. It's my friends' fault. We go out for lunch and they keep buying me cakes and puddings. I am really good all week and then they just ruin it for me.

3. You are the only person in the world I trust. I can't tell my doctor that I've found a lump. I'm too scared. I'm sure it's nothing. Please tell me it's nothing.

4. I just can't do it. I'm not clever or educated. Everyone else will be so much better than me. It's been so long since I've even been to a job interview. I've volunteered for ages and the people in the care home seem to like me. I've learnt so much since I've been there. I definitely know I would love to do this work for a living but I just know I'll make a fool of myself in the interview. Who would pay me to work?

5. I feel so sad and lonely. I feel silly saying that but it still hurts me so much. Every year at this time I remember him and wish he were still here. I loved him so much.

6. I think it's disgusting that people come over here from other countries and then tell us how to live. They should go back to where they come from. Then there's all this same-sex marriage. Bloody disgusting, if you ask me.

7. I can't leave my marriage. I really want to, as I'm sick of the violence, but my husband would never let me go.

Do you find any of the scenarios more difficult to respond to? If so, what makes them more difficult for you?

 That's really made me think. I'll remember that game show quote you mentioned, 'say what you see', to help me formulate a challenge.

 That little saying might be quite helpful in working with another skill: the skill of immediacy, which involves a twist on 'say what you see' to 'say what you feel'.

 That sounds really confusing; what do you mean by that?

IMMEDIACY

Sometimes the skill of immediacy is known by other names. In certain counselling approaches, it is called interpreting the transference.

Now I'm really confused.

OK, let's keep it simple. Immediacy is simply about acknowledging what's happening in the helping session between the helper and the helpee. It's about noticing what is happening in the present moment and reflecting that back to the helpee. It's about what is happening between the two of you. It takes courage and honesty to use the skill of immediacy. It can be used to explore any tensions between you: the proverbial 'elephant in the room'; the something that's often ignored or not talked about. Immediacy is about intimacy, about honest communication between two people working to understand what's happening when they are together.

Sometimes the relationship between the helper and the helpee can mirror or replicate other relationships in the helpee's experience. For example, the helpee might have a very critical mother and that can translate into them believing that other people will be critical, or the helpee might feel criticised and childlike in other situations.

USING IMMEDIACY 1

Helpee: I'm sorry, I'm just talking rubbish.

Helper: You were talking about some very difficult issues and then apologised and said you were talking rubbish.

Helpee: You must think I make a drama out of nothing.

Helper: I wonder what just happened between us then. We were talking quite freely and then you seemed to clam up. I felt quite angry when that happened and wondered how you were feeling. I think it's important for us to look very carefully at what's going on between us.

Helpee: I just felt you would think I was stupid and you've just said you are angry with me, and now I feel like a child and I hate it.

Helper: So when you feel someone is angry with you, you feel like a child.

Helpee: You looked as if you were bored with what I was saying and so I apologised.

Helper: It's very interesting that I felt angry while that was happening. I wonder whether I might have been picking up on your unexpressed anger at talking to someone who appeared bored. What do you think?

> Helpee: I don't know. I just felt judged and ashamed and I don't even know why but it reminded me of being with my mum; she always made me feel that way.
> Helper: Judged and ashamed …
> Helpee: Yes.
> Helper: Shall we talk more about those feelings and how they might affect our relationship?

 That seems a bit hard for me to understand. I don't think I'm ready to use this skill.

It can be even easier than that. It can simply be acknowledging what's happening in the here and now. For example, the helper might notice the helpee's body language change. They might fold their arms and cross their legs, and avoid eye contact. The helper could mention this to the helpee:

> Helper: When you closed your arms across your chest, I got the impression that you became quite defensive then.

This might help the helpee become aware of what is happening for them and then their feelings could be brought into the open and worked with. Or even:

> Helper: You seemed quite cross with me then; am I right?

Immediacy, therefore, is the ability of the helper to use the immediate situation to invite the helpee to look at what is going on between them in the relationship. It often feels risky and unfamiliar. It implies the use of the present tense. It is one of the most powerful skills in counselling. In its fullest sense it involves:

- revealing how you are feeling
- sharing a hunch or sense of what the helpee may be feeling in the here and now (and possibly linking this to the helpee issue)
- inviting the helpee to explore what is going on between you.

USING IMMEDIACY 2

> Helpee: (looking down at her knees)
> Helper: I notice that you haven't looked at me all session, which is leaving me feeling rather shut out. It feels as if you want to stop me getting too close … I wonder if that's how it feels to you?

When to use immediacy

1. To address the helpee's patterns of relating that may be being repeated in the helping relationship, in order to help them understand and deal with it:

Helper: I notice that you are responding defensively to what I am saying even though I feel very accepting of what you are telling me. I wonder whether this is because ... (link to helpee's issue).

Helper: I am aware that you have said that you never get angry, yet I am sensing that you are very angry with me even though your voice is quiet.

2. To deal with difficulties that arise which may be to do with anything going on in the session. For example:

i. *Lack of trust:*

Helper: You told me when you first arrived that you have never trusted anyone in your life. I wonder whether this is influencing how you feel towards me, because I sense that you are not finding it easy to trust me.

ii. *Boundary issues:*

Helper: I am finding it difficult to concentrate on what you are saying because I have just realised that I know the person you are talking about ... I wonder whether you have noticed my reaction and this is somehow affecting your ability to talk freely.

3. To deal with an issue of difference that might be affecting the relationship:

Helper: I am aware that you are a black female and I am a white male, and I wonder how easy you find it to tell me about your experience of racial discrimination at work. Can we talk about this?

tip

- Be direct, clear and honest about your own internal response.
- Be sensitive to the helpee, being aware of what is difficult, and choose your words carefully.
- Be very aware of timing and the possible impact of your intervention.
- Ask yourself who the immediacy is for: Why am I saying this? Will it help the other person?
- Be prepared to take the risk and follow through whatever emerges.

The following activity will help bring this all down to earth by inviting you to look at concrete examples of what you would do in practice.

ACTIVITY

In the following five examples, practise immediacy by:

- identifying how you would feel in each situation
- developing empathic understanding (how do you think the other person is feeling?)
- tentatively and gently offering your insight to the other person.

1. Your helpee said they wanted to make a donation to the church as a gesture of good will and gratitude for the time you spent listening to them. You are not comfortable with this but don't do anything about it. You meet several times and the helpee often talks about money problems and how people take advantage of his generosity and good will. These comments are not addressed to you directly but you still feel uncomfortable.
2. Your helpee talks about the same thing over and over again, and you are feeling weary and bored.
3. Your helpee is very different to you, in terms of disability, age, race, sexuality, etc.
4. The helpee is very late for a session which you have both arranged. This has happened before. You start to feel angry.
5. Your helpee gets very angry with you and shouts that you don't understand them.

The examples above are very challenging situations. How might immediacy help you support the helpee in these circumstances?

 I notice that when using the skill of immediacy, the helper sometimes talks about their own thoughts and feelings. Is that the right thing to do?

 That's a very interesting point which leads us on to another counselling skill – self-disclosure.

SELF-DISCLOSURE

Self-disclosure is a very valuable skill but, if it is not used appropriately, it can be unhelpful and sometimes damaging.

There are times when talking about your own thoughts, feelings and experiences can greatly enhance the helping work. In some agencies, volunteers and workers may have chosen to work there because of their own experiences, and they use that experience to offer help and support to others in a similar situation. This could be around, for example, substance misuse, homelessness or being a carer, and this 'experts by experience' approach can be therapeutically valuable because of the shared identification between the helper and the helpee.

EXAMPLE

Helper: I remember feeling incredibly guilty when my mother had to go into a care home.

Helpee: Oh my goodness, thank you so much, that's exactly how I feel. I hate myself but I just can't take any more. I think everyone will judge me and think I should have done more.

Helper: I remember feeling and thinking very similar things.

Helpee: What did you do about it? How did you get over it?

Helper: I'm not sure that would be helpful to you. We certainly have a shared experience and there are many similarities between us. However, my solution might not be your solution. How about we talk about how you are feeling and what's happening for you a little more and see if we can help you find your own solution?

When using self-disclosure, it is important for the helper to only disclose what is relevant to the helpee in the helping session. Too much self-disclosure risks the focus of the session moving away from the helpee to the helper, or it may burden the helpee with concerns and worries about the helper which get in the way of them speaking freely together.

Also, self-disclosure should not be used as a covert way of offering advice and guidance.

ACTIVITY

Helpee: My partner has always been quite an angry person but just lately it seems to be getting worse. He pushed me against a wall last night during an argument. He was very upset and apologetic afterwards but I was left feeling quite shaky.

Helper: I was in a violent relationship too and had to leave; it sounds like that's what you need to do.

In this example, what other response could the helper have offered the helpee?

What are the risks of using the counselling skill of self-disclosure?

What are the benefits of using the counselling skill of self-disclosure?

Why should the skill be used carefully and only when the helping relationship is fully formed?

SUMMARY

- Listening is the most important counselling skill.
- Non-verbal communication is critical in helping work.
- Key listening and responding skills include reflection, paraphrasing, summarising and appropriate use of silence.
- Skills of challenge, immediacy and self-disclosure are helpful but need to be used carefully.

7
Using Reflection and Feedback to Enhance Counselling Skills

In the previous chapters, we explored the skills, techniques and qualities needed to facilitate a helping session using counselling skills. In this chapter, we look at the importance of reflecting on our work as helpers and looking at how we can grow and develop in this role.

WORKING REFLECTIVELY

 To begin to understand why working reflectively is an important aspect of growing and developing as helpers, let's explore what 'reflection' means. As you know, the skill of reflection is a particular counselling skill (see Chapter 6) but it has many different meanings in different contexts. For example, it is:

1. something reflected back
2. when light or heat is returned after hitting a surface
3. what we see in a mirror
4. thinking deeply and carefully about something
5. a considered idea
6. a critical comment
7. suggesting a negative association.

In the above list, 1 and 4 are the most relevant when using counselling skills and facilitating a helping session effectively. We fix our thoughts on a helping session we have facilitated and give careful consideration to how we could improve on our performance. Often, when we give careful consideration, a thought will occur around how we could improve.

 What about definitions 6 and 7, which suggest it's about thinking of something negative – all the things I've done wrong. I don't really like the sound of that.

Mmm … it's important that we look at areas for growth and things we can improve on but it's also important to acknowledge what we did well and what our strengths are. I agree with you – if it was all negative, it could affect our confidence and make things worse rather than better.

 OK, so how do I reflect on what I've done? What if I am not sure what's good and what's bad? I'm only just beginning to learn about this subject and I might simply have insufficient knowledge and understanding to accurately reflect on what I do.

TOOLS FOR REFLECTING

 This is why we need input from others to support our growth and development. However, let's begin by looking at some methods we can use to reflect on our work as a helper using counselling skills.

INTERPERSONAL PROCESS RECALL (IPR)

Interpersonal Process Recall is a technique developed by Norman Kagan (1975) and his colleagues. It was originally developed for mental health workers and, later, for teachers but it has become widely used in counselling, supervision and helping work. It is a reflection tool that enables the helper to become more self-aware by using a form of structured reflection on what happened in a helping interaction. It brings things to mind that the helper was unaware of in the actual session. The helper can then take this increased self-awareness and insight into subsequent helping sessions. By reflecting on certain questions straight after a session, a helper is able to recall some of their own personal processes – in other words, what was actually going on – which they might not have been fully aware of at the time. Also, doing this exercise strengthens the helper's ability to be more self-aware during the actual session. It requires practice to develop this ability. It can be helpful to reflect on and respond to the following list of questions (a simplified version of Interpersonal Process Recall) after any helping interaction. It can also be useful to keep a journal of your reflections and observations.

As you recall the helping interaction:

- How did you feel?
- What did you think?
- What did you sense in your body? Where?

(Continued)

(Continued)

- What did you want to do?
- What did you think the other person was thinking about you?
- Was there something you wanted to say but felt unable to?
- What stopped you?
- What were the risks involved in speaking out?
- What did you imagine the other person really wanted of you?
- What did you want the other person to feel about you?
- Did you have any fantasies or images about the other person or about the outcomes?
- Was there anything you did during the session that pleased you?
- Was there anything you did which is normally difficult for you?
- What enabled you to do it this time?
- Is there anything you would like to have done differently?

Below is an example of how a helper can use tools to reflect on a helping session in order to improve and develop their skills. The questions in Table 7.1 can be used to reflect on a single session.

TABLE 7.1   Self-reflection tool

Comment on your management of the helping session:
Comment on how the helping interaction was established and maintained:
Comment on your use of counselling skills:
Record the main learning points of the session:

 I think I will find this very useful. It helps me to focus and reminds me to set clear boundaries and keeps me mindful of the counselling skills I use.

 It is important to find a tool for reflecting on your work that is right for you; one that over time will become almost second nature. You will begin to become a reflective practitioner and will automatically review any work you have done to look at how you can grow and develop.

 It's interesting. After using the reflective questions for a while, I almost look back over my helping sessions automatically. They have given me an internal checklist to run through in my helping work.

FEEDBACK

 That sounds very helpful. Continual improvement and learning are so important. There are other ways to improve your helping work and use of counselling skills. This is through giving and receiving feedback, particularly from your peers in counselling skills training and your tutor. Feedback from the helpee is also an important source of learning and reflection.

> Question: What is the shortest word in the English language that contains the
> letters ABCDEF?
>
> Answer: FEEDBACK. Don't forget that feedback is one of the essential elements
> of good communication.

tip

CRITICAL THINKING

In Chapter 5, you were introduced to the Johari window as a tool for increasing your self-awareness. Now we can use it to reflect on helping work.

The OPEN area is known to both self and others.

The BLIND area is known to others but not to self.

The HIDDEN area is known to self but not to others.

The UNKNOWN area is not known to self or others.

	Known to self	Not known to self
Known to others	Open	Blind
Not known to others	Hidden	Unknown

FIGURE 7.1   The Johari window

(Continued)

(Continued)

Using the four areas of the Johari window, think about why this might be a useful tool for reflecting on helping work:

Is feedback from others always helpful? If not, why not?

How do you feel about a helpee knowing things about you which are in your Blind area?

Through the process of feedback and development, more and more will move from 'hidden' to 'open' as you incorporate the useful elements from this process to broaden your understanding and use of helping skills and increase your awareness of those parts of yourself that you bring to the role of helper.

So that leads us to the question of what kind of feedback is 'good'. Good feedback is useful or constructive. This is why it is essential to learn how to give and receive constructive feedback.

Giving feedback

The aim of feedback is not to judge or belittle. It is to offer objective and specific observations on what you have seen. It can be very easy to hurt someone's feelings by giving clumsy, subjective feedback. The aim of giving feedback is to affirm and build confidence while making suggestions for continued growth. A useful acronym for remembering how to give feedback is BOOST:

B – Balanced

O – Observed

O – Objective

S – Specific

T – Timely

Balanced: The feedback should include both areas of strength and areas that need further development. When giving 'negative' feedback, be sure to include constructive points and be tentative when suggesting what could have been done differently. All feedback that focuses on areas to change or reflect on must be given sensitively and with respect.

Observed: The feedback should be based on what was actually observed in the session rather than on an interpretation of what happened. For example, it is more helpful to say 'I noticed that you found it difficult to maintain eye contact with your client', than to say 'You seemed really intimidated by your client'. The first opens up the subject so that it can be explored, while the second involves a judgement that closes down any exploration. It is also likely to leave the helpee feeling defensive.

Objective: To be useful, the feedback has to be objective. It is very nice to hear feedback that simply says how wonderful and marvellous we are but actually that doesn't help us to grow and improve. Therefore, it is important to give and receive honest feedback. It can be very difficult to give honest feedback for a variety of reasons and we will explore this later in the chapter. Feedback should be about the skills and techniques used in the helping session. It is not relevant to get involved in the content of the session and to offer opinions about what was going on for the helpee.

Specific: It is very important to be specific when giving feedback. If the feedback is vague, the helpee won't know what they need to do to improve and grow. 'You didn't listen' is not helpful at all. A useful and specific way of communicating this to the helper might be: 'I noticed you looked away and fidgeted a little when the helpee talked about problems with her child. I could be wrong but you seemed to lose focus then and I wondered what that was about.' Specific feedback does not make assumptions.

Timely: It is important for the feedback to be given while the helping session is fresh in your mind. This allows any concerns to be identified and explored immediately. Similarly, it is also good practice to acknowledge and affirm any skills that you have seen practised well at the time.

---

tip

RULES FOR GIVING FEEDBACK

To be helpful, feedback needs to be given in a careful and supportive way. Good feedback will:

- Focus on the actual skills and content of the helping session rather than on the personality of the helper.
- Use adverbs rather than adjectives in order to describe rather than judge, e.g. 'You spoke quickly' (adverb) rather than 'You were hasty' (adjective).
- Contain specific observations about exactly what was witnessed rather than make assumptions about what went on.
- Be specific rather than general, and focus on something the helper can proactively work on.
- Share ideas and information rather than giving advice like 'You should ...' or 'You shouldn't ...'
- Contain only the amount of information the helper can make use of rather than the amount we would like to give.

It is useful to offer an area for growth (negative feedback) between two things the helper did well (positive feedback). This is known as a feedback sandwich, as illustrated in Figure 7.2.

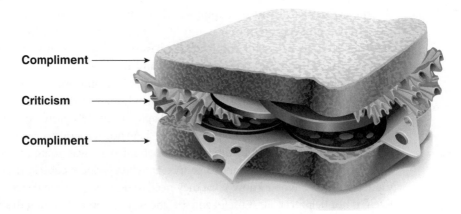

Compliment

Criticism

Compliment

FIGURE 7.2   Feedback sandwich

The critical feedback that might be difficult to swallow can be sandwiched between delicious bread, making the whole thing easier to digest and take on board. Also, when feedback has been given, it is useful for the helper receiving it to give a summary of what has been said, to ensure they have heard it accurately.

ACTIVITY

Below are a few examples of helpful and unhelpful feedback. Add to Table 7.2 some examples of your own.

TABLE 7.2   Examples of feedback

Helpful feedback	Unhelpful feedback
'I felt that you listened attentively, with good eye contact.'	'You were so lovely.'
'I noticed that you asked a lot of questions.'	'You were really intimidating.'
'Your body language was quite closed; I noticed you had your arms folded and legs crossed.'	'You seemed to be distracted.'
'Twice in the session you gave the helpee advice, which didn't really help him find his own solution.'	'You seemed very cold.'

There's a lot more to feedback than I thought but I can see how it is necessary to be specific rather than just generalise. I think I would find it hard to be honest all the time. What if I got it wrong? I don't know very much and my feedback could be wrong. That would be awful. Also, I'd hate to hurt someone's feelings by pointing out critical things. I think it would be easier for me to receive feedback than to give it. I thought it would be the other way round but I feel quite nervous about giving feedback now. In the past, I have just told people how well they have done, even if I didn't think they had done well. That's really dishonest, isn't it?

You have picked up something very important. Earlier in the chapter, I mentioned the challenges of giving honest feedback. Yes, it is difficult for a number of reasons. Sometimes there is a tendency to be too nice or overly critical, which can be influenced by our own personality and even how we are feeling at the time. There may be a fear of getting it wrong or of being hurtful. In addition, it is a human trait to want to be liked and approved of, and if we give feedback that could irritate or cause resistance in someone, we risk being disliked and disapproved of.

It is important to use your empathic qualities when giving feedback. Put yourself in the other person's shoes and imagine how it would feel to receive the feedback. This will help you frame feedback that will be well received and effective.

ACTIVITY

Complete the spider diagram below, identifying your personal blocks to giving honest feedback.

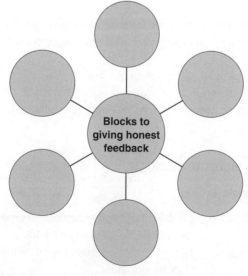

FIGURE 7.3 Spidergram

The main challenge for me in giving feedback is my fear of not being liked and this leads me to be overly nice.

 That reminds me of the saying: 'Nothing grows in honey.' Honey is sugary sweet but it does not contain the right nutrients for growing anything.

 I have just realised that when I have a decision to make or there is a problem in my life, I choose certain people to go to. I have friends who I know will agree with me, whether I am right or wrong, and I go to them to feel better and have a good moan or cry. I have other friends who I know will tell me the truth, even if I won't like it. I love the friends who tell me what I want to hear but I trust the ones who tell me the truth.

 An important realisation: It also highlights the need for you to be able to accept feedback. If you are non-defensive and open, people will meet you in a similar way and be honest and support your growth. If you are defensive and argumentative, they will be less likely to be so honest on other occasions.

Receiving feedback

Just as giving feedback is an important skill, it is also important to be able to receive and use feedback. It isn't pleasant to be given challenging feedback as we might feel hurt or defensive.

 I tend to just keep quiet when people give me feedback I don't like. I just accept it but inside I feel quite resentful and angry towards them.

 That's a pattern to be aware of and you need to find a way of challenging and working through it in order to utilise feedback more effectively. Below are some examples of how we might respond to feedback in ways that aren't too helpful!

RESPONDING TO FEEDBACK

Example 1

Observer: I noticed your body language seemed quite closed and you looked away from the helpee quite a lot.

Helper: I only did that because I sensed they felt uncomfortable; it felt the right thing to do.

Observer: You asked quite a lot of questions at the beginning of the helping session.

Helper: No, I didn't.

Observer: You paraphrased really well but I noticed you focused a lot on the details rather than on the helpee's feelings, and I wondered about how you could communicate your empathic understanding in future helping sessions.

Helper: Thank you, that's useful feedback.

[But helper thinks: You're only saying that because the tutor is listening and you want to sound clever.]

Let's look at how the helper might have responded to make more constructive use of the feedback.

Example 2

Observer: I noticed your body language seemed quite closed and you looked away from the helpee quite a lot.

Helper: I hadn't realised I was doing that. Can you tell me a little more – perhaps about when you noticed I did that?

Observer: I noticed it a couple of times when the helpee stopped talking and there were a few seconds of silence.

Helper: Yes, I think I remember more clearly now. A couple of times I was really struggling to think of something to say. Maybe that was when I shifted my focus away from the helpee, because of my own anxiety around getting things right and being good enough.

Observer: You asked quite a lot of questions at the beginning of the helping session.

Helper: Can you give me an example of when I did that, please, so that I can reflect on what was happening in the session at that point?

Observer: You paraphrased really well but I noticed you focused a lot on the details rather than on the helpee's feelings, and I wondered about how you could communicate your empathic understanding in future helping sessions.

Helper: Can you give me an example of that, please?

Observer: The helpee was talking about how her partner got really angry during an argument and punched the wall, which really frightened her. You paraphrased well but you focused on the argument rather than on her feelings of fear. Does that make sense to you?

Helper: Yes, it does. It's interesting but I wonder if my own experience got in the way then. My father was very aggressive and sometimes violent towards my mother and I used to feel really scared when he got angry. Maybe it was my feelings I didn't want to feel and that made me keep the helping session factual.

So it's OK to ask questions about the feedback and not just accept it?

Absolutely. The feedback must be meaningful to you in order to be useful. There are some guidelines for receiving difficult feedback. Before receiving feedback, take a few moments to prepare yourself. It is important to listen to what is being said without interrupting, even if you disagree. Give yourself time to reflect on the feedback but certainly ask for more information or ask questions about the feedback, or request more information or ask for examples, if necessary. You may have to work hard not to take the feedback personally and become defensive or make excuses for why you did what you did. Sometimes it is all too easy to have selective hearing and only hear some of what is being said. To counteract this, summarise what you have heard and ask if your version of the feedback is accurate. Move the focus to what can be done and how you can address and work on the issues which have been raised.

So, when you invite feedback from others: take what you need, try on the rest for size; check the validity of certain feedback with others you trust and if it doesn't belong to you, let it go. Aim to be engaged with both your personal and professional development. Make a commitment to be open and willing to learn.

SUMMARY

- Reflecting on feedback and on practice are essential for growth and development as a helper.
- Giving and receiving feedback are import aspects of reflection.
- Feedback needs to acknowledge good practice as well as identify an area for growth.
- Giving and receiving feedback are skills in their own right.

8
Preparing to Work within an Ethical and Legal Framework as a Counsellor

This chapter looks at how to prepare yourself to work within an ethical and legal framework as a counsellor entering into a counselling contract with clients. Working ethically includes understanding assessment and referral in an agency context.

 But I thought we had already covered ethics in Part I?

 Yes, you are right, but that was about exploring an ethical framework for people who use counselling skills as part of another role – 'helpers' working with 'helpees'. There are a lot of new things to think about when we look at ethics for counsellors working with clients. We need to explore the relationship between ethics, the law and agency policies and procedures, and to revisit issues about working within your limits or ability. We also need to look at how to refer clients for further help, how to manage ethical dilemmas, etc., but let's take one step at a time.

ETHICS FOR COUNSELLORS

The main difference here is that you have to show that you know how to apply your understanding of ethics to the counselling context – to a situation where you have entered into a formal contractual relationship with a client for counselling. This part of the book is about being properly prepared to take this next step and about practising in the classroom with your peers to make sure you are ready when the time comes.

> Remember, you still won't be a counsellor at the end of this course but you will be prepared for the next step of your training, which includes a placement in a counselling agency where you will work with real clients.

I think I get it. From this point on, I have to imagine that I am a counsellor and demonstrate that I understand counselling ethics while practising being a counsellor – but I still won't *be* a counsellor.

Exactly – that's why we will use the terms 'counsellor' and 'client' throughout this part of the book.

So, the first thing a counsellor needs to do is identify an ethical framework in which to work. We have already mentioned the BACP Ethical Framework for the Counselling Professions (2016), but there are other frameworks to choose from. At the end of the day, you have to find one that feels right for you, and the first step to working ethically is to sign up as a member of a professional body that offers an ethical framework. Most professional bodies offer student membership and provide resources and support as part of this membership.

ACTIVITY

Research four counselling professional bodies with ethical frameworks or codes of ethics. Two suggestions are offered below:

1. BACP – Ethical Framework for the Counselling Professions
2. Association of Christian Counsellors – Ethics and Practice
3. ....
4. ....

Have a look at a couple of different counselling ethical frameworks and compare them. How are they the same? How are they different?

Have a look at an ethical framework for another kind of organisation. How is it the same? How is it different?

The next step is to consider how you would actually apply ethical principles to counselling. Here is a quick reminder of them from the BACP Ethical Framework for the Counselling Professions:

Being trustworthy – honouring the trust placed in you (also called 'fidelity')

Autonomy – respecting a person's right to make their own choices

Beneficence – acting in the best interests of the person

Non-maleficence – not doing any harm

Justice – being fair and impartial

Self-respect – having integrity, self-knowledge and taking care of yourself.

Take the BACP ethical principle of 'non-maleficence', for example – what would that actually mean if you were working as a counsellor and how would your client know that you were working to this principle?

OK, I guess I need to think about this a bit. 'Non-maleficence' means not doing any harm … so it would mean things like not being physically aggressive or coming on to a client sexually. It would mean having a safe consulting room with a fire exit. It would mean not messing with their brains and making them feel worse … I suppose that could be a risk if I didn't know what I was doing. I suppose that if I was a counsellor charging for my services, it might also include things like not charging too much.

All these things are important and you are certainly along the right lines. What about turning up for a counselling session when you are hung over after a night out? Or what if you were worried, depressed or low yourself? That might not be a good time to be working with a client. What about insurance? Are you insured to work as a counsellor? Also, what would you do if you discovered that your client was related to someone you knew after the counselling had started? As you can see, the potential problems are almost endless, and, in some circumstances, the 'ethical' thing to do can be quite hard to fathom.

No code of ethics can ever anticipate every possible situation, which is why the BACP moved towards 'principles', 'values' and 'moral qualities' alongside 'commitment to clients' and 'good practice' which help counsellors grapple with 'the right thing to do'. Look at the case examples below and reflect on how you would behave in these situations.

ACTIVITY

The following are examples of ethical dilemmas for consideration.

Example 1

Cal works as a counsellor in a GP surgery. She is due to see three clients that afternoon at the surgery but has woken up with a migraine, is feeling very unwell and

(Continued)

(Continued)

has been vomiting. One of her clients, Jake, was very low and vulnerable when she saw him last week and has only engaged in counselling very reluctantly. Much of the last session was about trusting that Cal would be there for him.

Consider each of the following ethical principles and how they might help Cal reflect on what she should do:

Being trustworthy

Non-maleficence

Autonomy

Justice

Beneficence

Self-respect.

What would you do and why?

Example 2

Peter has been seeing a client, Jenny, for six months. The work has been focused on her lack of self-belief and self-worth, and has been very intense. The client comes in and tells Peter that she has lost her job. Her confidence is shattered. She tells Peter that she will have to stop counselling because she can't afford his fees. Peter has struggled to get to the point where he can charge for his work as a counsellor after years of voluntary work as a trainee. He has expenses associated with the service he offers and is stretched financially himself.

Consider how the ethical principle of self-respect might help Peter reflect on how he should respond. Would it make any difference if he was not under financial pressure himself? What would you do and why?

Essentially, a counsellor needs to develop ethical mindfulness. It is important for counsellors to be aware of how ethics informs counselling work and how ethics can help us to make decisions about counselling practice. But no ethical framework provides all the answers; rather, such a framework provides a structure which you can refer to in order to make difficult ethical decisions. Sometimes different counsellors come to different decisions.

 Different decisions? Can you give me an example?

Counsellors work within different theoretical modalities and this may be important when reaching an ethical decision. For example, the BACP Ethical Framework considers the notion of duality within the counselling relationship. Duality here means when a counsellor might have a relationship with the client in another context – in other words, a dual relationship. From a classical psychodynamic perspective, knowing the client in another context could be considered a cross-contamination of the therapeutic relationship and is therefore taboo. However, a more person-centred counsellor might argue that this could be beneficial in some counselling settings and could be worked through as part of the therapeutic relationship. It could even enhance the work. Both arguments hold weight, but you would still need to justify your position in terms of the ethical principle of non-maleficence, for example.

I get it now: ethics is not a set of rules, but a set of guidelines that help counsellors make decisions in the best interests of their clients.

Yes, it is important that counsellors work in the best interests of their clients and ensure that they are fit to practise. In addition to the ethical principles and personal moral qualities which we looked at in the first part of this book, the BACP Ethical Framework offers a set of underpinning ethical values which counsellors are expected to commit to.

REFLECTION: BACP ETHICAL VALUES

1. Respecting human rights and dignity
2. Alleviating symptoms of personal distress and suffering
3. Enhancing people's well-being and capabilities
4. Improving the quality of relationships between people
5. Increasing personal resilience and effectiveness
6. Facilitating a sense of self that is meaningful to the person(s) concerned within their personal and cultural context
7. Appreciating the variety of human experience and culture
8. Protecting the safety of clients
9. Ensuring the integrity of practitioner–client relationships
10. Enhancing the quality of professional knowledge and its application
11. Striving for the fair and adequate provision of services

Reflect on each of these ethical values. What do they mean to you? Do you agree with them all?

(Continued)

(Continued)

For example, is counselling always about 'increasing personal resilience and effectiveness' (5)? Should counsellors be responsible for 'improving the quality of relationships between people' generally (4) or for 'striving for fair and adequate provision of services' (11)?

How would you ensure that you practise as a counsellor in a way which takes account of each ethical value?

At this stage of your training, you are not working with clients but it is important to start considering how to apply an ethical framework to counselling practice sessions.

Let's look at an example and consider the ethical principle of client 'autonomy'. Autonomy means respecting the client's right to make their own choices and to be self-governing. This means allowing the client to be autonomous and not imposing your own agenda or strategy on them. It sounds straightforward, doesn't it? Most counsellors would have no trouble agreeing to the principle of 'autonomy', whatever their counselling approach.

 But what if the client is making the wrong decisions? Well, I don't mean 'wrong' exactly, but maybe deciding to do something which is not in their best interests.

 That poses an interesting ethical question. Does the client have the ability to make that decision? Who decides what is right? Under what circumstances might you feel you want to take direct action contrary to the client's wishes? All these kinds of questions can be considered within an ethical context in order to help the counsellor to make an informed decision. Generally, a counsellor would also use clinical supervision to help make decisions and to ensure that they are working in the best interests of the client. Engaging in clinical supervision is another ingredient of safe and ethical practice, which will be explored in more detail in Chapter 14.

AUTONOMY

Example 1

Benita has been referred for counselling at a women's refuge after being beaten up by her boyfriend. She is struggling with being alone and misses having a partner. Her boyfriend is acting sweet and putting pressure on her to return. She tells you that she thinks he has turned over a new leaf and is planning to move back in with him.

Example 2

Max is living with his new partner who is very jealous of his two-year-old daughter by a previous relationship. Max has her to stay every other weekend but it is causing rows and friction with his current partner, and his ex-partner is making it increasingly difficult by messing him around about the access arrangements. His daughter seems stuck in the middle and gets anxious and upset. Max tells you that he thinks it would be easier for everyone – and for him – if he stops having contact with her. She is so young she will soon forget him anyway.

What is your response to these scenarios?

How easy would you find it to trust in the client's autonomy?

If you felt the need to challenge the client's decision, which aspect of the ethical framework would you draw on to do this?

Would it make a difference in the first scenario if Benita had young children who were also at risk from her partner's violence?

COMPLAINTS

When a counsellor becomes a member of a professional body, they agree not only to work within that organisation's ethical framework but also to abide by its complaints procedure. If a client feels that they have not been treated fairly or have been abused in some way by the counsellor, they can make a formal complaint to the professional body that the counsellor belongs to. This is an important protection for the client.

 I get it. When we become a member of a professional counselling body, we are signing up to their ethical guidelines. By being a member, we are agreeing to work in a particular way. If we cause harm to the client or do not work professionally, the client can then seek redress by bringing a complaint to the professional body. The professional body will then reach a judgement as to whether you have acted appropriately or not.

 Precisely. The professional body you belong to will make a formal investigation and find in favour of either the client or the counsellor. If the counsellor is found to be at fault, a sanction may be imposed. The severity of the sanction will be in proportion to the nature of the transgression. Sanctions might include one or more of the following:

- requiring the counsellor to apologise to the client
- requiring the counsellor to do further personal development to fill a gap in their training

- requiring the counsellor to seek further supervision
- requiring the counsellor to make financial reparation
- suspending the counsellor from the professional body register
- removing the counsellor from the professional body register.

All these sanctions could have serious implications for future employability. It is important to remember that there is no statutory body that can prevent a counsellor practising or prevent someone calling themselves a 'counsellor' without appropriate training. Therefore, belonging to a professional body and being on a recognised counselling register does provide the client with some confidence that the counsellor has an appropriate level of training, that the counsellor is practising within an ethical framework and that they have an avenue to make a complaint if the counsellor behaves unethically.

LIMITS OF PROFICIENCY

In Part I, we looked at the limits of being a helper. Counsellors also have professional limits of ability depending on their training and experience. Some of these limits are more obvious than others. For example, although most counselling courses offer some training and understanding of common medications, this does not mean a counsellor can give advice to clients on medication that they may be taking, unless, of course, the counsellor is also medically trained. For example, it is important that a counsellor does not collude with clients if, say, they want to come off anti-depressants.

But is that not the client's choice?

Yes, of course – ultimately it is their choice – but a counsellor needs to point out that they are not medically trained and strongly urge the client to seek advice from the prescribing doctor/nurse-practitioner. In some cases, when clients are taking anti-depressants they may need to come off them slowly by reducing the dose over a period of time, and this may also be dependent on how long the client has been on the medication.

So, what other limits are there? I thought that once I was trained I could just work with anyone?

Not at all. It is crucial that you are aware of which issues and which clients your training allows you to work with. Some training courses are quite specific, such as training to work only with bereavement or young people, while others are more generic, but there will still be limits in terms of scope of training and experience. As you gain experience, you will be able to work with deeper and more complex issues. In a sense, your training provides you with the first foundation on which to build your professional ability to work with clients. It's a bit like a driving test. Everyone knows that a newly qualified driver still has an awful lot to learn and this only comes from actually being out on the roads and getting the experience. Also, if someone wants to drive an HGV or a 100-seater coach or manoeuvre a military tank, they would have to do further specialised training. The key thing here is that it is the counsellor's responsibility to monitor and recognise what their personal limits are and to make these limits clear to the client.

Different kinds of limits might be around:

- the setting and client group, e.g. bereavement, young people
- the type of counselling being offered or needed, i.e. individual, couple, family or group
- personal issues; for instance, if the counsellor has recently had a bereavement, it is not wise to work with bereaved clients until the counsellor has had time to work through their own grief
- specialist training being needed for certain issues, e.g. sexual dysfunction, trauma, eating disorders, adoption
- the counsellor's own lack of training and/or experience in relation to the client's need, complexity and depth of work required.

ACTIVITY

Make a list of some client groups or issues you feel are beyond your limits of proficiency in terms of your training at this time, considering the following questions:

Why is working within limits an ethical issue for both the client and the counsellor?

Could harm come to a counsellor if they worked beyond their limits, or is it just the client who might be harmed?

In terms of limits of proficiency, is it enough for a counsellor not to harm the client?

In an ideal world, trainee and newly qualified counsellors should only be asked to work with clients within their scope of experience but in the real and complicated world of clients and their lives this is very difficult to do.

EXAMPLE

Ben is a recently qualified counsellor in a GP surgery. He is seeing a client who was referred for mild anxiety and low mood. He establishes a strong and trusting relationship with the client despite her initial misgivings about working with a male counsellor.

(Continued)

(Continued)

In the fourth session, the client discloses that she was raped by her stepfather and is now experiencing flashbacks and panic attacks. Ben is worried that he has had no special training in working with sexual abuse or anxiety and is concerned the client seems to be getting worse.

Ben takes his fears to supervision. What are the issues he should take into account when deciding what to do?

 I am not sure I could work with Ben's client.

 Not at this time, although counsellors sometimes support clients until they get access to more appropriate help, almost in a 'holding' role, as long as these limits are clearly explained to and agreed with the client. It is good that you recognise your limits now. When you start working with clients in a placement, you will be supported to work initially with clients presenting with issues appropriate for your level of experience. A good placement will assess your suitability for working with each client as a trainee counsellor. As you progress in your training and placement, you will be supported to start working with clients with deeper issues.

AGENCY POLICIES, PROCEDURES AND THE LAW

 As well as working within an ethical framework, a counsellor has to work within the specific policies and procedures of the counselling agency where they are seeing clients, and also with conscientious consideration of the law. All these aspects help to keep the client safe and ensure that you work safely. Good agencies will have comprehensive policies and procedures that are updated on a regular basis to take account of good practice and changes in the law. It is also important to remember that if something goes wrong, not knowing your agency's policies or not having legal knowledge is no defence in the eyes of the law.

 What sorts of laws do I need to be aware of? Are there particular laws that govern counselling? Why do I need to be worried about the law if counselling is not a statutorily regulated profession?

 A good question. It would be difficult to cover every aspect of the law but you can get advice and help from your professional body and some, such as BACP, publish specific information on counselling and the law. What would be useful here would be to look at the kinds of legal and ethical issues that inform how agencies operate and what policies and procedures need to be in place.

LEGISLATION WHICH IS LIKELY TO IMPACT ON AGENCIES AND COUNSELLORS

1. Health and safety legislation
2. Control of Substances Hazardous to Health (COSHH)
3. Fire regulations
4. Data protection
5. Equal opportunities legislation
6. Anti-discrimination legislation
7. The European Convention on Human Rights
8. The law and confidentiality
9. The Children's Act and child protection
10. Disability legislation
11. Adoption legislation
12. Prevent Duty in the Counter-Terrorism and Security Act 2015

- What do you know about the areas of law listed above?
- What do you think you need to know?
- What role do these laws play in keeping clients and counsellors safe?

The types of policies and procedures that an agency adopts will reflect the nature of the agency itself and the service that they offer clients. It will be easier for you to get a feel for the different agencies by investigating a few examples.

ACTIVITY

Make a list of a range of counselling agencies in your area. Visit or research a particular agency that interests you:

- What ethical framework does the agency work with?
- What client group does the agency work with?
- What policies and procedures does the agency have?
- How would you feel about this agency as a potential placement?

Consider your responses to the idea of working in each of the different agencies you have on your list. Be aware of what you are thinking and feeling while you do this.

If you are drawn to a particular agency, spend a few moments reflecting on whether this is telling you something about yourself. Are you particularly drawn to this client group or service because of personal experience? If you are averse to certain agencies, what might this mean for you?

ASSESSMENT

'Assessment' means lots of different things in different contexts but essentially it is about evaluating and reaching a judgement about something in order to determine what is appropriate. In a learning context, it could be understood as determining the quality and level of work, while in medicine it might mean reaching a diagnosis in order to prescribe a treatment. In counselling, assessment is about determining whether the counselling being offered is right for the client.

There are lots of tools for making assessments and it is beyond the scope of this book to provide an in-depth list of mental health screening and assessment tools. Many have been developed to cover a range of mental health issues such as those specific to substance abuse, children and young people, anxiety, depression and behaviour problems. What these assessment instruments have in common is a means to determine the type and severity of the client's presenting issues and their appropriateness for the service being offered. Many agencies have their own 'intake forms' but there are also an increasing number of assessment instruments which are used to collect data in standard formats and which offer a way of measuring client outcomes for the individuals and for the agency.

EXAMPLE

An agency intake form might use a simple set of questions to find out:

- the level of the client's distress
- what kind of support network the client has
- when the problem began
- how well the client is functioning in everyday life
- whether there is any risk of harm or suicide.

An example of a standard assessment form which is used nationally is the CORE (Clinical Outcomes in Routine Evaluation) therapy assessment form. This form collects data on the client's relationships and support, current and previous psychological problems, medication, nature and duration of the problem and level of risk at the beginning of therapy. Other CORE forms have been designed to collect outcome data – in other words, what progress (or not) the client has made at the end of therapy. The CORE forms and associated data can be used by individual counsellors free of charge. Alternatively, organisations can pay a fee for a more comprehensive service from CORE which includes data collection and analysis aimed at measuring progress and outcomes in therapy. (You can find out more by visiting the CORE website at www.coreims.co.uk.)

Woah! That all sounds very clinical; I thought counselling was about the relationship we form with the client rather than about classification, diagnosis and treatment.

That is an interesting point, and I guess you could say that there is a medical and a humanistic model of treatment for mental health.

The medical model of assessment

The medical model is based on the idea that the therapist is the expert who knows what is best for the client. They are the expert on mental health issues and psychological problems and therefore know how to treat those problems. Once a diagnosis has been made, this will lead to a specific treatment. This approach comes from the field of medicine where psychiatrists use standard classifications to diagnose what is 'wrong' with the client. One common tool which is used to make such diagnoses is the *Diagnostic and Statistical Manual of Mental Disorders*, now in its fifth edition (DSM-5) (American Psychiatric Association, 2013).

REFLECTION

DSM-5 is sponsored by the drug companies. Do you think it is relevant that research into classifications and drug treatments is done by those who have a vested interest in clients taking medication as part of their treatment?

Why might it be important to reflect on the fact that the number of classifications for mental disorders rises each time a new edition of the DSM is published?

The humanistic model of assessment

The humanistic model of assessment aims not to categorise the client or take the position of expert. This approach is based on a central belief in the client's subjective and inter-subjective experience, the client's own personal feelings and opinions and how these are shared with others. Humanistic practitioners believe that the therapist's role is to work with the client's own language for describing their difficulties rather than giving them a label or diagnosis.

I think I prefer the humanistic model; it sounds more like what counselling is about.

Part of the current debate is how these two diametrically opposite models can be unified in some way. Both have their merits. From a counsellor's point of view, we are not in a position to medically diagnose and as such we are not in a position to advise clients on medication. It is important to recognise that medication has its place in the treatment of mental health problems alongside talking therapies. Whatever your views on the subject, you should always refer your client back to whoever is responsible for their physical health.

 But what exactly are mental health problems? How many people suffer from mental health problems?

 Well, not all counselling approaches would even use the term 'mental health problems', but given that this term is widely used it is important to understand what it means. We all have off days and feel depressed or low in mood, and most people will have periods in their lives when they just don't want to get out of bed or they feel like crying for no apparent reason. The mental health charity Mind suggests that something like one in four people in the UK suffer from common mental health problems, and the incidence continues to rise.

 But how would I know if someone is suffering from a mental health problem?

 Well, as we said, counsellors are not qualified to make a medical diagnosis – this responsibility belongs to doctors and mental health practitioners; but counsellors do need to know about the most common mental health categories which clients present with. Table 8.1 lists some of the most common mental health problems.

It is also useful to consider the effect of mental health problems on the individual. There is still a social stigma attached to mental illness, and those that suffer mental illness experience discrimination in society, in the family and in the workplace. The stigma and discrimination associated with mental illness can compound the condition and delay recovery. People may not seek support and treatment because they fear how others will view them.

Additionally, some cultures and older generations may frown upon help such as counselling. If someone suffers from a long-term mental health problem, they are more likely to have difficulties finding work, sustaining adequate housing, holding down long-term friendships and relationships or being part of mainstream society.

TABLE 8.1   Common mental health problems

Depression	Depression can be experienced at different levels from mild to severe. The common factor in depression is a lowering of mood which can manifest in feelings of worthlessness or lack of motivation and feelings of exhaustion. Depression can occur due to specific life events such as postnatal depression or after the death of a loved one, or it can appear from nowhere. There are many explanations for the causes of depression.
Anxiety	Anxiety, sometimes along with panic attacks, relates to a constant and often unrealistic worry about something. Physical symptoms may manifest such as feeling sweaty or having a dry throat.

Eating disorder	An eating disorder is often symptomatic of other life issues or as a way of managing emotions and feelings. There are a range of eating disorders, the most common being anorexia, bulimia and compulsive eating.
Obsessive compulsive disorder (OCD)	OCD is made up of two elements: *obsessions* relating to constant thoughts which are negative or unrealistic, such as a constant fear of being afflicted by dirt or germs; this then results in *compulsive* behaviours, such as constant cleaning or hand washing.
Bipolar disorder	Although there are different degrees of bipolar disorder, the common factors are mood swings from periods of feeling low/depressed to feeling high/overactive.
Phobia	A phobia is a fear of an object or situation which the sufferer goes to great lengths to avoid. The fear is characterised as irrational and disproportionate, such as arachnophobia (fear of spiders) and agoraphobia (fear of open spaces).

REFLECTION

- How do you feel about mental health problems?
- Do you know anyone that has been diagnosed with a mental health condition and how did you respond?
- Have you ever suffered from a mental health problem?
- How do people you know react to people with mental health illnesses?
- How do the media portray people with mental health conditions?

But let's get back to what this might mean for you beginning counselling work in an agency context as a trainee counsellor.

CRITICAL THINKING

Once a client has a 'diagnosis' for depression, anxiety, mood disorder or any other common mental health problem, they also have a 'label':

- What are the likely advantages to the client of having a diagnosis and a label?
- What are the possible disadvantages of having a diagnosis and a label?
- What would be/has been your own response to having a diagnosis and a label?

Some people would argue that a person with a psychotic mental illness just has a different view of reality. What is your response to this statement?

In an ideal world, clients should be assessed by a more experienced counsellor before being passed to you to work with as a trainee, in which case you would not need to worry so much about initial assessment. However, this does not always happen and it is important that you have an understanding of what client assessment means in a counselling context. As we have said, counsellors do not undertake clinical assessments because counsellors are not medically trained to diagnose clients or to make any clinical decisions. Nonetheless, counsellors do have to make an assessment as to whether a client is able to engage in the process of counselling and whether the client is suited to the model of counselling being offered, and also the level of experience of the counsellor who will undertake the work. The counsellor additionally needs to be able to assess the client's ability to hold themselves together between sessions and be as confident as possible that the client is not in need of a more specialist kind of help.

Sometimes it transpires that the client needs practical support rather than counselling – such as help with a housing or debt problem. It could be that the client is presenting to the wrong agency and needs to be referred to a specific agency that will meet their needs.

It is important to emphasise here that you would not need to make these decisions on your own but would have the support of your agency and supervisor to discuss any issues or concerns you may have.

 I am confused – are you saying that different types of clients benefit from different models of counselling? Is that why we do an assessment?

 Not exactly, but the model of counselling might determine the kind of assessment that the counsellor does, both in terms of what they are trying to assess and what tools they may use to do this. It also helps to determine whether there is a good fit between what the client is seeking and what the counsellor can offer.

ASSESSMENT IN DIFFERENT APPROACHES

- A behavioural counsellor might undertake a behavioural analysis to determine what the client may be trying to avoid.
- A cognitive therapist might make an assessment of the client's patterns of thoughts and behaviours.
- A person-centred therapist might make an assessment based on whether the client is able to form a relationship in which the client can feel the counsellor's acceptance of them.
- A psychodynamic therapist might want to assess the client's ego strength and their ability to cope with working with unconscious processes.

 Oh dear, this is all straying into territory about different approaches that we haven't yet covered, but in a general sense the counsellor is making some form of judgement as to whether the service being offered is going to be right for the client, because there needs to be a match between what the counsellor can offer and the type of intervention the client expects and needs in order for the counselling to have the best outcome. In all cases, whatever the approach, the counsellor needs to establish whether the client is able to form a therapeutic alliance because without such an alliance the counselling is unlikely to work.

SUMMARY OF THE PURPOSE OF INITIAL ASSESSMENT IN COUNSELLING

- To give the client an experience of counselling and enable them to find out how it might help them. A client can ask questions and make a choice whether to go ahead with further sessions.
- To give the counsellor an opportunity to explore whether what they can offer meets the client's specific needs.
- To assess the strength, motivation and resilience of the client and their ability to engage in the counselling process.
- To enable both the counsellor and the client to decide whether they can work together.
- To refer the client to another kind of help if what you can offer is not right for them.

REFERRAL

 I can see that there will be times when I might need to refer the client to another source of help, but how would I know what is the best help for the client? How would I refer a client I feel I am not suited to work with?

 Just as a helper needs to be aware of other sources of support in their area, it is important for a counsellor to build local knowledge of the different counselling agencies and types of support available. These could, for example, include the local women's refuge for domestic violence, children and adult services, housing and benefits, employment agencies, day-care facilities, local support groups, local doctors and the Citizens Advice Bureau.

You will also need to be aware of other counsellors, therapists and agencies and understand the roles of other relevant organisations, such as the local mental health team and the Child and Adolescent Mental Health Service (CAMHS). It is important, not to mention ethical, to be mindful of when you have reached your level of expertise or proficiency and to know where you can refer a client on to, either at the assessment stage or later on in the course of the counselling work.

 It might be a good idea to compile a resource book of all the agencies, counsellors and support organisations in my area so that I have the information to hand, but how do I actually make the referral?

This needs to be handled sensitively and carefully. It is always important to ensure that you do not make the client feel that it is their fault that you cannot work with them or that they are being passed from pillar to post.

CRITICAL THINKING

- **Case example 1**: Steve was rejected by his father at birth and thrown out of the house by his mother in his teens. He does not have close friends.
- **Case example 2**: Laura blames herself for everything and suffers from low self-esteem.

   How might the process of referral be experienced by these two clients?

   How might you respond to being referred yourself?

You need to discuss with the client your reasoning behind wanting to make the referral. This would include highlighting the benefits of the referral and explaining why it would be in the client's best interests. You need to leave space for the client to explore their feelings and responses and to work through all the possible consequences for them.

 But if I was working with a client who needed help with housing, for example, would this necessarily mean that they did not need counselling too?

 That is a good point and maybe I have confused you here. Some referrals are for additional support and your role can include working with the client to empower them to seek that additional help. However, if there are other reasons why it would not be advisable for you to work with or continue working with a client, you need to make a referral.

When you are working in an agency, the organisation might take responsibility for making the referral, but sometimes this can take time and you might go on working with the client until this can be arranged.

KEY POINTS WHEN MAKING A REFERRAL

1. Discuss the need to make a referral with your supervisor and/or agency manager to get help and support and reach the best possible decision.
2. Discuss the reason and purpose of the referral with the client.
3. Obtain the client's consent for the referral wherever possible.
4. Obtain the client's permission to share any notes and records that may support a clear transition where appropriate.

I had not thought of the issue of confidentiality, but that seems to be very clear.

It is important to be clear of the process with the client and how the referral will benefit them. Part of that benefit may be sharing the work you have done so far with the client, though it is likely that the other agency will also do their own assessment.

Once counselling has begun and long after the assessment stage, there may still be occasions when clients need to be referred for other kinds of help. This might be because they become more fragile or show signs of more severe or complex mental health problems, or because an issue requiring specialist intervention comes to light. In such cases, the client may need to be referred back to their GP initially and then on to a psychologist or psychiatrist to receive appropriate help and/or medication. In addition, there may be more practical or logistical reasons why a referral is necessary. Here are a few examples:

- The client might be moving to another part of the country.
- The counsellor might be leaving the agency.
- A client in individual counselling might decide to start couple counselling to work on their relationship.

I am sure you can think of a few examples of your own! Let's draw this all together by reflecting on an example.

REFLECTION

Jackie is a senior supervisor at a busy agency and has agreed to manage Rose, who has just started her placement at the agency. Jackie is responsible for assessing all new clients and Rose is keen to start working with clients. Jackie has not had time to find a suitable client for Rose but suggests that Rose has a quick look at some of the new files to see if there are any clients coming with issues that could be defined as common life events. Rose reads one file about a client, Jack, who is 26 and has been referred by his GP with mild depression after his long-term partner left him for a younger man. Rose shares this with Jackie and Jackie gives the go-ahead for Rose to arrange a first session with Jack.

The work with Jack starts well, though Rose is taken by surprise that Jack was in a relationship with an older man and is finding some aspects of what she is told uncomfortable. In session six, Jack reveals that he can no longer cope with being on his own, that he just wants to end it all. Jack also reveals that he has a history of

(Continued)

(Continued)

depression and takes medication to manage his bipolar disorder. Rose panics and tells Jack that she will need to make a referral. Jack gets very upset because he feels that Rose is rejecting him; he leaves, saying, 'What's the point?'

1. What do you feel went wrong here?
2. Whose responsibility was it that this issue arose?
3. How should the client have been assessed?
4. If you were Rose, how would you have approached the need for a referral with Jack?
5. What lessons could Rose and the agency learn from this?

SUMMARY

In order to work within an ethical, procedural and legal framework as a counsellor, you need to:

- Adopt an ethical framework for counselling and abide by relevant legislation.
- Monitor and work within your personal and professional limits of proficiency.
- Understand the legal and procedural framework of specific counselling agencies.
- Understand the process of assessment and referral within an agency context.

9
Understanding the Counselling Relationship

This chapter looks at the role of the counsellor in different counselling settings and what this means for the client. It explores how to establish and maintain the boundaries of the counselling relationship, how to manage the stages of the relationship and the counselling process, and how to make good endings.

THE COUNSELLOR ROLE IN DIFFERENT SETTINGS

In Part I, we examined how to establish a helping relationship and how to work within the boundaries of your role as a helper and within the specific context of each situation. We now need to consider how the whole issue of boundaries, roles and relationship are relevant to a counsellor working in an agency setting.

What exactly do you mean by an agency setting?

Counselling organisations are often referred to as 'agencies'. Different agencies offer different services and have different purposes and aims, and this may mean that as a counsellor you will have different expectations and limitations placed on you. There may also be other professionals working with individual clients you are seeing. The counsellor needs to work within the remit of a particular agency.

For example, if you are working within a substance misuse agency, the focus of the counselling will be on the substance misuse and steps to recovery. You may have to work within a particular theoretical model and there may be constraints on the number of sessions and the focus of the counselling. You may also be obliged to share your work with other professionals, which will have a direct effect on the boundaries of confidentiality. In other words, you will have to consider what information you are obliged to share and when you might have to breach confidentiality.

Does that mean that I cannot just work with what a client chooses to bring to the session?

Well, you are quite right that client issues can't just be put into categories and dealt with separately – human beings are just not that simple! In most cases, all client issues are muddled up and confused but certain agencies may be funded or set up for a particular purpose and you would need to consider the terms and conditions of the particular agency that you work in. It is possible that the counselling service being offered in a particular setting may not be able to address all the client's needs, especially where the number of sessions is limited. However, the most important thing is that the client understands what is being offered and is able to make an informed choice about whether they want to engage in the counselling or not.

I would certainly want to be clear before I put my trust in someone.

Quite. It is also important to consider what expectations the client has of the counsellor. The client should be able to expect the counsellor to be appropriately qualified for the work being offered in a particular setting. This will include the level of training and the focus of that training. Some agencies offer specialised training to counsellors who are studying on a general counselling course. Some agencies train volunteers just to work within their particular agency with a single focus. So it is important for both parties to find out about each other at the beginning of the relationship.

Consider how the counsellor's role and the client's expectations may be affected by a counselling service being offered in these different settings. Some examples are given in Table 9.1.

TABLE 9.1   Counselling agencies and counsellor role

Agency focus	Counsellor's role
Bereavement	To support clients coping with the death or loss of someone close to them.
Women's refuge	To support clients to deal with violence against them.
Sexual abuse	To support clients to come to terms and deal with the effect of past or present sexual abuse.
Adoption counselling	To support clients to work on adoption issues, as well as offering support in all related issues, e.g. access to birth family, contact arrangement, access to legal records.
Rehabilitation centre	To support clients to manage issues and lifestyle around substance misuse. Some agencies may focus on abstinence while others may support safe use.
Relationships	To support clients to work on and manage their close relationships.
Children and young people	To support children and young people. This requires specialist training and knowledge of child protection and safeguarding.

Leaving aside all the different expectations of the counsellor and the client in different agencies for a moment, what would you expect from counselling in general?

Well, I would hope it would be about talking to somebody who could give me some solid advice and point me in the right direction, or perhaps make some suggestions about how to sort things out.

Hmm … that is probably the most common expectation of all – that counsellors will give advice and make suggestions, but this is not really what they do, which can be quite a hard thing to explain to someone who is desperate for help. This takes us to a really basic question – what is counselling? Let's look at a couple of definitions:

> Counselling is a type of talking therapy that allows a person to talk about their problems and feelings in a confidential and dependable environment. (NHS, n.d.)

> Counselling and psychotherapy are umbrella terms that cover a range of talking therapies. They are delivered by trained practitioners who work with people over a short or long term to help them bring about effective change or enhance their well-being. (BACP, n.d.a)

Woah! Hang on a minute: 'talking therapies', 'psychotherapy', 'counselling' – what's the difference, or are they all the same? And while we are on the subject, I have always been confused about 'psychiatrist'/'psychologist' too – anything beginning with 'psych' freaks me out.

I was rather hoping you would not ask that question because the answer isn't simple. Practitioners and their respective professional bodies have been arguing about whether there is a difference between counselling and psychotherapy since the words were first used, without coming to any agreement. However, there are some things we can say for sure. Both counselling and psychotherapy are 'talking therapies' and both are focused on helping the client talk about their problems or issues in a safe and confidential space with a trained person to help them come to a better place in their lives. The term 'therapist' or 'practitioner' is often used to avoid getting bogged down in this argument, and whatever the finer points, there is definitely a considerable overlap between the roles. We can leave it there for now but I will try to explain the other roles you asked about because they may also deliver 'talking therapy'. Table 9.2 gives a brief overview of all the words you have just mentioned.

It is also important to clarify what counselling is not. Counselling is not about giving advice and is not about bringing a client round to the counsellor's way of thinking. It is not just a cosy chat between two people, such as you might

TABLE 9.2   Definitions of terms

Therapist (Counsellor or Psychotherapist)	A lay person who is trained to work in a professional therapeutic relationship with clients. There are many different models and approaches, and trainings can vary in depth and length. Those who identify a difference between counselling and psychotherapy argue that psychotherapy training is longer, at greater depth and equips the therapist to work with more complex issues. Those who do not accept a difference point to the fact that experienced counsellors and psychotherapists do the same kind of work with the same kinds of clients.
Psychologist	A lay person who has undertaken a psychology degree. A psychologist can then train at doctoral level to be a 'counselling psychologist' or 'clinical psychologist' and deliver talking therapy.
Psychiatrist	A medical person who has completed a medical degree and then specialised in psychiatry, which includes the ability to prescribe medication and treat patients with severe mental illness. Some psychiatrists also train as psychotherapists.

have with a friend. It is not the same as 'befriending', although befrienders might use counselling skills in their befriending role. Counselling is not the same as mentoring or coaching or peer support, all of which have different roles and purposes. Counselling is about a formally contracted agreement where a person (who generally has no other role or relationship with the client) works with the client (or clients in the case of couple or group work) to empower them to make decisions, come to terms with life events and find solutions to their own issues without bias from the counsellor.

 What you just said about generally 'no other role or relationship' and 'formally contracted' sounds pretty essential. How do you go about creating this relationship?

 Well, it all starts with setting the boundaries.

ESTABLISHING THE BOUNDARIES OF THE COUNSELLING RELATIONSHIP

Being clear about all the elements needed for the counselling to take place is usually referred to as 'setting the boundaries' and 'agreeing the contract'. This means having a discussion and agreeing certain details with the client. Some counselling agencies require the client to sign a written contract.

The areas you would normally need to include in the discussion are:

- clarifying your role and limits of ability
- clarifying the boundaries of confidentiality (including note taking, client records, agency policy on sharing information, legal limitations)

- explaining and agreeing the time boundaries of the session, the number of sessions and where and when the sessions will take place
- clarifying any procedural issues, e.g. cancellations, contact arrangements between sessions
- clarifying the client's expectations of counselling in relation to what the counsellor can offer
- making a formal agreement to work together.

We have talked about clarifying the counsellor role in some detail already, so let's move on to confidentiality.

Confidentiality

As we saw in helping work, it is important to make the limits of confidentiality clear, not only because it is vital for building trust but also because any breach of confidentiality can have serious consequences. Unlike helping work, which can take place in many informal settings with variable boundaries, the boundaries for counselling work should be clear from the outset and remain constant.

Although there is a general obligation that counselling be confidential, there are some important exceptions which the counsellor must explain to the client as early as possible. Some of these exceptions are legal and universal and others may relate specifically to the context in which the counselling is taking place.

Counselling trainees are often taught to say that 'Everything is confidential unless there is a serious risk to self or others', because this broadly covers the exceptions; but it is important to bear in mind that if this were put to the test, a court would probably uphold the client's case for a breach of confidentiality if the counsellor could not reasonably evidence that the client or others were actually at serious risk.

 It sounds like a bit of a minefield.

 It is certainly complex and not something to be done lightly, because in essence a breach of confidentiality has to be established as legally defensible. Bond (2002) sets out three types of disclosure that could be deemed defensible in law:

1. where consent to disclose has been obtained
2. where information is already public knowledge
3. where the balance of public interest would favour disclosure.

If the client consents to the disclosure (e.g. for the counsellor to discuss particulars with their doctor), then formal consent has been given to disclose. Bond further points out that a counsellor would be unlikely to risk making a disclosure assuming prior public knowledge. The third reason, that the disclosure is in the public interest and therefore justified, would assume that others were at significant risk.

 Is there anywhere I can go for help if I want advice on whether to breach confidentiality?

 You can consult the most recent guidance from your professional body or give them a ring and ask for advice. You would also discuss any concerns with your supervisor, who could help you interpret the relevant information and understand the law. For example, there are some exceptions where there is a duty to breach confidentiality. These obligations fall into several categories:

> **Crime**: a counsellor can breach confidentiality if they reasonably suspect or know that a client is engaged in criminal activity under S115 of the Crime and Public Disorder Act 1998.

> **Public interest**: a breach of confidentiality may be defensible in preventing serious harm, either to the client or others, or if it would be in the public interest to prevent serious harm.

> **Statutory obligations**: there are several statutory laws where a counsellor would be obliged to breach client confidentiality; these include the Terrorism Act 2000, Counter-terrorism and Security Act 2015, Drug Trafficking Act 1994, Proceeds of Crime Act 2002 and Money Laundering Regulations 2007.

> **Child protection**: counsellors have a statutory duty to breach confidentiality when working within a statutory agency, but also would be supported in breaching confidentiality under Public Duty.

> **Court orders**: a counsellor may be ordered to release any records they have on a client or attend and answer questions on a client in court.

It is important to remember that when considering a disclosure you need to have accurate information and not make unjust claims that you cannot support. A client about whom you make false claims could sue you for defamation.

A good source of information on breaches to confidentiality is *Standards and Ethics for Counselling in Action* (Bond, 2015).

In addition, the BACP's Policy and Public Affairs Department has published a range of briefings on the Prevent Duty and its implications within a variety of settings where counsellors may work:

- Health and social care
- Specified local authorities
- Higher Education sector

- Further Education sector
- Registered childcare providers
- Probation systems.

 Woah! I have heard about Prevent Duty but I am not sure what it is all about. I think it is something to do with terrorism!

 You are on the right lines. It is part of the Counter-Terrorism and Security Act 2015 for specified authorities to assess the risk of a person being drawn into terrorism; this includes being exposed to extremist ideas or terrorist ideology. If the counsellor was working in one of the settings listed above, it would be their responsibility to check what the counselling agency's policy is on safeguarding, including the Prevent Duty. BACP offers some help and advice on their website (BACP, n.d.b).

As you can see, there is a lot to think about in terms of when you can and cannot breach confidentiality. It is important for you to remember that you are not alone, and you will have the support of your agency and a supervisor with whom to discuss the pros and cons if you felt you had an obligation to breach confidentiality. BACP also has a legal helpline which is part of its membership service. Let's look at some examples:

CASE EXAMPLE 1

A counsellor is working with Gary in a GP surgery and Gary discloses that he has decided to stop taking his medication. Would you feel it necessary to inform Gary's GP and what would your reasoning be? How might this affect the counsellor's relationship with Gary?

CASE EXAMPLE 2

A counsellor has been working with Sian (aged 15) for five weeks and gradually built a trusting relationship. During the fifth session, Sian pulls up her sleeve and shows the counsellor multiple razor-blade cuts on her arms – both scars and fresh incisions. Would you need to tell anyone? What effect might this have on the therapeutic relationship?

As you can see, issues relating to harm are not always clear-cut. Even at the extreme end, if the client states that they are suicidal, some counsellors from some theoretical backgrounds would argue that they had a duty of care to disclose this information to protect the client. Conversely, others would argue that it is the client's right to choose and not for the counsellor to decide. Another consideration would be whether you could justify a breach of confidentiality on legal grounds as the legal system could support the client's right to confidentiality unless such a limit to the confidentiality had been carefully contracted.

 So what you are saying is that the law is not black and white and that I may have to make a judgement on a case-by-case basis? That seems an awful lot of responsibility for the counsellor to carry. I am not sure I would know how to act in the client's best interests but I think I can understand both sides of the argument.

 This is why it is important to make the boundaries of confidentiality as clear as possible right at the beginning when you agree the contract with the client – always remembering that different agencies have different confidentiality boundaries. It might be particularly important to explain exactly what notes or information you will be recording about the client and explain where these will be kept and who will have access to them. This includes being familiar with data protection issues. But don't panic – this will all be explained in the agency's policies and procedures.

CRITICAL THINKING

John is working with Marina in a young person's counselling agency for 16–25-year-olds. Marina discloses that she was systematically abused by her stepfather when she was in her early teens. Marina now lives away from home with her boyfriend but flashbacks are causing problems in her physical relationship with him.

At the beginning of counselling, John made a general statement that he would have to breach confidentiality if Marina disclosed harm to herself or others:

- Does John have a duty to disclose Marina's abuse to the agency manager?
- Would it make a difference if Marina said she still visits home occasionally?
- Would it make a difference if Marina was 17 or 25 now?
- Would it make a difference if the setting was a GP practice rather than this agency?
- Would it make a difference if agency policy was that all instances of abuse – historic or current – must be disclosed to the agency manager?

How might your answers to any of these questions affect what you said about confidentiality at the beginning?

For now, it is important to realise that there are limits to confidentiality and that, the clearer you can be at the outset, the less likely it is that you will have to break your word if something unexpected is disclosed. It is also important to consider that the client's ability to make a rational decision may be diminished because of the state of their mental health.

I am beginning to understand why a trainee counsellor has to start off in an agency placement rather than seeing clients in their own home or in a rented room. This all feels like a huge amount of responsibility to carry on my own and it feels reassuring to think that somebody else is sharing the load and offering support. So once confidentiality is sorted, what happens next?

Setting the boundaries of time and place

Do you remember we said that helping sessions could be quite informal and probably not regularly spaced or of a fixed length but simply agreed each time? Well, in counselling it is quite different. Sessions are usually of a fixed length and the overall number of sessions will be either fixed by what the agency offers or formally agreed during the 'contracting' stage. There will also usually be a dedicated counselling room in a safe confidential place where the sessions will happen. All this needs to be explained and discussed at the beginning.

I am starting to wonder how on earth it is possible to remember all these issues, discuss them and agree them before even getting down to talking about the client's problems. Are counsellors allowed to use checklists to help them remember?

Well, it can certainly help to have an information sheet to give the client which covers everything that you have discussed. This is why some agencies have a written contract, but I haven't quite finished the boundary-setting stage – there is more to come! Have you considered the importance of being clear about how the client cancels a session if they need to; whether they still have to pay if they miss a session (if money is involved); and whether or not they will be offered another session if they don't turn up? By the way, when a client doesn't turn up, it is usually called a DNA which stands for 'Did not arrive'.

Well, that's one to remember, but on this 'making contact' issue I would have thought it would be OK to phone, text or email to let the counsellor know … but then I would not want a client phoning me on my mobile during a family meal or while I'm at work or with another client.

The important thing is to try to get all this clear during the contracting stage so that you can focus more on building the kind of relationship that will be therapeutic for the client. It also helps to practise finding the right words in different counselling settings and to check with the client that they are OK with what is being offered and agreed.

> **ACTIVITY**
>
> Imagine you are working as a volunteer counsellor for an NHS agency which offers up to three sessions of counselling to support women who are making a choice about having an abortion. The agency policy is that information can be shared with other NHS personnel, and records of the client's attendance and final decision are kept on the computer system. No other notes are kept. There is a dedicated room for counselling and times are agreed with the client for all three sessions at the outset. There is a waiting list so missed sessions can't be made up. Any messages about appointments or cancellations can be sent by email or telephoned through and are handled by the central admin team.
>
> Practise to see if you can find the words to set the boundaries for a counselling relationship with a client – remembering that it is not just a lecture but a negotiation!

Now, let's look at why the counselling relationship is so important.

THE COUNSELLING RELATIONSHIP

The counselling relationship is fundamental to the counselling process and the outcome of counselling. Research shows that the counselling relationship, especially the 'working alliance' aspect of the relationship, is one of the factors that contribute to therapeutic change (Cooper, 2008: 125). The counsellor will be used to working with clients and familiar with the type of relationship that is being offered, but it is helpful to explore the client's understanding of the counselling relationship, their expectations and any previous experience of counselling.

Different therapists work from different theoretical models of counselling which place a different emphasis on the nature and quality of the relationship as a factor for therapeutic change. These models fall broadly into three types of relational category:

1. **Person-centred and experiential models**: the relationship is considered central to the therapeutic process. The aim is to create an atmosphere where the quality of the relationship, founded on empathy and non-judgemental acceptance of the client, enables them to accept themselves and find their own solutions.
2. **Psychodynamic traditions**: the relationship focuses on working with the client's unconscious processes. As an 'expert', the counsellor may offer a number of interpretations, including those about the relationship, as a way of shedding light on the client's difficulties and helping them to make links between past and present.

3. **Cognitive-behavioural therapies**: the relationship is more like that of a teacher and student. The therapist's role is to challenge and break down irrational beliefs and guide the client towards more realistic goals and expectations.

This is a simplification of what is a very complex field and we will revisit these ideas in Chapters 12 and 13, but you can see that these different kinds of relationships can result in very different ways of working. It is therefore important to establish the client's previous experience of counselling and their expectations. Clients who have engaged in counselling before may have had good or bad experiences which will affect their involvement and motivation, but it is also an opportunity to clarify whether there is a fit between what the client is looking for and what you are offering.

REFLECTION

If the client had a bad/good experience with their last counsellor, how might this affect the development of the relationship with you?

If the client is expecting a counselling approach which offers them strategies and homework, how might they react to you offering a relationship that is non-directive?

If the client finds it generally difficult to trust people, how might this affect their ability to trust you?

Contemporary research (Cooper, 2008) shows a number of factors that contribute to effective outcomes for clients receiving counselling. It has been suggested that perhaps as much as 30% of effective counselling is based on the relationship, but this is not something that is given to the client by the counsellor; rather, it is developed through the course of counselling. Although different theoretical models emphasise different types of relationship, at the core of the relationship there needs to be a positive working alliance where both parties are working together towards the client's objectives.

DEFINITIONS

The *therapeutic relationship* is a unique relationship that fosters an intimate connection between the counsellor and client, where the client is able to explore their feelings, thoughts and beliefs in a safe environment where they do not feel censored or feel the need to conform.

Working alliance is the agreement made between the counsellor and client, along with the agreed focus of the work to be undertaken and how that work will be done.

Alongside the relationship, other factors contribute towards change. Crucially, research suggests that the client is the most important single factor in effective counselling, accounting for up to 70% of a successful outcome for client change. This recognises that the client's active participation in the process of counselling, their willingness to engage in therapy and their desire to change are far more important than the type of counselling being offered.

 So, let me see if I can understand this: the two most important things for effective therapy are the relationship with the client and the client wanting to engage in counselling. It makes sense really – if the client does not want to be in therapy or does not believe it will work, then it will not really be effective, but where does the therapist or the theoretical orientation come into it?

 Current research shows that different types of counselling therapy are probably equally effective but there is something about the characteristics of the therapist that can also contribute to change. It is suggested that the more self-aware the counsellor is, the more effective they are, and this factor alone can contribute up to 10% towards effective therapy.

 So, a counsellor who is not self-aware will have less of an impact on the counselling relationship?

 That would seem to be the case. See Chapter 5 where we explored this further. For now, it is important to understand that the centrality of the counselling relationship is one of several factors that contribute to change.

> Factors that contribute to therapeutic change:
>
> - The type of therapy offered has the least impact on outcomes.
> - The counsellor contributes up to 10% (depending on their self-awareness).
> - The therapeutic relationship contributes up to 30% towards change.
> - The client's own motivation and willingness to engage in therapy accounts for 70% of the outcome and is the most crucial factor in therapeutic change.
>
> You will find more information on the research findings in Chapter 20 in Part III, which draws on work by Mick Cooper (2008).

THE STAGES OF THE COUNSELLING RELATIONSHIP AND THE COUNSELLING PROCESS

Setting the boundaries is the first stage in beginning a counselling relationship but like all relationships it is made up of different stages. As such, it can be helpful to think in terms of the different stages of the relationship and the different stages of the counselling process.

Counselling process? What does that mean?

'Process' is a key word in counselling. It includes the relationship between the counsellor and the client but it means more than that. It means, literally, anything that is 'going on' in the counselling experience. This includes:

- what's happening for the client
- what's happening for the counsellor
- what's happening between them (spoken and unspoken)
- what stage the counselling is at
- what progress is (or is not) being made.

No matter what the client's issues are or what theoretical orientation informs the work, or whether progress is being made, there is always something 'going on', even if that something is 'stuckness'! So 'process' is the word we use to describe what's happening and how one thing leads to another. The idea of process is common to all counselling approaches but what you are looking at, how you describe it and what is significant will depend on what models and theories you use to:

- explain what you do
- do what you do
- reflect on what you do.

So the counselling process and the counselling relationship go through common stages. A simple but elegant way of structuring the process and the relationship is to think in terms of a Beginning, Middle and Ending.

Stage 1: Beginning – establishing the relationship and agreeing how to work together

The most important part of this stage is building the relationship. From the start, it is important that the counsellor provides a safe place for the client. The client needs to feel heard in their own terms and feel that they can trust the counsellor to hear and understand what they are saying. In a sense, the counsellor is helping the client to make contact with what is happening for them right now and clarifying what the client wants from counselling and how they are going to work together.

During this stage, the counsellor will be carefully checking their understanding of the client's story through empathic reflections and questions to seek clarification. The counsellor may also start to hear what is unsaid or unacknowledged by the client, perhaps feeding back the 'blind spots' or implied meanings that the client is not engaging with or aware of. Throughout this process, the client is supported in seeking a fuller picture for what is going on for them. With this clarity, the counsellor can then support the client to identify their objectives and choose the focus for their work together.

Stage 2: Middle – working with the client on their issues towards change

Once the client has clarified and understood their issues and is clear what the focus of the work needs to be, the counsellor uses their knowledge, understanding and skills to actively facilitate the client's progress towards their objectives using skills and interventions consistent with their way of working. Client objectives may vary from specific concrete changes in the external world to more intrinsic internal changes, such as self-acceptance or healing. This will depend on the client, the therapist and the nature of the therapy. The Middle stage is often turbulent and Experienced as more ambivalent than the other two stages, as the client struggles with the process of change and responds to the increased depth and challenge of the work. This response is only possible if trust is established and the working alliance is solid.

Stage 3: End – working towards an ending

During this final stage, the counsellor supports and encourages the client in making and living with the changes or finding strategies to achieve their objectives. The counsellor is also preparing the client for the ending so that the client is able to sustain change and manage without the support of counselling.

The client is the centre of this process model, which can also be applied to each individual counselling session in microcosm. However, it is important to remember that the client will not necessarily work through these stages in a linear way. If there are any breaks or ruptures in the counselling relationship (planned or unplanned), or there is a loss of trust, or an unexpected introduction of new issues into the work, then it might be appropriate to revisit Stage 1, but it is always important to pay attention to the end stage.

 Why is the end stage so important?

Issues to reflect on when ending the counselling relationship

 In Part I, we looked at some of the skills needed to manage the ending of helping sessions but there are additional factors to consider when ending a counselling relationship. Ideally, the relationship will end with some time and consideration given to the journey undertaken, how the client has moved forward, what has been achieved and what is still left to do. Both counsellor and client will approach the agreed ending in a planned way with all the loose ends tied up neatly. However, the reality is very different. Here are some possible scenarios:

- The client may end the relationship unexpectedly by not turning up.
- The client may need more sessions but has used up the agency allocation.
- Something may prevent the counsellor from being there at the ending.

Ending a relationship is more complicated than ending a single session.

I don't much like endings. I don't even like the word 'ending' really. It always sounds so final.

Most people find endings difficult, so it is not surprising that clients do too. That is why it is important to try to find out about the client's experience of endings and to factor this in when anticipating endings in counselling. This is a huge subject but I want you to get the feel of the kinds of ways that understanding the client's personal history of endings can be important when making a 'good' ending in counselling. Let's look at a few examples.

ACTIVITY

Take a few moments to think about what might be important when ending with the following clients:

Case 1: Charlie

Charlie has been working on issues of low self-esteem and confidence. He quickly formed a trusting relationship with his counsellor and can never remember how many sessions he has left. He still lives at home with his mother.

Case 2: Corrie

Corrie has found it difficult to trust the counsellor. Her experience is that people always let her down so she usually ditches friends and partners before they ditch her.

Case 3: James

James is very practical and task-focused and finds it difficult to show his feelings. He has been working on how to allow himself to be more vulnerable in close relationships.

Now it's time to turn the spotlight the other way and ask a few questions about you and your own experience of endings.

REFLECTION

Take a moment to think about how you would react to the following ending scenarios:

- A client you worked well with does not turn up for the final session.
- A client says, 'It's not really an ending because I know I can always come back.'
- A client bursts into tears in the closing moments of the session and says he cannot cope without counselling.
- You have worked towards an ending with a client who arrives at the final session to say that her GP has given her permission for six more sessions.
- A client says the counselling has not helped at all but thanks you for your time.

Be aware of your thoughts and feelings and consider how your own experience might impact on your ability to make 'good endings' with clients.

I don't think I know what you mean by a 'good' ending. Why do clients have to have good endings? If everyone is different, how can a counsellor learn to do a good ending? And how on earth do you make a good ending with someone who does not turn up to say goodbye?

These are all good questions. The key here is to factor in what the ending might mean for the client and to give them the opportunity to express and explore their feelings about their ending. The counsellor can use their knowledge of the client to be sensitive to what the issues are likely to be and gently probe to facilitate the client to talk about what is relevant for them. Let's revisit the examples above.

EXAMPLES

The following is the kind of thing the counsellor might say to each of the clients above, bearing in mind what the counsellor knows about the issues and being sensitive to endings.

Case 1: Charlie

Charlie, you seem to be finding it difficult to remember how many sessions you have left and I am wondering whether you are finding it hard to think about leaving here.

Case 2: Corrie

Corrie, I know that you try to deal with endings by putting the boot in first so I want to check out whether you will be able to face coming to our last session together or whether you will do a runner.

Case 3: James

James, we have been talking about how difficult you find it to express your feelings so it might be particularly important to explore how you feel about ending counselling with me.

Counsellors cannot know what happens to their clients and are often left with the 'unknowing'. Even after the best ending, the counsellor never really knows what happens next. This is the nature of the work but it is much harder for the counsellor if the client abandons therapy and does not return. It is worth remembering that we can never know if a client will return each week so each session should be seen as an ending in its own right. For this reason, it is often helpful to end a session with some sort of summary about what has been explored, clarified and discussed during the time together. Sometimes doing a 'good ending' is the most important thing you do for a client because it can heal past experiences of difficult endings.

SUMMARY

In order to understand and work with the counselling relationship, you need to:

- Understand the role of the counsellor and the context in which they work.
- Understand the importance of setting boundaries for the counselling relationship, especially confidentiality.
- Reflect on the importance of the counselling relationship as a significant factor in therapeutic change.
- Understand the stages of the counselling relationship.
- Understand the importance of making 'good endings' with clients.

10
Understanding Difference and Diversity to Develop Empathic Understanding

We explored why an understanding of diversity and difference was important when using counselling skills in helping roles. We are now going to broaden that understanding and consider difference and diversity within our own personal relationships and in the wider social context in order to understand how this impacts on counselling.

DIFFERENCE AND DIVERSITY IN RELATIONSHIPS

 So, how is diversity relevant to my personal relationships? I mean, I choose my own friends, don't I?

 That is a good point but I guess we need to look at the kinds of people you have in your friendship group. It would perhaps be safe to say that your friends are people that you have something in common with, such as shared interests or beliefs, or a similar cultural background or education.

 But not all my friends are the same as me. Many of my friends are different from me in lots of ways.

And you would be right. We have already explored that we are all individual and that we are all different. But a wider question might be: what draws us towards certain people? Why do we feel more comfortable around some people than others?

REFLECTION

- Who are your friends?
- Who are your closest friends?
- What draws you towards your friends?
- What are the qualities and similarities that you share?

That might have been an easy exercise to do but reflecting on what draws us towards certain people is important. Conversely, we also need to explore what keeps us more distant from some people. What makes us wary of some people? What makes us feel unsafe? Whom do we avoid? These types of questions are relevant to the counsellor. Counsellors have to work with a diverse range of clients and enter each client's unique world. Clients will present with many different values, ideals and beliefs. A good counsellor will be able to set aside their own preferences and enter the client's frame of reference and subjective view of the world. The term *frame of reference* is one you will come across a lot in the counselling world.

But that feels really hard. How can I just set aside my own opinions and enter another person's frame of reference?

First, you need to understand yourself. An integral part of becoming a counsellor is trying to understand who you are and what makes you tick: what are your viewpoints and where have they come from? We will explore much of this in Chapter 12 but for now it is enough to consider that we need to understand ourselves in order to understand how we relate to the world around us. This will help us appreciate why we feel more comfortable around some people than others. It is not just about why you don't get on with some people, but also about why you feel closer to certain people.

REFLECTION

The BACP Ethical Framework for the Counselling Professions (2016) highlights 'identity' as a personal moral quality for counsellors on the basis that a sense of self in relationship forms the basis of responsibility, resilience and motivation. (Ethics clause 12, BACP Ethical Framework, 2016)

- Why might the counsellor's sense of self in a relationship be important in the counselling relationship?
- Why might a strong sense of self be important to resilience in relationships?
- Why is it important to recognise our own motivation in relationships?

Even here we have to be careful because the degree to which we can understand and empathise with another person may be both a help and a hindrance.

 What do you mean – help or hindrance? Surely being able to empathise is always a bonus?

 Yes it is, but if a counsellor's own experiences, background or beliefs are very similar to those of the client, this can get in the way of seeing things from the client's perspective. This is sometimes called 'identification' in counselling terms. Identifying with the client presents as much risk of making assumptions about them as not being able to identify with them at all, because no two people's experiences are the same.

EXAMPLE

Irem is a counsellor who is married with two children. She found herself unexpectedly pregnant while still breastfeeding her second child. At the time, her job was the only source of family income and very reluctantly she and her husband wrestled with the decision of whether or not to have an abortion because of their economic circumstances. They both agreed in the end that an abortion was the right decision for their family. They did not tell anyone else for fear of being judged. Irem does not regret this decision but she has struggled with some of the repercussions, especially with imagining who her third child would have been and whether it was her fault that she was not more careful with her contraception.

Irem starts working with a client, Sally, who has coincidently just been through a very similar experience. Irem realises that women are likely to have many different reactions to having had an abortion, and she tries to focus on Sally's experience. Consider this section of the counselling session:

Sally: I know it was the right decision but I am ashamed to tell people all the same and my partner did not want me to tell anyone either.

Irem: So you both felt ashamed that you would be judged for what you had done?

Sally: Yes, I certainly felt that I would be judged as a mother. Having an abortion seems to go against what people expect of a mother and that can leave very difficult feelings. It has left me with very difficult feelings.

Irem: Difficult feelings … about the decision you have made and some unresolved issues within yourself about what you have done?

Sally: (irritated) No, I have no bad feelings about what I have done. I just feel very angry that I am expected to be struggling with what I have done. This is just part of other people's expectations. I am happy with what I have done. Why can't this just be enough for other people? (Sally looks annoyed and looks at her watch)

- At what point did Irem make an assumption about Sally's feelings?
- What effect did this have on the counselling relationship?
- What could Irem have said instead?

Irem was trying to understand Sally and was aware from her training of the danger of making assumptions, but she heard what Sally said through the prism of her own experience, without even realising it.

How would your own experience have coloured your responses to both Irem and Sally if they had been your clients?

It is not the client's fault if the counsellor feels unable to work with them, but it is a real challenge for every counsellor to be able to work with any client or any presenting problem.

 Woah! Hold on a moment. Is that realistic? I am not sure that I could work with everything or anyone. I am not sure that is possible. Does that mean I would not make a good counsellor?

 Well, as I said, this is a challenge. Counsellors are human beings and there may be good reasons why you could not, or would not, choose to work with a particular client or particular issue. But I think there is also something here about seeing beyond the obstacles and making a commitment to look beyond the things that are difficult in order to engage with the person.

 So it's not so much about being able to work with anyone or any issue, but about being willing to look beyond the behaviour or type of person in order to really know that person?

 Yes, I think that is right. We as counsellors must have a willingness, a curiosity, to know the person so that we can form a relationship with that client, so that they feel valued and heard on their own terms. Do you remember that we explored this when looking at the concept of empathy using counselling skills? The question for the counsellor is: can I really enter this person's inner world so that they feel fully heard, accepted and understood? It is a challenge sometimes for counsellors to accept certain behaviours but we must reflect on what stops us entering that client's world. This is one of the key reasons we also commit to continual self-reflection, as well as engaging in clinical supervision and our own personal therapy – as a means of continually challenging our views and attitudes as they emerge. You can never fully be aware of what might 'trigger' an adverse reaction to a client. We use the term 'trigger' because the moment of reaction can come quite suddenly and out of the blue.

EXAMPLES

1. Donna started working with a client who looked like her stepfather. The client reminded her of the years of violence and bullying behaviour towards her own mother.

2. Felicity was working with a university student who belonged to the Christian Union. The client said that she had met a nice boy but was struggling with her feelings because her boyfriend wanted a physical relationship whereas she wanted to save herself for when they got married.

3. Phil's client, a policeman, had lost his job after irregularities in his expense claims. Phil has spent time in a Young Offender Institution.

4. Fay's client came to her about a relationship problem. He mentioned in passing that his way of earning a living was selling women's 'used' underwear on the internet.

- What might trigger a reaction in the counsellor in each of these examples?
- What is your own reaction to each of these examples?
- How easy would you find it to enter the client's frame of reference?

The critical point here is that the counsellor needs to be open and honest about their own feelings and responses so that they are in touch with their own triggers – both those which are known to them and those which happen unexpectedly. In his book *Love's Executioner and other Tales of Psychotherapy* (1989/2012), Irvin Yalom openly explores his experiences with a series of clients. Critically, Yalom, an experienced existential therapist, highlights his own journey and process as he encounters different clients and explores and documents what each bring up for him. Without the courage and wisdom to acknowledge and explore our own blocks as we become aware of them, we cannot meet the client in their own realm and reality. If we are unable to acknowledge and work with prejudices or pre-judgements, we will be unable to empathise with the client. This can interrupt or destroy the therapeutic process.

So essentially what you are saying is that I have to be continually aware of what is happening for me and check if this is preventing me from developing an empathic understanding of the client?

Yes indeed, but more than that – this commitment to exploring what blocks me from fully entering the client's world becomes in itself a rich source of self-awareness and growth. The more I understand myself, the more I am able to set aside or 'bracket' my own stuff and be with my client. The idea of being able to put things in 'brackets', in order to set them aside, is a useful concept in counselling.

ACTIVITY

Students often arrive for a training session with their heads and hearts full of the worries and stresses of their personal lives: getting children to school, traffic problems, work problems, money problems, and so on. This can make it very difficult to fully focus on the group and the training.

Try inviting everyone in the group to write down their immediate concerns on a piece of paper and put these into a single large brown envelope. Ask the course tutor to keep this safe until the end of the training session. This is a physical way of 'bracketing' personal preoccupations and concerns in order to focus on another task.

At the end of the training session, the students are invited to take back their concerns. You will be surprised at how many people prefer not to collect them! You can then ask the tutor to destroy any remaining bits of paper safely.

This idea of bracketing is particularly useful for your own values, prejudices or experiences, all of which can get in the way of relating to particular clients.

 But sometimes it is difficult to understand or empathise with a client, not because I hold a prejudice or preconception, but just because their experience is completely outside my own. In fact, now I come to think of it, that is really quite likely with many clients.

DIFFERENCE AND DIVERSITY: A WIDER SOCIAL CONTEXT

 This leads us onto looking at difference and diversity in a wider social context. A basic idea we explored in Part I of this book is that everyone is unique and individual. As we go through life, we meet a wide range of individuals and groups but there may be certain individuals in certain groups that we never come across and where we have little understanding of the world as they experience it.

 You are talking about groups rather than individuals and suggesting that they all have something in common. Is this not straying into the dangerous territory of stereotyping?

 I am glad you thought of that but there may be some things that are common to individuals in a group that we have a responsibility to know about, and this includes being aware of how certain groups experience prejudice and oppression on a social level.

Despite equalities legislation and whatever we may want to believe as individuals, not everyone is treated equally. As counsellors, we may strive towards equality in relationships and between people but counselling may become part of the problem if we do not recognise how unequally people are treated outside the counselling room. Part of this realisation is that counselling cannot solve things that are happening at a social level, however much we might hope it can. Counselling cannot stop prejudice or racial abuse or secure someone a job.

The counsellor has a duty to work with and acknowledge the client's reality and to constantly ensure that what is going on in the counselling room does not become part of the client's problem. This could mean exploring your assumptions about the client – conscious or unconscious – but it might also mean checking out the assumptions the client is making about the counsellor. The challenge is to bring this into the room so it can be talked about and understood. This can be difficult, but there are times when it is necessary to be honest about what is going on and what may be blocking one or both parties from fully engaging in the counselling process.

Unfortunately, we live in a world where individuals experience discrimination, oppression and prejudice on a daily basis, based on race, sex, age, sexuality, disability, and so on. These experiences negatively impact on individuals' sense of being valued in society.

EXAMPLE

Jerome is an Afro-Caribbean teenager living in London. His mother works in a local supermarket and has a strong work and moral ethic. Jerome is predicted to get eight good GCSE grades and has been accepted to do four A Levels at the local college. He is also a keen football player. However, Jerome has been stopped 25 times within the last three months by the police, questioned and searched.

How might Jerome's experience of the police impact on how he views himself within society?

It is incumbent upon the counsellor to become aware of how prejudice affects different groups within society and this will also include the history that different groups have experienced. An example may be the oppression experienced by the Jewish community during the Second World War or the experience of the black community and the slave trade. The historical experience of any group will have an effect on how they view themselves within the wider social context, which is re-enforced by how society continues to discriminate, even in the present day.

 But how can something from a historical perspective affect how you feel today?

That is a good question, but I think the easiest way of explaining it is to think about your own history. If, for example, you come from a wealthy, privileged, educated white family, you may be predetermined towards careers that foster privilege. If you have been educated within a particular school or gone to a certain university, such as Oxford or Cambridge, these social networks will open certain doorways for you, such as access to the political arena. The Cambridge Footlights alumni include such notables as Germaine Greer, Stephen Fry, Clive Anderson, David Baddiel, Peter Cook, Griff Rhys Jones and Emma Thompson. UK Prime Ministers Margaret Thatcher, Tony Blair and David Cameron all went to Oxford University. The social sphere that you grew up in may have a significant impact on your future and on how you view yourself.

A lack of good education may not be the only barrier holding someone back or determining or limiting their opportunities. A regional accent, skin colour or even a particular style of dress can impact on a person's chances of employment. The social/cultural background of the client may impact on how they view themselves and on the opportunities available to them. Experiences of racism, sexism and homophobia can severely affect how people value themselves in a social context. All these factors may have a direct effect on a person's mental health.

 Are you saying that the mental health of a person will be affected by how society treats them?

 Definitely, but let's broaden this out even further. Let's consider difference from a Western and Eastern perspective. On a basic level, Western models of thinking and counselling generally emphasise the individual and the individual's right to freely express themselves and to strive for personal self-fulfilment. On the other hand, many Eastern cultures place primary importance on the inter-dependence between people and unity within society and family. These traditions see the well-being of the collective group as being more important than that of the individual.

There are also different views of 'mental health'. Western models have developed a tradition of valuing talking therapies as a way of relieving the distress of mental health problems, whereas Eastern cultures might consider mental health in a more spiritual way. Western doctrine sees mental health as something that needs to be controlled or, at best, something that needs to be understood and treated, whereas Eastern cultures might consider it more important to find some kind of resolution within the self (e.g. a search for harmony and balance between the different parts of the self). This understand-ing is expressed through practices such as meditation instead of talking therapies and psychological help.

This sounds like a pretty fundamental cultural difference. How on earth would I know how to work with such a difference?

 It is about bridging the gap, working with the client to find a space that they can engage in, rather than forcing our way of experiencing upon the client. Accepting that there are different routes to mental health is perhaps the key to building successful relationships with clients, and not assuming that one size fits all. Being open to the full experiences of individuals is in itself a means of starting to meet the client within their own 'frame of reference'. Again, the BACP highlights the need for 'valuing each client as a unique person' in the *Ethical Framework for the Counselling Professions* (2016). To do this we need to be aware of our own values and beliefs but also be open to understanding and respecting our clients' world views. It is only with these two things in mind that we can start to form a relationship with clients and find responses that are culturally appropriate.

Experiences of prejudice and oppression start from a young age and are still present in schools, despite a concerted effort to eradicate discrimination, but these kinds of factors also have an impact on who actually gets access to counselling and the kind of counselling that is on offer.

ACCESS TO COUNSELLING

 How can who you are affect your access to counselling?

 Colin Lago, in *Race, Culture and Counselling: The Ongoing Challenge* (2006: 37), looked at access to therapy in the USA. Studies conducted there suggested quite strongly that if you were white, you were more likely to be referred to talking therapies, and if you were black, you were more likely to be put on medication. Interestingly, Lago (2006) did not suggest that the medical profession in America was full of racists; rather, that these decisions were being made at a subconscious level. Lago also discovered that, within therapy, issues and experiences of racism were likely to be addressed between a black counsellor and black client but unlikely to even be considered between a white counsellor and white client. Within mixed combinations, this was also a rarity.

The way we use language and the legal framework in society can go some way to addressing these issues but the roots of inequality are very deep and take time to eradicate – even where this is possible. Counsellors need to be aware of the issues that affect individuals within different social groups. We have a duty to inform ourselves as counsellors of known areas of ignorance to try to get a picture of how different social and cultural groups may have experienced discrimination and prejudice.

CRITICAL THINKING

- How much is it the counsellor's responsibility to find out about things which are unfamiliar to them or outside their own experience?
- Does the focus on individual experience mean that counsellors should never research the impact of social factors on certain groups?
- Is it enough for the counsellor to say to a client: 'I don't know anything about your culture; please tell me about it'?
- How might you feel if you belonged to a cultural group that was characteristic of communities in your local area?

We cannot fully know what it is like to be something different – to be another gender or have a different sexual orientation, or to belong to another race or culture. But we can have the humility to acknowledge that we can never truly know what that experience is like for another and attempt to work towards moments of understanding.

ACTIVITY

Consider the following groups in society. What five things could you do to find out more about their experience within your society today?

- Afro-Caribbean
- Jewish
- Muslim
- Christian
- Buddhist
- Disabled
- Women/men
- Second-generation Asian youth
- Asylum seekers
- White middle-class
- Lesbian/gay/bisexual/transgender

So I hope I have got you thinking about how important it is to proactively investigate areas of difference that you might not know much about. You may be surprised to find 'white middle-class' in the list above but clients from well-off backgrounds often feel judged by counsellors who are less privileged, and this not only denies them a safe space to explore their concerns but is clear discrimination. Depression, anxiety, grief and all common mental health problems affect all levels of society.

Believing that you know about an area of difference has its own challenges too. Consider the following example.

EXAMPLE

James, a trainee counsellor in placement, had just done a workshop in class on the experiences of disability. James believed that he now knew more about what it was like to be disabled. The following week he saw a new client who was experiencing relationship issues with her partner. The client arrived in a wheelchair. James spent the session focusing on how the client felt about being in a wheelchair and her experiences in the wider social context. He was surprised that the client did not return for the next session.

- How might this client have felt?
- What assumptions did James make?
- How might the session have contributed to the client's feelings about how society views them?

 This feels like a lot to take on board. I am not sure that I, as one person, can understand all the discrimination and oppression that someone can experience. But I can see we need to be open to the experiences and social context that clients come from.

EXAMPLE

Another good example here is the work done by Jane Elliott (www.janeelliott.com), an American white woman, famous as an anti-racism activist and educator, who has spent the last half-century teaching about the prejudice still experienced by black people. In her now-famous 'blue eyes, brown eyes' experiment, she proved the harmful effects of discrimination by conducting an exercise with her third-grade students after Martin Luther King was shot.

She divided the class by eye colour (blue and brown) for one day and was surprised at how quickly the children became discriminatory towards their fellow classmates and friends. Furthermore, she showed that being discriminated against had a tangible effect on the children's self-esteem, self-confidence and in turn their academic performance. The following day the experiment was reversed and the brown-eyed children were given privileges over the blue-eyed children. The children were filmed during the experiment and again when they were adults. The adult interviews showed that the effects and lessons learned during this experiment stayed with these children into adult life. What the exercise demonstrates is how easy it is for anyone to succumb to discriminatory behaviours if given the message that it is acceptable. It is easy to see how propaganda has supported crimes against groups throughout history, including the discrimination and degradation of others in the slave trade, in the extermination of the Jews during the Second World War and in the persecution of Christians under Emperor Nero.

So, our words and deeds can be swayed by others. If we hear something often enough, we will start to believe it.

 I feel weighed down by these thoughts and will need to reflect more on how I have been influenced by what I have heard. But in terms of counselling, how do I actually work with someone who is different?

WORKING WITH DIFFERENCE AND DIVERSITY

 I guess it is always a work in progress and there will always be a challenge in finding the balance between knowing more about difference and diversity within its wider context, versus the need to understand and honour the unique experience of the individual client. But difference is not always a barrier in counselling work.

A good counsellor will 'pick up' on anything that seems to be blocking the therapeutic process and invite the client to comment on, feed back on and explore the issue. Although it is sometimes helpful to look at obvious differences at the start of counselling work, such as 'I notice you are a man and I am a woman and I wonder if that will be a problem', this does not in itself go far enough to address diversity issues and does not take into account the many layers of difference that exist between people.

The client's ability to open up and be honest about who they are in therapy is key. The counsellor needs to be aware of the impact of diversity within the room, both in their ability to respond and to enter the client's world, and in the client's ability or willingness to open up. The client needs to feel that they will not be judged or experience a repeat of the prejudice and discrimination that may be familiar to them outside the counselling room. Exploring any difficulties with the client and their experience of oppression or discrimination may be a valuable part of the work.

Working with difference and diversity is a challenge but also rewarding. We need to be open to working outside our comfort zone and to learning about different perspectives on the world and about cultural norms and experiences that are unfamiliar to us. Almost like an anthropologist, we are entering a different world. It is not for us to judge the merits of another way of life or other areas of difference. We need to keep an open mind and be willing to engage with and learn about not only the individual's experience, but also how that experience resonates within cultural norms and expectations, history and social experience.

SUMMARY

- Understanding yourself is part of being able to work with difference.
- Working with difference requires the counsellor to enter the client's frame of reference.
- Inequality in society has an impact on how clients experience and access counselling.
- Counsellors have a duty to proactively widen their understanding of difference.
- Counsellors have to actively address issues of difference.

11
Working within a User-centred Approach to Counselling

Working with a user-centred approach is essential in counselling work. The term 'user-centred' is not elegant but it is useful for thinking about who actually uses the service being offered. It is also a term which is widely adopted outside the field of counselling wherever services are being offered.

I have heard the terms *client-centred* and *person-centred*. Are these the same as *user-centred*?

No, although they obviously have something in common. *User-centred* just means focused on the needs of the user, where the user could be in all kinds of contexts and accessing all kinds of services. On the other hand, the term *client-centred* is a theoretical term which comes from the *person-centred* approach to counselling developed by Carl Rogers (1951). If a counsellor is *client-centred* or *person-centred*, it means that their way of working is founded on establishing a particular kind of client–counsellor relationship and using a particular range of non-directive skills which leave the client in the driving seat all the time. You can read more about Carl Rogers in Chapters 12 and 13 but the point here is that while all counsellors should be user-centred (even those who employ more directive approaches), not all counsellors are *client-centred* or *person-centred*.

Hmm … I think I get that but it is pretty confusing.

Just think of user-centred as keeping the client and the client's needs at the heart of the work at every stage of the counselling process.

USER-CENTRED CONTRACTING

So the first stage of being user-centred is agreeing the contract and establishing the focus of the work in a user-centred way. If a counsellor simply lectures the client on all the boundaries, number of sessions and agency requirements, the client can feel as if something is being imposed on them rather than being part of a shared agreement. It is helpful to think of agreeing the contract with the client as a negotiation rather than simply giving them information.

In Chapter 9, we looked at all the elements that need to be agreed when setting the boundaries of the counselling relationship. As you probably discovered, it can be quite daunting trying to get all the information across at the start of a new counselling relationship but *how* you do this is the bit that needs to be user-centred.

EXAMPLES

Here are a few questions and phrases which will help you work in a user-centred way. When agreeing the contract:

- Do you have any questions about what I have just said?
- Do you have any worries about how I have outlined confidentiality/record keeping/ how to book appointments/make cancellations?
- Is this what you were expecting when you came here today?
- Let me know if I am going too fast or saying anything that is not clear.
- How are you feeling so far?
- Does that seem OK to you?
- Are you OK for me to go on?

When agreeing the work together:

- Have I captured your reasons for coming today?
- Does that sound like something we could work on together?
- Is that a fair summary of what you would like to focus on?

These examples show how it is possible to involve the client right from the start, and it also helps the process of building a relationship.

All this presupposes that the client actually wants to come to counselling but there are times when it is not really the client's choice. This could be because they are under pressure from a partner or family member to 'get help' or 'sort themselves out'.

Sometimes counselling is recommended by a GP, an employer, a social worker or a probation officer in response to particular problems. Or sometimes counselling is built in as part of a package of help/support relating to a particular treatment plan. For example, clients being treated for eating disorders or addictions are often required to attend counselling as part of the treatment programme.

I hadn't really thought about a client not wanting to be in counselling. That would surely make the whole venture tricky or doomed from the start.

Well, it certainly makes the first stage more problematic and it can be difficult for the counsellor as well as the client. It is not easy trying to help someone who does not want your help. But in a funny sort of way this is the time when it is all the more important to be 'user-centred' – to stick with what the client wants. Let's look at an example.

EXAMPLE

Simone's GP practice has referred her for counselling after several visits where she complained of abdominal pain. Extract from the counselling session (after a frosty start):

Counsellor: I am getting the feeling that you really don't want to be here.

Simone: (hostile) Well, to be frank, I don't think I should be here. I don't believe that my problems are in my head … which is what my doctor is suggesting by sending me to see a counsellor.

Counsellor: So you feel you have been sent against your will for a problem which you are sure is physical not psychological? You sound fed up and even angry.

Simone: I am angry. It's f*****g insulting. He has just got fed up of me turning up in his surgery and wants to fob me off with someone else. No offence … it's not personal but I am wasting my time and your time.

Counsellor: Well, you are not wasting my time and I won't take it personally … but … (pause) I can hear that you don't feel this was your choice and you feel that your doctor is not listening to you and not responding to what you really need. Maybe we can use this time to look at what you want to do about the fact that he won't listen?

Simone: (looks surprised and visibly relaxes) Well, I hadn't thought of that. (pause) I suppose as I am here anyway, that might be quite useful actually. (pause) I really am very angry … and scared. My aunt died

(Continued)

(Continued)

of stomach cancer and she had all the same symptoms as me. I want my GP to give me an MRI scan but he says there is no justification for it.

Counsellor: It sounds like there are two things that might be important here. First, to find a way to go back to your GP and explain to him why you want the test and ask again whether it would be possible. We could look at exactly what you want to say and how you might say it … but perhaps more immediately we could look at your fear … your fear of cancer and dying. It sounds like both parts are important to you.

Simone: (eyes fill with tears) Yes, I would like to do that.

- What did the counsellor do that changed Simone from being angry and hostile?
- Why was the counsellor's reaction a surprise to Simone?
- In what way was the counsellor's response user-centred?

Trainee counsellors often lose confidence when a client is hostile and does not want to engage. That is why a counsellor has to be willing and able to respond to where the client actually is, not where the counsellor hopes they are.

There are other reasons why a client might be unwilling to work with a counsellor, even if they arrive willingly. This can also be tricky, especially for an inexperienced counsellor.

EXAMPLES

1. Doris, a client in her early 70s, took one look at the counsellor, who was in her early 30s, and shut up like a clam. The counsellor started to discuss the boundaries and the contract, at which point Doris said it was a mistake to come and got up to leave.
2. Peter, a teenager from a mixed-race family, sat opposite his white, middle-aged female counsellor and felt she could not possibly understand him. When the counsellor asked if he was OK, he was too polite to be honest and said, 'Yes, I'm fine'.
3. Kim, a client who finally plucked up the courage to go to counselling to talk about deep-seated scars from sexual abuse when she was a child, was horrified to find that the agency only offered six sessions. She couldn't really see the point of starting.

These are just a few examples of reasons why the client may not be ready to start talking about the contract, boundaries and future sessions.

- What might you say to each of these clients to try to address directly their feelings about not wanting to work with you?
- How difficult would you find each of the above examples?
- How would you usually respond in your everyday life?
- How would you remain user-centred as a counsellor?

So, in summary, here are a few tips for trying to work with clients who are reluctant to engage in counselling at all or in counselling with you.

> - Acknowledge the client's reluctance if it is evident.
> - Acknowledge the client's feelings, especially hostile feelings, towards the counsellor or towards counselling.
> - Meet the client where they are in their process, not where you expect/want/hope them to be.
> - Listen to what the client wants at that moment.
> - Listen for underlying issues that you can work with.
> - Be prepared to accept that even after you have tried this approach it may not be what the client wants.

tip

ESTABLISHING A USER-CENTRED FOCUS

So, let's move on. You are now fairly sure that the client wants to be there and the boundaries have been agreed. The next step is to identify why the client has come for counselling and what they want to focus on. Some of this has been covered in Chapter 3 when looking at needs and wants in helping work, but when there are going to be further sessions, especially if there are only a limited number of sessions being offered, it is important to agree a focus. Again, this is part of being user-centred.

Do clients always know what they want to focus on?

Well, sometimes the focus may be opaque and not fully clear at the start. A client might not know exactly what they want but may have a feeling that counselling could be helpful. This is a good starting point. A client who is anxious or depressed, for example, might want to feel less anxious or depressed without knowing exactly why they are depressed. This is where the counsellor's own approach becomes relevant. One counsellor might use techniques to help the client feel more 'positive' or 'less anxious' without going in to the 'why', whereas another counsellor might focus on trying to help the client understand the reasons why they are feeling depressed or anxious as a way of facilitating change.

Different theoretical models will also place a greater emphasis on the importance of agreeing an explicit focus. Counsellors working in non-directive approaches, such as the person-centred approach, would not use an overt goal-setting technique but they might end the first session with a summary of what the client has spoken about and reflect back the client's key concerns as a way of agreeing the work together. The method itself does not define whether the process is user-centred but it is important that it matches the client's own wishes and preferences.

 So, how you work may well guide the type of focus that you expect from the client. But what would you do if you did not agree with what the client wants from counselling? That could be tricky. Does that happen? Supposing my client wanted to slim down to a size zero or have plastic surgery or an abortion?

 Well, this can be a personal challenge because it touches on our own values and ethics and on client autonomy, which we discussed earlier, but the challenge here is to focus on what is in the best interests of the client. This is not always easy.

CRITICAL THINKING

Zinna comes to counselling saying she wants to lose two stone in weight. Her mood is low and her self-esteem at rock bottom. She says she has tried every known diet without success and thinks the problem is in her head.

Is the therapist's role to help and support her to achieve the goal of losing two stone or is it the therapist's role to help her reach a place of greater confidence and self-acceptance?

- Would it make a difference if the client was overweight?
- Would it make a difference if the client was already visibly underweight?

In what ways is your own relationship with weight and size likely to affect the way you view Zinna's goal of losing weight?

Sometimes the challenge of agreeing a focus for the work is about knowing where to start because of the sheer number of issues that the client presents with. Imagine a client who arrives saying that their partner has left them, they are behind with the rent, the car has failed its MOT, they have had a final warning at work and the cat has disappeared.

I'm not sure where I would start with all that, but it seems the car and the cat are the least important!

Are you sure about that? Remember that people are different and diverse. We cannot assume what is more important for the client. The cat disappearing may be the starting point and the initial focus of the work. It may not be realistic to work on all these potential issues, especially if there are a limited number of sessions, so we would need to invite the client to consider, or rank, what they would find most helpful to work on. It is also important to remember that counselling is usually only one hour a week but if a client is able to work on and resolve one issue, it may help them cope better or find answers in other areas of their life.

STAYING USER-CENTRED

Agreeing a focus for the work is challenging but even if you are able to agree a focus at the start of the session, it may change as the work progresses.

But you just said that the client has chosen the focus for the work – why would we not stay with that?

Clients' needs can change and life events may change between sessions, and this may mean shifting the focus of the counselling. In some ways, it will depend on the work but as counsellors we sometimes have to act a bit like chameleons, changing to fit in with the client.

One common reason why the client's focus may change is that, as trust develops, the 'real' issue or a deeper issue emerges. The challenge for the counsellor is to try to keep track and make sure that the work is still focusing on what the client needs.

There are different ways of doing this. In some approaches, the counsellor would stay with what the client is bringing to the work in the belief that any other issues discussed will re-emerge if they become more relevant for the client. Another way would be for the counsellor to reflect to the client that they had noted a change in the focus of the work and then check that this is the direction the client wants to follow.

I think I understand. We either sort of trust the client and go with the flow or check out that the client wants to change direction. Is this what you mean by staying user-centred throughout the counselling work and not just at the beginning?

Yes, but this does not just mean checking whether the focus is right but more generally checking how things are going. When you are practising skills in class, you have the advantage of getting feedback from fellow students and from your tutor. When you are working with a real client, there are only two people in the room. Therefore, it is very important to check with your client what they are thinking and feeling about the counselling sessions and your relationship, and whether it is meeting their needs. Of course, you also need to facilitate a space where the client feels able to be honest about their experience.

 But what if you didn't feel able to be honest? I would probably just not turn up at the next session.

 I quite understand – which is why it is important to look at the reasons a client might not feel able to be honest.

REFLECTION

Reasons why a client might feel unable to be honest with their counsellor could include:

- fear of hurting the counsellor's feelings
- fear of the counsellor being angry
- shame and/or guilt
- wanting to be liked
- wanting to be a 'good' client
- wanting to 'get better' so the counsellor doesn't feel bad
- loss of focus
- feeling stuck
- not liking the counsellor
- loss of trust.

How might a counsellor acknowledge these potential challenges to the counselling work?

As a client, would you be more honest if your feedback was invited in the session itself or via a paper questionnaire or an online feedback portal?

In open-ended counselling, it is good practice to have regular reviews to check back with the client and offer an opportunity for them to give feedback. Some counsellors offer their clients a structured feedback space at the end of every session. Other counsellors argue that the increased use of structured feedback is driven more by agency requirements for collecting data on client progress and outcomes than because it meets the needs of the client. There is probably an element of truth in both points of view.

It is also worth bearing in mind where the counselling is taking place in relation to staying user-centred. If the counselling agency is set up to deal with a specific issue such as bereavement or employment, it may be necessary or appropriate to refer the client to a different agency which can better meet their needs.

The only other thing to mention at this point is the vital role of supervision in making sure the counsellor remains user-centred. This subject is so important that supervision has a whole chapter to itself (Chapter 14).

SUMMARY

In order to work within a user-centred approach to counselling, you need to:

- Agree the focus of the work when negotiating the contract.
- Recognise, acknowledge and work with any client resistance to counselling.
- Monitor and remain focused on the client's changing needs throughout the counselling work.
- Ask the client for feedback on how the work is going.
- Make use of supervision to make sure you are remaining user-centred.

12
Using Theory to Increase Self-awareness

In this chapter, we are going to explore how counselling theory can be used to develop self-awareness by applying concepts from different theoretical approaches to understand our internal self, our personal history and our patterns of relating. In Chapter 13, we will take these ideas further by looking at how theory helps us understand and work with clients.

 Hold on, what has theory got to do with my self-awareness? And what has theory got to do with understanding the client? I thought that now I had learned counselling skills, I could work with clients.

ROLE OF COUNSELLING THEORY

 Let me explain. Understanding theory and working within a coherent theoretical framework is one of the central ingredients for working as a counsellor. All counsellors need to be able to explain what they are doing and why, and theory helps us do that. But let's start with a definition of the word theory:

> a set of principles on which the practice of an activity is based; an idea used to account for a situation or justify a course of action. (*Oxford English Dictionary*)

So counselling theory is a set of ideas and principles based on practice and experience which has been systematically put together to try to explain what counselling is and how it works. In that sense, theory underpins the work that counsellors do, and every theory is a further attempt to provide a better description and better understanding of counselling and how it works.

You said 'every theory' not 'theory'. How many theories are there?

 There are somewhere between 400 and 600 theories of counselling and new theories are being developed all the time. The purpose of this book is not to attempt to describe every theory, or even the nuances and depth of all the main traditions which inform counselling today. What we aim to do is provide a brief overview of the three main schools of counselling and offer a framework for looking at different theories.

 Woah! That's a lot of theories – are they all really necessary, or even new? We don't have hundreds of theories for, say, relativity or gravity! Why are there so many theories in counselling?

 I think it is because when something is well understood, you don't need hundreds of theories to explain it, but when something is unknown, people constantly try to find different ways, or in this case develop new theories, to explain it. That's why there are lots of different theories about climate change or the origins of the universe – to give just two examples. Perhaps another answer to your question is that no single theory satisfactorily explains who we are, what makes us tick, what goes wrong and how we can put it right. Human beings are very complex so it is not surprising that there are many theories about how best to work with psychological problems. All theories have elements of truth and provide a map which helps us understand what might be happening and how best to address the needs of different clients.

Research shows that working within a coherent framework of theory and skills is important for good therapeutic outcomes – exactly which theory you work with is less important, as long as it is a *bona fide* theory.

 What does *bona fide* mean?

 Bona fide is Latin for 'with good faith', in other words 'genuine' and 'sound'. In this context, it means theory which has a tried–and–tested track record backed up by evidence that it works. Not all theories are *bona fide* and some come in and out of fashion very quickly. Others remain but are not widely adopted by others in the field.

One helpful way to think about the role of different theories is to imagine a diamond where every facet of the diamond offers a different angle for sending down a shaft of light which illuminates the mysteries of what it is to be human.

 So if one theory cannot provide all the answers but having a theory is important, how do I choose what theory to study and work with?

Well, one of the reasons for introducing you to a range of theories at this stage of your training is to give you a flavour of the different theories that are out there.

At this juncture, what is really important is to realise that a theory is not something to be frightened of, nor something abstract which sits outside the actual work of counselling. Think of theory as something that you might need if you were a car mechanic. If your car needs an oil change, you cannot just go to buy a carton of oil and put it into the car. You have to choose the right type of oil for the make and model of your car. In a similar way, if your car needs a new tyre, you need to have the right type of tyre fitted to match the car specifications. So a mechanic needs to understand the language of different car specifications and different makes and models in order to provide the car with what it needs.

I suppose it's up to me what make or model of car I buy, so it is up to me what theory I choose.

You will probably find that you can relate to some theories better than others because they fit well with your own ideas and values about what makes people the way they are and how they can best be helped. That's why we invite you to 'try out' theories on yourself before you try to apply theory to clients. If the theory makes sense to you, it will probably help you make sense of client issues. Different theories appeal to different people for different reasons and this means we have a rich landscape of different theories to draw on. However, all theories share some common characteristics and these can be summarised as follows:

- an underlying philosophy
- a language for looking at the self:

    o how we relate within ourselves (internal self)
    o what happened in our past (personal history)
    o how we relate to others (patterns of relating)

- a theory for describing what 'goes wrong' for people
- a theory about how the counsellor can work with what 'went wrong' to help the client and bring about change.

This gives us a kind of template for looking at the many different theories which we can choose from.

Let's start by looking at the three main theoretical traditions or the three main 'schools' of counselling. These three approaches form the bedrock from which all other approaches stem. They are:

- psychodynamic counselling
- humanistic counselling
- cognitive-behavioural therapy (CBT).

PSYCHODYNAMIC COUNSELLING

Origins of the psychodynamic approach

The psychodynamic tradition began with psychoanalysis and Sigmund Freud (1856–1939). Freud is widely considered to be the father of psychotherapy, as well as a key influence on Western thinking about the mind, especially the role of the unconscious. He originally trained as a doctor in Vienna but gradually broke away from the establishment and started experimenting with hypnosis and the technique of 'free association' (letting the patient say whatever comes into their mind while lying on a couch) to work with emotionally disturbed patients suffering from hysteria. He found that if patients talked about past memories and buried emotions (often of a sexual nature), they seemed to get better. This was the origin of the 'talking cure' and the beginning of a wide vocabulary of language for talking about the mind.

Basic philosophy of the psychodynamic approach

The basic philosophy here is that people are driven by unconscious drives and shaped by early unresolved childhood experiences. If these early experiences can be brought into consciousness and worked with dynamically in therapy, then a person has more choices in the present and will be less unhappy or less neurotic.

Woah! I can barely remember what I was doing last week, let alone years ago, so I'm not sure that the past is really affecting me that much. It does not sound very optimistic either – just trying to be less neurotic!

Well, you won't necessarily be able to remember things without help but Freud would argue that the past affects you unconsciously, whether you like it or not. So, let's look at his ideas about the unconscious.

Think of the unconscious as being like an iceberg where the bit you can see above the water is just a fraction of the complete iceberg and the rest is submerged or hidden. Freud actually divided the mind into three layers of consciousness, which are illustrated in Figure 12.1.

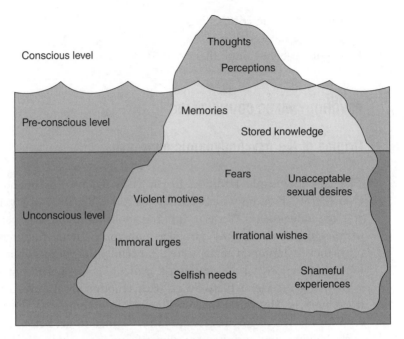

FIGURE 12.1   The iceberg metaphor of the mind

Conscious mind: this part of the mind contains all our thoughts, perceptions and things that are in our awareness. This includes feelings and dreams.

Pre-conscious mind: this is closely linked to our conscious mind. It consists of all the things that we are not consciously thinking about in the present but which we can call to mind without difficulty. This includes memories and stored knowledge.

Unconscious mind: this larger, submerged part of the iceberg holds all the memories that the conscious mind does not want to remember or acknowledge. Freud believed that the unconscious holds significant information which is so disturbing that we have to keep it out of our awareness because it would be damaging to the self if it was fully known.

 That kind of makes sense, but if something is unconscious why do we need to worry about it?

 Both the conscious and pre-conscious areas of the mind contain material that we are aware of and can handle. We keep unconscious material out of awareness because it is too hard to handle, but it still has an important influence on who we are and how we behave.

Although we may be unaware of the powerful information that is held in the unconscious, it can still 'slip out' in what is termed the 'Freudian slip', such as calling your partner by your ex's name or saying the wrong word. Freud believed that such 'slips' provide a link to the unconscious mind. He also believed that dreams were the 'royal road' to the unconscious because they offered a means of expression for the unconscious if they could be interpreted and worked with.

REFLECTION

Have you ever had a dream that seemed to be telling you something about your unconscious?

Have you ever made a Freudian slip that revealed something about your true thoughts?

How might your unconscious mind influence your everyday life?

Psychodynamic view of the internal self

Alongside the notion of different levels of consciousness, Freud developed a theory about how the psyche or mind is structured. He saw the mind as being divided into three competing parts: the id, the ego and the super-ego.

CRITICAL THINKING

A definition of the psyche is *the human soul, mind, or spirit*, which comes from Latin via the Greek *psukhe*, meaning 'breath, life, soul'. One criticism of the psychodynamic approach is that it does not encompass the spiritual dimension of the psyche. Given that a spiritual life is important to many people, does this limit the usefulness of this approach? Would not having a spiritual dimension matter to you?

The *id* is the early instinctual part of the mind which is intent on self-gratification (the 'pleasure principle') and driven by unconscious drives both towards life, love and sex on one hand and death on the other. The id has no morals, no core values and no concept of danger or excess. The id just wants to party and to hell with the consequences!

Oh, I like the sound of the id; I can really relate to that when I go out on a Friday night and there are times when I have no real idea what I have done. But I then feel guilty the next day because I have been excessive and drunk too much and have vague memories of doing stupid things.

That indeed sounds like the id in action. But I think you may have also introduced us to another part of the mind – the super-ego.

The *super-ego* is your conscience where all the messages that you have received from your parents and significant others are stored. It is that little voice inside you telling you not to do something because it is wrong, which echoes the morals, values and social conventions you learned as a child. Whereas the id is all about self-indulgence, the super-ego is all about doing what is right and sensible. The super-ego tries to check risky impulses and acts like a censor to the id.

 Yes, I often get that voice in my head that tells me not to do something because it is dangerous or bad, but it seems that this voice does not want to have fun. It is like having to be on your best behaviour at a funeral when all you can see is the funny side. This seems like two extremes – either do what you like or don't do anything bad.

 Quite right, but this is where the ego comes in!

The *ego* acts like a mediator between the two voices of the id and the super-ego. The ego sees the whole picture and draws on logic and reason to work out how to balance the demands of the other parts and arrive at a reasonable response based on the reality of the situation.

 So it is like when I want to go rock climbing. I could just climb the rock face but that would mean if I make a mistake or slip, I could fall and injure myself. My super-ego is telling me it is too dangerous, so don't do it, but I want to do it. Then my ego analyses what my id and super-ego are saying and comes up with a compromise. I can go rock climbing but I must use all the safety equipment.

I think that is a pretty good explanation of how they work together.

EXAMPLE

Id, Ego and Super-ego go to the pub on a Friday night

Id: Thank God, it's Friday night. It's been a long hard week and I am in the mood for letting my hair down and having some fun. Let's get hammered! I'll get the first round in.

Super-ego: Well, is that really a good idea? You've got that essay to write before Monday and you promised to go round and help your mum in the garden tomorrow. Anyway, you can't drink because you've got to drive home and if you get wasted you won't be any good to anyone tomorrow.

| Id: | You are such a killjoy. I don't want to be thinking about that now. It's time to party – get lost! |
| Ego: | Hang on, guys – it doesn't have to be one thing or the other. What about having a couple of drinks then getting a taxi home? You can always pick up the car in the morning and drop in on your mum on the way back. |

- Can you think of a time you let your id take over and later regretted it?
- Can you think of a time when your super-ego stopped you doing something you wanted to do?
- Can you think of a time when your ego successfully found the middle ground?

Ego defences

The id and the super-ego are in constant conflict and there are times when the ego is unable to cope with the competing demands. Freud suggested that the ego develops a range of defences to stave off difficult feelings like depression and anxiety. Ego defences are like the walls around a castle keeping the ego safe from the constant attacks of the id and the super-ego. Here are some examples of common defence mechanisms:

Repression: this literally means 'subduing someone or something by force' (*Oxford English Dictionary*). It works at an unconscious level to stop uncomfortable thoughts or feelings from bubbling up. The thoughts and feelings do not disappear completely as they lurk in the unconscious and still affect what we do but repression helps us deal with the immediate discomfort. An example might be repressing guilty feelings of attraction towards your friend's partner but unconsciously flirting with them anyway.

Projection: this is when you project onto someone else your uncomfortable thoughts or feelings because you don't want to face the fact that these are actually your own thoughts or feelings. An example might be when you take a dislike to someone but rather than admitting to disliking that person you persuade yourself that they don't like you.

Denial: this is when you block the reality of a situation from your awareness: 'I do not want to hear this!' A classic example would be a smoker denying that smoking is bad for their health.

Displacement: this is when we take out frustration or anger on something else rather than the real object of our frustration. An example might be coming home after a bad day at work and taking it out on your partner or yelling at the TV.

Intellectualisation: this is when you try to explain your feelings away in a cold and detached way, rather than deal with the rawness of your emotions. For example, you might focus on all the practicalities of splitting up with your partner, rather than engaging with how you are feeling about the end of your relationship.

Rationalisation: this involves the person explaining away a situation rather than acknowledging the reality. For example, a student might blame their poor mark for an assignment on the teacher's bias, rather than facing the fact that they have not done enough work.

REFLECTION

Do you recognise any defence mechanisms that you use?

What are these defence mechanisms helping you to avoid?

Psychodynamic view of personal history

Freud and all psychodynamic approaches propose that early development has a direct effect on who we are and the kinds of psychological problems that we are likely to encounter in later life. These early childhood experiences, which Freud divided into five psychosexual stages of development, shape our personality by the age of five. He suggested that each psychosexual stage needs to be successfully negotiated and that if any particular stage is not well negotiated, a person becomes stuck, or fixated, at that stage as an adult.

Why is it called psychosexual – is it all about sex?

It has been argued that Freud was obsessed with sex, but what he proposed was that there is a link between each stage of our psychological development and a particular erotic pleasure centre in the body. As we grow, different areas of our bodies become either a source for pleasure or frustration, and life is a constant battle between frustration and pleasure. Table 12.1 gives a brief summary of the five psychosexual stages.

Freud seems to be obsessed with sex and heterosexual sex in particular, but what if you are gay or transgender or single? What if you have been brought up by one parent or two parents of the same sex?

These are valid points. We must remember that Freud was a product of his time. His ideas about development and his assumptions have been challenged and adapted over time. The modern-day practice of psychodynamic counselling can accommodate difference and diversity in social structures as well as in sex and gender preferences.

TABLE 12.1   Freud's psychosexual stages of development

Stage	Successful negotiation	Problematic outcome
Oral Stage: Birth to 1 year During this stage, the infant's mouth is the source of pleasure and frustration.	If I am fed and nurtured during this stage, I will develop a sense of trust in others.	If I am not cared for or well nourished, I may lack trust in myself and distrust others. If I remain fixated in this stage, I may exhibit problems with eating, drinking or smoking.
Anal Stage: 1–3 years During this stage, the toddler learns to control his bowel movements.	If during this 'potty training' period my parents and carers praise my efforts, I will have a positive experience and will develop a sense of competence and ability to achieve.	If I am humiliated, punished or forced to use the potty before I am ready, I may struggle with issues around criticism, power and independence. If I remain fixated at this stage, I may develop compulsive behaviours or obsessions.
Phallic Stage: 3–6 years During this stage, children start to develop an awareness of gender difference. Freud also identified the Oedipus and Electra complex. Essentially, children develop an unconscious desire for the parent of the opposite sex, e.g. 'daddy's girl' and 'mummy's boy', coupled with a destructive desire towards the parent of the same sex. The parent of the same sex is seen as a rival for their affection and these unconscious feelings have an influence on sexual development in later life.	If I successfully negotiate this stage, I will be able to identify with the same-sex parent and start to adopt their characteristics. I will also be able to start to comply with social norms and mores.	If I am inappropriately encouraged to identify with the opposite-sex parent or do not negotiate this stage successfully, I may struggle with issues around gender, sexuality, identity and relationships.
Latency Stage: 6 to puberty This stage is a quiet period free from sexual activity. Children go to school and start to develop relationships with their peers and start to develop interests and hobbies while learning about the world.	If I successfully negotiate this stage, I will develop relationships and interests and also develop good social skills and self-confidence.	If I struggle to make friends or don't develop interests and hobbies, or if I don't successfully achieve things, I may lack social skills and have poor confidence in later life.
Puberty This is the final stage of sexual development and Freud believed this is where there is a strong desire for sexual pleasure with the opposite sex, rather than self-pleasure.	If I successfully negotiate adolescence, I will settle down in a loving relationship and enjoy a range of interests.	If I don't successfully negotiate this stage, I may develop sexual perversions and deviant sexual interests.

CRITICAL THINKING

All theories and all theorists are the product of their own times. Freud's clients were predominantly middle-class Jewish women with emotional problems living in late 19th-century Vienna, which was a strongly patriarchal society. How might Freud's ideas on sexuality and human development have been influenced by his milieu and the client group that he worked with?

But how does Freud's psychosexual model help me understand myself if it is flawed or outdated?

Well, let's think of an example. Suppose you had an eating disorder which meant that you could not control your eating. Your GP has told you that you need to lose weight but you have struggled with doing this because eating gives you comfort.

That would place me in the oral stage?

Yes, that's what Freud would suggest. Now let's suppose that during therapy your therapist helps you uncover a buried memory that when you were born you were separated from your mother for six months because she was unwell and you were left in the care of various relatives. How might you understand this?

Oh, I get it. Even though I don't remember this event, I may have learned not to trust people because I was being passed from pillar to post and did not develop trust with one reliable person. My overeating is a way of comforting myself because I was not properly nurtured during the oral stage.

Exactly. Although the model is biased towards heterosexual ideals, it can still provide a useful framework for helping you understand yourself as a person and what may have gone wrong.

REFLECTION

Think of a behaviour or habit you are struggling with in your life today. Can you relate it back to any of Freud's psychosexual stages of development? Does this help you make sense of your situation?

The psychodynamic view of patterns of relating

Freud's fundamental idea was that our relationships with our parents and 'significant others' set the pattern for how we relate to others as adults. These patterns, which are laid down in early childhood, are unconsciously carried through into present-day relationships in ways that are unhelpful and repetitive. The most important concept he developed to explain this phenomenon was 'transference'. Transference is when the client unconsciously relates to someone 'as if' that person was someone from the client's past. In other words, the client 'transfers' thoughts, feelings and behaviours from a significant past relationship onto a present-day relationship without even realising it. You will be amazed how common this is and how useful it is to explore this as part of your self-development.

REFLECTION

- Think of someone who has been or currently is in authority over you such as your boss, a teacher or a group leader.
- What is, or was, the pattern of your relationship with this person?
- Are there any elements in the way you relate(d) to this person that echo patterns in the way you related to one of your parents or main care-givers?

'Transference' often occurs in relationships with people in authority over us because our parents/care-givers were in authority over us when we were children. This is when the blueprint is laid down.

This brief look at Freud is like putting a toe in the water of the many theories that make up the psychodynamic tradition. Freud's ideas have since been developed and moulded by others in ways which are very different and more appropriate for our time, especially his views on women and sexuality. Other key people you might want to read about and apply this template (for looking at theory) to, include: Carl Jung, Alfred Adler, Melanie Klein, Sandor Ferenczi, John Bowlby, Otto Rank and Karl Abraham.

THE PERSON-CENTRED APPROACH

Origins of the person-centred approach

A key development in counselling was the emergence of humanistic approaches, – also called 'the third force' in psychology – in particular the person-centred approach, which was developed by Carl Rogers in the 1930s. Rogers trained in the psychoanalytical tradition but then became dissatisfied with the psychoanalytical and behavioural models which seemed to 'reduce' human beings to either machines that go wrong or people unconsciously repeating patterns from their past.

> Man does not simply have the characteristics of a machine; he is not simply a being in the grip of unconscious motives; he is a person in the process of creating himself, a person who creates meaning in life, a person who embodies a dimension of subjective freedom. (Rogers, 1964: 129)

Rogers developed an optimistic and holistic approach which valued the meaning and subjective experience of each client. This approach is based on the idea that if a certain quality of therapeutic relationship can be established, the client will be able to change in ways which foster their growth and potential.

Basic philosophy of the person-centred approach

The key philosophical idea underpinning this approach is that all humans have the capacity to grow and, given the right conditions, can reach their full potential. Rogers called this positive and constructive urge the *actualising tendency* and he likened it to the way a potato puts out shoots towards the light, even when it is kept in dark, unpromising conditions. He saw humans as essentially trustworthy and capable of finding their own direction. You may remember that we mentioned 'self-actualisation' in Part I, Chapter 4, when we looked at Maslow's hierarchy of needs. Maslow is often seen as the forerunner of Rogers in developing humanistic and person-centred ideas.

 I must say, I like the idea of being in control of my own destiny.

Person-centred view of the internal self

Rogers wasn't particularly keen on the concept of the self but he discovered that his clients were. They liked to talk about the self and it seemed to make sense to them so he accepted this as useful. Rogers saw the self as being composed of the *organismic self* and the *self-concept*.

 Organismic self? That sounds a bit dodgy!

Yes, you have to say it and spell it very carefully. The *organismic self* is the early, true, honest and uncontaminated self which does not have to conform to the expectations of others or be moderated or changed to fit in with social norms. Rogers believed that essentially we can rely on our organismic self to tell us what we need from the world around us and from other people. If we have received unconditional acceptance from others, we will be able to trust our organismic self and flourish.

REFLECTION

Imagine a newborn baby. When a baby wants something, she simply expresses that want without censorship or premeditation. If a baby is hungry or wants its nappy changing, she will cry. If these needs are met, then the baby comes to trust the world and its own instincts and desires. This is the organismic self.

When a toddler is angry and upset because another child takes away his toy, the toddler's instinct might be to bite the other child in anger. But the child learns from the reactions of those around that this is not acceptable and may begin to doubt his own instincts and wants. This is the organismic self beginning to adjust to the expectations of others.

A teenager may feel angry with her girl friend for going to a party with another friend and not including her. The teenager may have adjusted to the idea that anger is not acceptable and instead feels sad, withdrawn or depressed. She does not recognise her true feelings as anger.

The *self-concept* is the idea of the self that we develop over time in response to the expectations of others and because of pressures to fit in and behave in certain ways. When we are young, our self-concept is fairly fluid and changeable but it becomes more fixed over time. Sometimes the self-concept is based on reality but often it is formed by the ideals, expectations and social pressures of others. The self-concept is far removed from the organismic self.

So, if we have a fairly good sense of self based on the reality of who we are, we are more likely to be acting from an authentic sense of self. If what we believe about ourselves is not based on reality, we will be living with an inauthentic sense of self.

 What exactly does 'authentic' mean here?

 'Authentic' can be defined as being of 'undisputed origin and not a copy; genuine' (*Oxford English Dictionary*). A good example here would be contestants in a singing competition like *The X Factor*. Some contestants really have talent and can sing while others believe that they are fantastic singers but have absolutely no voice.

 I think I get that. So if I have a good sense of myself, my self-concept will be based on reality. I will know what I am good at and what I am not good at. Whereas if I have no real sense of who I am, I will have a false, delusional idea of who I am and what I can do.

REFLECTION

Let's look at your own self-concept:

- Think of something you know you are really good at.
- Think of something you are not so good at.

Let's look at a time when your self-concept has not matched reality:

- Think of something you thought you were better at than you really were.
- Think of something you thought you were not good at doing but actually were able to do well.

Person-centred view of personal history

Rogers believed that our self-concept is formed by the *conditions of worth* put on us by other people. He also believed that the tension between a person's organismic self and their self-concept is what causes unhappiness and emotional difficulties.

 What do you mean by conditions of worth?

 Most people want to be accepted and loved and look to others for approval and acceptance. This in turn helps each of us develop a positive sense of self, especially if the love and approval are given unconditionally. The message you will receive might be: 'I will love you no matter what you do.' But whereas unconditional love is both necessary and appropriate for a newborn baby, it is not realistic or appropriate in the adult world. Just imagine a world where everyone did exactly what they wanted whenever they wanted and received approval for it. It would be chaos and full of hedonistic egotists!

What happens instead is that love and approval become increasingly conditional on what is acceptable and valuable to others. Rogers gave these messages about how to be the term *conditions of worth*. In this case, the message might change to: 'I will love you if …'

Conditions of worth are necessary because eventually we all have to become socialised in order to live together in an ordered world that respects the rights of others. However, conditions of worth act as a restriction on our organismic self because, instead of doing exactly what we want, we have to adjust our behaviour to meet the conditions that bring us love and approval. This not only sets up an inner tension and alters our self-concept but also creates the patterns for the way we behave in relationships with other people.

Some of these conditions are social and cultural messages about how to be, while others are specific messages received from our own families of origin.

Person-centred view of patterns of relating

So let's look at how the conditions of worth and the formation of a self-concept might influence how you are in relationship with others.

> **REFLECTION**
>
> Examples of social and cultural conditions of worth are:
>
> - Big boys don't cry.
> - Girls are caring and look after others.
> - Boys are competitive.
> - Girls are cooperative.
>
> Considering each of the above messages:
>
> - How might each message act as a restriction on a child's developing sense of self?
> - How might a child alter their behaviour to fit in with what is expected of them?
> - How might this affect their relationships with others?
>
> An example of a specific condition of worth from a parent to a child might be:
>
> Parent: I will kiss you and read you a story if you stop having a tantrum and go straight to bed now.
>
> *(Continued)*

> *(Continued)*
>
> - What might be the message to the child?
> - How might this become a condition of worth?
> - Why might this message result in the child having difficulty expressing anger in an adult relationship?
>
> Let's think about your own conditions of worth:
>
> - Do you behave in ways that seek to gain approval from others?
> - Where have these conditions of worth come from?
> - How has this affected your relationships with others?

I think that was quite challenging for me. I realise that I try really hard to do what other people want. Sometimes when I do get the chance to choose something for myself, I don't even know what I want. That's a bit sad, isn't it?

Well, it is certainly not uncommon. The constant process of looking outside yourself for confirmation and reassurance that what you are doing is right and trying to fit in would mean you get increasingly out of touch with your organismic self. Rogers called this having an *external locus of evaluation*:

- *external* – outside yourself
- *locus* – Latin for 'place'
- *evaluation* – making a judgement about something.

In short, this means looking to a place outside yourself in order to make a judgement about something. One of the goals of person-centred counselling is to develop an *internal locus of evaluation* – in other words, to find a place within yourself that you trust, to reach your own judgements. You can imagine that a person who has an *external locus of evaluation* would probably defer to their partner when it came to decision making because they wouldn't trust their own judgement. This then becomes their default position which, over a long period of time, erodes their confidence and self-esteem.

Rogers is still a monumental influence in counselling – he even invented the word 'counselling' – but, as with all theorists, his ideas have been further developed and shaped by others into new ways of working. Some of the key figures within the person-centred family of counselling include: Dave Mearns, Brian Thorne, Eugene Gendlin, Mick Cooper, Margaret Warner, Robert Elliott, Les Greenberg, Campbell Purton, Keith Tudor and Mike Worrell.

COGNITIVE-BEHAVIOURAL THERAPY (CBT)

Origins of cognitive-behavioural therapy

Cognitive-behavioural therapy is a blend of two different approaches which are now usually put together and referred to as 'CBT'. Let's briefly look at where they came from.

The origins of the behavioural approach come from the work of people like Pavlov (1849–1936) and Skinner (1904–1990).

I remember learning about Pavlov's dogs at school.

That's right. If you remember, he conditioned dogs to start salivating at the sound of a bell because they associated the ringing with the arrival of food. In essence, the work that Skinner did was all about looking at how people respond to external stimuli and how this then becomes a learned pattern. He believed that human free will was an illusion as we all react in predictable, learned ways.

Definition of behaviour:

> The way in which one acts or conducts oneself, especially towards others.
> (*Oxford English Dictionary*)

The cognitive strand comes from the work of Aaron Beck (1921–) and Albert Ellis (1913–2007). Both men were interested in how our thoughts influence our feelings. They did not work together but they shared a belief that our thought processes and the meaning that we give to events are the key to understanding ourselves and changing the way we feel. The word 'cognitive' comes from 'cognition'.

Definition of cognition:

> The mental action or process of acquiring knowledge and understanding through thought, experience and the senses. (*Oxford English Dictionary*)

In a nutshell, the 'cognitive' part is how we think and the 'behaviour' part is what we do. CBT, therefore, looks at how the way we think informs what we believe and in turn how we feel and behave.

Basic philosophy of the CBT approach

The philosophy behind this approach is that humans create their own meaning by the way they think about things and the meaning they derive from experience, and this in turn affects the way they feel. Therefore, looking at how we think can change how we feel and how we behave.

The CBT view of the internal self

CBT does not have a language for the different 'parts' of the internal self but it is very focused on the relationship between what we think and what we feel – in other words, between our 'cognitions' and our 'emotions'. You might think of this as the relationship between the left and right brain. The thinking part of the brain attributes meaning to experience and this in turn affects the emotions. Although humans are capable of rational thoughts (i.e. thoughts based on fact and reason), we develop irrational thoughts that are not based on either, and these irrational thoughts distort how we feel and how we behave.

For example, someone might be afraid of rejection or failure and tell themselves: 'I can't do this big project or piece of work.' Another person might say: 'People will not like me because …' By holding onto mistaken beliefs like these, people become frightened of living and blame themselves, or others, when something goes wrong or someone rejects them.

 So are you saying that the way I think makes me feel distressed, not the event itself?

 Yes, that's right. Aaron Beck described these as 'automatic thoughts'.

 Automatic thoughts? So I have no choice, as they just happen inside my head?

 Yes, but there is a positive side to this too. If I have positive and rational automatic thoughts, this will support me towards achieving my goals and ideals. I will be able to adapt to new situations and remain flexible about how I respond to the world. On the other hand, if my thoughts are irrational or negative then the opposite will be the case. I will tend to have an unrealistic and distorted view of reality, and my thoughts and therefore behaviours will work against me in achieving my goals, and I will struggle to adapt to different situations.

 So I can talk myself into a bad place and then feel bad, and this then becomes a habit?

 Think of your brain as being a bit like a computer where the wiring is not quite right. If we can find the faulty connection in how we think and respond, we can rewire ourselves so that we have a more realistic outlook.

> **REFLECTION**
>
> - Are you aware of any automatic thoughts yourself?
> - What *positive* automatic thoughts do you have?
> - How do these support you?
> - What *negative* automatic thoughts do you have?
> - How do these undermine you?

CBT view of personal history

Albert Ellis proposed that any irrational belief stems from a core 'must' statement or 'musturbation'. Ellis believed that there are three core 'must' statements that are irrational:

1. I must do well; if I do not perform well then I am no good.
2. Other people must be nice to me, and if they are not they are not good people.
3. I must have what I want and life must be easy, otherwise I cannot cope.

I can see why those could be irrational. It is not like I can do everything well all of the time, and not everyone will be nice to me.

I guess that is the point. A useful example here is an adolescent who believes that unless they have the latest fashion gear they may not find a boyfriend, or another who believes they did not get picked for the football team because the selectors are horrible people.

> **REFLECTION**
>
> 1. Can you think of a time when you felt you must do well because if you did not you would not be a good-enough person?
> 2. Can you think of a situation where you felt people must like you and if they did not like you they were bad people?
> 3. Can you think of a time when you believed that if you did not have something you could not cope with life?

The CBT view of patterns of relating

Like all approaches, the CBT view of how people relate is that they repeat the patterns they are familiar with in their responses to events and in their relationships with other people. In CBT terms, this means continuing self-defeating patterns that have to be examined and unpicked. One useful way of breaking down a repeating pattern is the ABC model.

ABC model

Ellis developed the ABC model to teach how irrational beliefs cause discomfort and self-defeating emotions in response to events. The ABC model broadly assumes:

- **A** = Activating event: something happens.
- **B** = Belief: your belief about the event or situation.
- **C** = Consequences: your emotional reaction to that belief.

OK, so I think I get this. So an event happens in my life, like I fail my driving test, which confirms my irrational belief that I am useless at everything, so then I get depressed and go home and end it with my girlfriend because she couldn't possibly want to be with a waste of space like me.

I think that is a very good example, but the outcome would depend on the belief that you held in the first place. If your belief was that you had to pass your driving test, otherwise life would not be worth living, the outcome might be that you stopped taking lessons and became too anxious to leave the house.

This is all very well, but what do I do about these irrational beliefs?

Once you have identified and understood the irrational thoughts, you have to work out why the irrational thoughts are untrue and replace them with a more rational explanation.

So, with the driving test example, I might construct a rational argument that says, 'It's OK not to pass my test first time, and although I am upset about it I can absorb the feedback from the examiner and use it to prepare for a retake.'

Exactly. CBT is about identifying irrational thoughts in order to change them for more rational ones. Part of the philosophy of CBT is to continually question what you think, and that only by thinking about my thoughts can I change the ones that disempower me. Our irrational, negative responses to events make us feel anxious and depressed but if we can learn to 'self-talk' ourselves into better ways of thinking, we can respond better to the world around us.

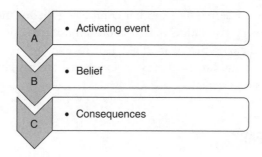

FIGURE 12.2   The ABC model

REFLECTION

- What irrational beliefs do you hold?
- How might these fit into Ellis's three 'musts'?
- Is there anything in your life that you could map onto the ABC model?
- What might you do to change the way you 'think' about a situation?

There are many different ways of increasing self-awareness but applying different theoretical concepts to ourselves is one way of becoming familiar with different counselling theories and while learning what these theories mean in practice. The template for looking at theory that is offered here can be applied to all the counselling theories we cannot cover in this book.

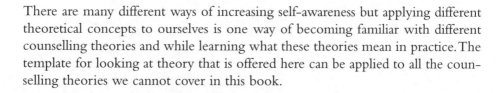

Counselling training courses offer a wide variety of different theories as part of the curriculum at this stage of your training, but in all cases you can apply the template for looking at theory that we have offered in this book. In other words:

- an underlying philosophy
- a language for looking at the self:

   o   how we relate within ourselves (internal self)
   o   what happened in our past (personal history)
   o   how we relate to others (patterns of relating)

- a theory for describing what 'goes wrong' for people
- a theory about how the counsellor can work with what 'went wrong' to help the client and bring about change.

Do some research into another counselling theory and see whether you can analyse the concepts and ideas of that approach using the headings offered in this template. Some theories that you might like to explore are Transactional Analysis, Gestalt, Bowlby's attachment theory or existential theory. This is just a glimpse of the 400 models on offer!

SUMMARY

- There are many different theories about the person.
- Theory helps us understand ourselves.
- No single theory holds all the answers.
- The psychodynamic approach is focused on bringing the unconscious into conscious awareness.
- The person-centred approach is focused on how exploring conditions of worth cause tension with the organismic self.
- CBT approaches are focused on identifying irrational beliefs and changing these to rational beliefs.

13
Understanding Theories of Counselling in Practice

In the last chapter, we looked at how to use theoretical concepts from the three main schools of counselling as tools for increasing our own self-awareness. In this chapter, we will look at:

- how to apply theory to understand 'what went wrong' for the client
- how counsellors coherently integrate theory and skills to work with the client towards change.

 That word 'coherently' sounds important. What exactly does it mean in this context?

 Well, there are inner tensions between the different approaches which can be confusing and even contradictory. Counsellors need to be able to explain what they are doing and why, and use skills and techniques that are consistent with their model for understanding the client's issues. It is not helpful if the counsellor is confused or sends out mixed messages about how counselling works or what they expect of the client.

REFLECTION

The person-centred approach is based on the philosophical idea that clients can be trusted to find their own answers and find their own direction – both in life and in the counselling process itself:

- Why might it be confusing for a person-centred counsellor to set the client structured homework tasks?

(Continued)

> *(Continued)*
>
> The person-centred approach sees total acceptance of the client as central to the therapeutic process:
>
> - Why might it be confusing for a person-centred counsellor to use the CBT technique of challenging irrational thoughts?

One way of becoming more familiar with the different approaches is to use case discussion and case examples to explore how counsellors from different theoretical approaches would understand and work with client issues. You will need to refer back to the concepts covered in Chapter 12 to make sense of this example.

EXAMPLE

Wayne is a 16-year-old client who has been referred to counselling by his GP. When Wayne was a premature baby, he spent the first six months of his life in intensive care. Throughout his life, Wayne has had a difficult relationship with food, either over-indulging or starving himself. He has a small circle of friends but is very body-conscious and wears baggy clothes to hide his shape. His favourite lessons at school are performing arts and dance. He recently collapsed during a dance class while preparing for the end-of-year performance. His father took him to the GP, who is concerned about his low weight. Wayne says he often skips meals because he is too fat but sometimes he just forgets to eat.

Let's look at how each of the approaches would explain 'what went wrong' for Wayne.

Psychodynamic perspective

There may be a conflict between Wayne's id and his super-ego. His id might be telling him that he needs to put all his energy into looking a certain way and that not eating is the best way of achieving his dreams. His super-ego might be telling him that he needs to look after himself and eat properly to achieve his goals, which he can do through hard work and practice. The counselling work might centre on how to balance these conflicting demands.

A psychodynamic therapist would be interested in Wayne's early childhood. Wayne's problems strongly indicate that he had developmental issues at the oral stage, which is when the child's focus of pleasure is on the mouth. Wayne may not have experienced sufficient consistent nurturing as a baby which might mean that he lacks trust in himself, which in turn could lead to a fixation on food. This may link to deeper unconscious processes that can be brought into consciousness and explored to give him insight into his internal conflict.

Wayne may also be employing various defence mechanisms, such as denial. He might recognise that not eating is bad for him but for some reason does not want to hear this and continues to starve himself.

CBT perspective

Wayne might have some irrational beliefs about how he should look and how and what he should eat. These thoughts may be automatic, negative and unrealistic. For example, Wayne might have an automatic thought such as 'If I starve myself, I will have the ideal body and that will help me get the roles I want in the performing arts'.

Wayne could also have what Ellis termed 'musturbations' such as, 'I must be thin' or 'I must succeed as a performer or life isn't worth living'.

We could use the ABC model to look at Wayne's responses:

A – Activating event: someone calls Wayne fat.

B – Belief: 'I am fat and being fat is the most awful thing in the world.'

C – Consequence: 'I must lose weight so I won't eat.'

Person-centred perspective

Wayne may have developed a self-concept that is based on conditions of worth. He may have been told that he has to look a specific way to be accepted – in this case to be thin. To be accepted by others, Wayne has dieted and probably received compliments about his weight loss. He may, therefore, have gone on losing weight in order to continue to receive 'positive regard' from others. In effect, the conditions of worth that he should look a certain way have gained him the approval and acceptance of others. Wayne may have lost contact with his organismic self in order to maintain his self-concept. He is out of touch with his internal locus of evaluation, and instead of trusting himself he looks to external influences to determine what is best for him.

As you can see from this example, there are a lot of 'mays' and 'mights' in the exposition of how each approach would view Wayne's problems. When we are trying to understand a client's issues, theory provides a potential framework for looking at what has 'gone wrong' and this in turn informs us how the counsellor might work with the client. Before we move on to examine how a counsellor would work with these issues, let's look at another case study. This time, see if you can apply theoretical concepts from each approach to frame what might be going on for the client.

EXAMPLE

Jeremy is in his first year of a medical degree. Both his parents are doctors and have actively encouraged him to become a doctor like them. Jeremy took science subjects and drama at A level and got A grades. He also joined the college amateur dramatic society and took leading roles in several productions during the two years he was at college. His parents did not attend any of the productions because they felt it was a 'waste of precious time' and disapproved of the hours he spent on his hobby. His two closest friends at university are studying dance and musical theatre and he hangs out with the 'thespian' set whenever he can. Jeremy got very poor grades for his first assignment and has been feeling depressed. He has the opportunity to change subjects but does not want to upset his parents. He worries that they will disown him and that he will no longer be the 'good enough son'. Jeremy has to make a decision to change subjects by the end of the first term.

Psychodynamic perspective

- Can you relate Jeremy's concerns to one of the psychosexual stages?
- Can you identify any possible defence mechanisms that Jeremy may be employing?
- What ego states might be at play inside Jeremy?

CBT perspective

- What might Jeremy's 'negative automatic thoughts' be?
- How might Ellis's ABC model help us understand Jeremy's situation?

Person-centred perspective

- What 'conditions of worth' might have influenced Jeremy?
- What might change if Jeremy got in touch with his organismic self?
- Where is Jeremy's locus of evaluation?

Don't worry if you found this exercise difficult. The important thing at this stage is to start to recognise how theory offers different perspectives on the client's self and the difficulties they are experiencing. Remember that theory does not provide the answers but it does offer a framework for what might be going on.

THE PROCESS OF CHANGE: THEORY AND SKILLS

As well as giving you a framework for understanding 'what went wrong', your theoretical model will also determine how you work with clients in the counselling process. All clients come to counselling because they want something to change, but change means different things to different people. It also means different things in different theoretical approaches, and this in turn has an impact on how the counsellor works with the client.

 OK, I understand that talking will somehow benefit me and that theoretical concepts will help me understand the client but how would counsellors from different approaches work differently in the actual session? Don't they all do the same sort of thing – listen and demonstrate empathy?

 Well, you are right that all counsellors listen and try to be empathic but that does not fully encompass what counsellors do, and even 'empathy' has a different significance in different approaches. Just as different theoretical models offer different ways of conceptualising client issues, they also offer different ways of working with clients. These differences will be evident in:

- the nature of the counselling relationship
- the goals and intentions of therapy
- the skills and techniques used by the counsellor.

Let's look at what this means in practice.

PSYCHODYNAMIC COUNSELLING

As we have already seen, psychodynamic theory is focused on how the client's past history impacts on the present. Most of the consequences of this early experience are acted out unconsciously, and therefore the aim of psychodynamic counselling is to bring past, unresolved issues or traumas into awareness in order to shed light on them and help the client change things in the present.

 But if this is all in the client's unconscious, how does the counsellor work with it?

 Good question. One reason why psychodynamic counselling is often longer term is that this takes time. Uncovering and working with unconscious processes and past trauma needs a lot of care and often the work can last two years or even longer. In classical psychoanalysis, the counsellor would also expect to see the client more than once a week.

 That sounds very intense.

 Well, it depends on the client's issues. Psychodynamic counsellors may also work on more short-term contracts but where the aim of therapy is to change things at a deep level, it will mean integrating learning or working through aspects of a key developmental stage that the client did not successfully negotiate. You may remember that Freud believed that each life stage needed to be successfully negotiated, otherwise trauma and stuckness would occur later in life.

 So how do you work to uncover these unconscious processes?

 The first thing to understand is the nature of the relationship in psychodynamic counselling. The psychodynamic counsellor aims to be neutral and keeps a certain aloofness or professional distance. I am sure you have seen films where the therapist sits behind the client, who lies on the couch talking into thin air. This is how classical psychoanalysis is carried out and not how most psychodynamic counsellors actually work, but the idea of staying neutral still applies.

 You mean they don't give anything away about themselves?

 Correct. The therapy room itself may also be neutral or clinical in appearance and the counsellor would probably not give the client so much as a glass of water, to ensure that there is no confusion of roles.

 But what is the purpose of this type of relationship? It doesn't sound very therapeutic.

 The idea is that by not giving anything away about themselves, the therapist becomes in effect a 'blank screen' onto which the client will unconsciously 'transfer' thoughts, attitudes and feelings which actually belong to past relationships with significant others. We looked at the concept of transference in Chapter 12 as being when you behave towards someone in the present 'as if' they were someone from your past.

 But I still don't understand why that would be useful or how the therapist would work with it.

 It is useful because the therapist can then interpret what is being transferred unconsciously onto them to help the client better understand themselves, their history and their patterns of relating. Transference can take many forms – positive, hostile or neutral – and this is all material which the therapist can work with. For example, the client might project positive feelings of the 'good mother' onto the counsellor or negative feelings of the 'bad teacher'. Transference can also be ambivalent (in other words, mixed or contradictory feelings) towards the counsellor.

 So what you are saying is that the counsellor is kind of assigned that role by the client.

Yes, but it is important that the counsellor does not actually take on that role but rather uses the information (from being seen in that role) to help the client examine what the transference is about and how it links back to the client's past. These transferred feelings and attitudes can then be analysed and interpreted to help the client understand how earlier childhood relationships are impacting on present relationships and present difficulties.

EXAMPLE

Georgia kept getting into arguments with her boss. Every time he asked her to do something, she found herself answering back or finding reasons not to cooperate. Despite being very capable, Georgia's behaviour was significantly affecting her chances of promotion at work.

Georgia's counsellor helped her to see that she was transferring unresolved issues from her relationship with her father onto the relationship with her boss. She was able to separate out past and present and develop a more appropriate employee relationship with her boss which reflected the present reality of their respective roles.

Here are some other skills and techniques that psychodynamic counsellors use. They are all focused on making the unconscious conscious.

Working with resistance and defence mechanisms

The counsellor will notice how the client is defending themselves from uncomfortable thoughts and feelings – in other words, what defence mechanisms the client is using both in the room and in their life – and bring these into the client's awareness.

Free association

The counsellor will invite the client to 'free associate' – in other words, to say whatever comes into their mind – as a way of seeing what unconscious material slips out without the client realising it. The counsellor will then interpret this or invite the client to reflect on it.

Dreams and fantasies

The counsellor will encourage the client to describe their dreams and fantasies because these less-guarded expressions of what is going on in the client's unconscious can reveal truths of which they are unaware. Freud was particularly interested in dreams as the 'royal road to the unconscious', but both dreams and fantasies contain disguised messages and symbols which signpost issues which the counsellor can work with.

As you can see, these skills and techniques all serve to bring unconscious material to the surface so that clients have 'insight' which they can then use to change things about themselves or their lives in the present.

One note of caution though: counsellors working within this approach need to be ever-mindful of their own responses and reactions to what is put onto them in the process of transference, to ensure that they do not react to the client unhelpfully because of unresolved issues from their own past.

REFLECTION

- How do you feel about the psychodynamic relationship?
- What is your response to the psychodynamic way of working?

One criticism of the psychodynamic way of working is that 'insight' does not necessarily lead to change:

- Would insight be enough to help you change something in your life?

In summary, the psychodynamic family of counselling and psychotherapy share a core set of beliefs that focus on the importance of the individual's unconscious and past experiences and how these impact on current beliefs and behaviours. There is a shared concept that the counsellor is able to facilitate change by making explicit the client's early childhood experiences and relationships, coupled with working with the client's defences against overwhelming unconscious pain.

CBT COUNSELLING

CBT aims to change self-defeating thoughts and unhelpful behaviours. The CBT counsellor does not focus on past events or childhood development but focuses instead on the client's current negative thoughts and behaviours. The counsellor works very much with present difficulties and, although they will recognise that the problematic thoughts and behaviours emerged from the past, they will see them as learned behaviours that can be unlearned. The therapist's task is to identify, challenge and work with the client to change irrational thoughts and behaviours to ones that will enable them to function more effectively. Essentially, CBT counsellors work at problem solving by teaching new ways of thinking and behaving.

TABLE 13.1 Psychodynamic family of therapies

Therapy	Who	Overview	What goes wrong	Goals of therapy	Therapeutic relationship	Further reading
Adlerian Therapy	Developed by Alfred Adler (1870–1937)	Adlerians are interested in how we develop our own individual, unique, private beliefs and lifestyle in childhood. This early map becomes a reference for the individual's beliefs, behaviours, and view of self, others and the world. If encouraged in childhood, we feel capable and connected with others and the world.	The individual develops feelings of inferiority based on early experiences which may depend on the individual's position within the family, and whether the individual experienced humiliation as a child, had a severe health condition or was generally discouraged. When we feel inferior or discouraged by others we may react by over-compensating or competing, withdrawing or giving up.	The goal of therapy is to challenge the individual's assumptions about themselves based on their own feelings of inferiority. The therapy encourages the individual to develop social interests and foster a sense of equality with others, coupled with seeking own personal goals, contributing to society and working with others.	The therapy initially focuses on developing an empathic relationship of equals that builds an atmosphere of hope to encourage the client to believe that things can change and be different. Generally, the therapeutic process centres on four processes: • Assessment of life-style. • Socratic questioning to explore the client's thinking, feelings and way of behaving. • Guided and eidetic imagery to access symbolic pictures and change negative scripts. • Role playing to explore and practise new behaviours.	Lundin, R.W. (2015) *Alfred Adler's Basic Concepts and Implications*. New York: Routledge.

(Continued)

TABLE 13.1 (Continued)

Therapy	Who	Overview	What goes wrong	Goals of therapy	Therapeutic relationship	Further reading
Jungian Therapy	Developed by Carl Gustav Jung (1875–1961)	Jung termed his theory 'Analytical Psychology' to differentiate it from Freud's psychoanalysis. Jung disagreed with Freud in key areas. On the theory of the libido, Jung believed it was the centre of psychic energy that influences our spirituality, intellect and creativity. The theory of the unconscious for Jung is where the psyche is made up of different interrelated systems including the ego, alongside our personal and collective unconscious. Core to Jung is the idea of archetypes: symbols, images and thoughts with universal meaning.	Jung postulates that below our unconsciousness is a deeper collective unconscious made up of patterns (archetypes) that are universal and are inherited and uncontrollable. These archetypes lead to behaviours and beliefs that we cannot break, such as addictions, anxiety and depression.	The ultimate goal of Jungian therapy is to bring balance within the psyche by making the unconscious conscious, and analysing our archetypes to understand who we are.	Therapy is intense and can last several years; it can be one or more times a week. The relationship is built upon authenticity, trust and equality. Common techniques used in therapy include dream analysis, word association and creative exercises.	Stevens, A. (2001) *Jung: A Very Short Introduction.* Oxford: Oxford University Press. Storr, A. (1986) *Jung.* London: Fontana Press.

Therapy	Who	Overview	What goes wrong	Goals of therapy	Therapeutic relationship	Further reading
Attachment Psychotherapy	Developed by Edward John Bowlby (1907–1990)	The relationship a child has with their primary care-giver provides a model for how the individual forms relationships with others. Based on our memories and expectations, Bowlby considers three patterns of attachment: 1. Secure attachments: The individual feels secure both with who they are and in their relationships with others, and does not avoid contact with others. 2. Anxious resistant attachments: An individual becomes clingy because they fear separation. 3. Anxious avoidant attachments: The individual seeks to become self-sufficient because they expect to be rejected.	When a child experiences maternal separation and deprivation in early life the individual will develop a lack of emotional development, concern for others and guilt, coupled with problems forming meaningful or lasting relationships with others.	By exploring and identifying losses and grief from childhood, the individual can work towards closure and learn to form secure relationships with self and others.	The therapeutic relationship is established by forming a 'secure base' for the client founded on building trust, listening and by responding to the client. The therapist aims to provide a secure attachment base with regular appointments. The therapy can use a variety of techniques, including dream analysis and free association.	Holmes, J. (2014) *John Bowlby and Attachment Theory* (Makers of Modern Psychotherapy). Hove: Routledge.

(Continued)

TABLE 13.1 (Continued)

Therapy	Who	Overview	What goes wrong	Goals of therapy	Therapeutic relationship	Further reading
Object Relations Theory	Melanie Klein (1882–1960) is considered the 'mother' of Object Relations theory, which later included theorists such as Ronald Fairbairn and Donald Winnicott.	Although there is a diverse range of ideas surrounding Object Relations, there is an overriding emphasis on the bond between the mother and child during the first three years of life as a key factor in the development of the child's psychic structure. 'Object' refers to our relationship with others, not with actual objects, but it can also refer to the relationship the child has to a specific part of a person, such as the mother's breast.	At the heart of this theory is the drive to form relationships with others; if we have not experienced good relationships in the family, and in particular with the mother, this will lead to problems in establishing healthy relationships later in life. The earlier the bad experiences the greater the damage that is done. Klein also hypothesised that the relationship the baby had with the mother's breast was important. The baby will feel loved and nurtured if the breast produces sufficient milk and is freely available. If the breast is not freely available and produces insufficient milk, the baby will hate the breast and become frustrated and project hostile thoughts onto the breast.	The goal of Object Relations therapy is to help the client to explore problems they have in their relationships by looking at how current emotions and relational patterns developed from childhood object relations. Therapy will also make conscious those aspects of self that have been split or repressed so that the client can have less internal conflict and be able to build more fulfilling relationships.	The therapy relies on initially fostering a relationship that is empathic and trusting for the client to feel safe and understood. The therapist will analyse transference as indicators of the client's object relations and defence mechanisms developed as an infant, bringing the unconscious conscious. The counsellor will help the client to greater self-awareness and develop a strong object relation with the therapist that in turn can be transferred onto relationships outside the therapy room.	Hinshelwood, R.D, Robinson, S. and Zarate, O. (2011) *Introducing Melanie Klein: A Graphic Guide.* Cambridge: Icon Books.

It feels very much as if the counsellor is the expert and is doing something to the client.

 Well, it might be better to think of it as a teacher–pupil relationship, but the CBT counsellor takes the lead by assessing the problem and agreeing a specific treatment plan with the client aimed at achieving the desired change in thinking and/or behaviour. The CBT counsellor will use different tools, techniques and prescribed homework tasks to facilitate this change.

 Does that mean that the client needs to have a clear idea of what they want to change?

 Yes. In CBT counselling, it is important that the client knows what they want to change for the therapy to work. This is why goal setting is an important part of contracting in CBT work. However, clients who are just feeling depressed or anxious will need help to explore what they want to change. The first session would typically include an assessment of the problems that the client is experiencing and a clarification of what thoughts and behaviours are causing problems in the client's everyday life.

Typically, CBT counselling is not long term (usually not more than 10–15 sessions), but organisations like the NHS offer as few as six sessions. This is because therapy does not involve an in-depth analysis of the history of the client's problems or any systematic exploration of their past development. Once a treatment plan has been agreed, the counsellor will use specific techniques and skills to help the client work towards change. These include:

- challenging irrational beliefs and automatic thoughts
- 'thought stopping' to break old patterns of thinking
- 'experimenting' with different ways of thinking and behaving
- using different measures and scales to track progress and change
- engaging in homework assignments, e.g. keeping a 'thought diary' or practising new ways of behaving.

EXAMPLE

Bella was asked to record how high her level of anxiety was when she went into social situations, using a scale of 0–100. At the beginning of counselling, she rated her anxiety levels as 89 out of 100. By the end of therapy, she was asked to repeat the exercise and this time scaled her anxiety at 11 out of 100.

I am not sure I like the idea of homework. It brings back bad memories of having to do homework at school, and even when I did it the teachers never seemed to bother to mark it or take any interest. It all seemed a bit pointless to me.

 In CBT counselling, it is crucial that the client takes an active part in their own therapy or treatment. The homework is designed to help the client actively engage with their issues between sessions – in other words, to keep the momentum going. For example, a client might be given the task of keeping a diary to record the 'activating event' – as it is called in Ellis's ABC model – and the thoughts and feelings that follow this event. Later on in the therapy, the client might be given the specific task of trying out new ways of thinking or behaving based on what they have learned during the session.

 Ah, so the homework is like practising the new way of thinking or behaving so that it becomes an automatic process.

 Precisely. It reinforces the new pattern of thinking or behaving. CBT is also noted for its focus on helping clients to prepare for and guard against falling back into old habits – in other words, relapse prevention. Clients are given techniques and tools for recognising the warning signs so that they can take preventative action.

Clients have to be quite robust to engage in some aspects of CBT therapy. CBT therapy can be challenging and the client may have to face situations that they find difficult. CBT has been shown to be particularly effective for treating phobias because phobic reactions are usually learned behaviours that are deep-seated but irrational. For example, a client with agoraphobia might be directed to take a certain number of steps outside their house as part of a homework assignment.

REFLECTION

- How do you feel about the CBT relationship?
- What is your response to the CBT way of working?

One of the criticisms of the CBT way of working is that it does not focus on the client–counsellor relationship itself. CBT counsellors work on the basis that a 'working alliance' is sufficient, but this leaves little scope for exploring the dynamics of what is happening between the counsellor and client, including dealing with issues such as transference.

- Do you think that this matters?

TABLE 13.2 Cognitive-behavioural family of therapies

Therapy	Who	Overview	What goes wrong	Goals of therapy	Therapeutic relationship	Further reading
Acceptance and Commitment Therapy (ACT)	Developed by Steven Hayes and associates in the late 1980s	Combines acceptance and mindfulness techniques to fully connect with the present moment and help the individual to create a meaningful life while being able to manage the stresses and pain that life brings. ACT focuses on three things: • **Acceptance** of how we experience in the moment. • **Choose** your values and goals that hold most meaning. • **Take** action.	A person gets stuck with negative thoughts and behaviours over situations they cannot control, overwhelming emotions or personality traits that are difficult to change. The person is left helpless by getting stuck and repeatedly going over, obsessing and worrying about the situation without accepting its reality.	The ultimate goal of therapy is to accept those things that are outside the client's control and commit to changing those things that can improve the client's way of being and quality of life.	ACT requires a firm, caring, therapeutic relationship which supports the client to fully engage. ACT teaches mindfulness-based skills and techniques to help manage painful thoughts and feelings more effectively, and works with the client to find and focus on those values that are held as most important and meaningful to them.	Harris, R. (2009) *ACT Made Simple: An Easy-to-Read Primer on Acceptance and Commitment Therapy*. Oakland, CA: New Harbinger. Hayes, S.C., Strosahl, K.D. and Wilson, K.G. (2011) *Acceptance and Commitment Therapy: The Process and Practice of Mindful Change*, 2nd edition. New York: Guilford Press.
Cognitive Analytic Therapy (CAT)	Developed by Dr Anthony Ryle in the early 1980s	Combines psychoanalytic therapy and cognitive behavioural therapies to explore the ways in which a person thinks, feels and behaves, and considers the events and relationships in the past that have informed them.	A person learns powerful behaviours and beliefs from the past which are negatively impacting on and contributing to current problems.	The aim is to identify the problems and the effect they are having on current well-being. The therapy examines how the client has learned particular ways of behaving and beliefs that are now holding them back; these were originally fostered to manage often-unmanageable feelings that have arisen from early life experiences.	The therapist strives to create an empathic therapeutic relationship to understand how past behaviours and experiences are impacting on the 'here and now', and explore how to make changes.	Ryle, A. and Kerr, I.B. (2002) *Introducing Cognitive Analytic Therapy*. Chichester: Wiley-Blackwell.

(Continued)

TABLE 13.2 (Continued)

Therapy	Who	Overview	What goes wrong	Goals of therapy	Therapeutic relationship	Further reading
				The ultimate goal of the therapy is to learn different ways of doing things which can make life better for the client and others close to them.		Ryle, A. (1997) *Cognitive Analytic Therapy and Borderline Personality Disorder: The Model and the Method.* Chichester: John Wiley & Sons.
Dialectical Behavioural Therapy (DBT)	Developed by psychologist Marsha M. Linehan in the late 1980s	Specific type of CBT to help treat borderline personality disorder. Dialectics is the way the mind understands different concepts by comprehending and recognising their polar opposites, such as 'love and hate'.	A person develops an extreme and rigid view of the self, others and the world which leads to intense feelings and unrealistic ideas, expectations and feelings about self and others that can fracture relationships and lead to health issues.	The aim is to work towards decreasing self-destructive behaviour and provide positive reinforcement to motivate change in the individual. This teaches a person more balanced coping strategies and helps them to identify and build their strengths.	The therapy requires the client and counsellor to develop a collaborative relationship where the client is encouraged to work through relationship issues with the therapist. Skills and tasks central to DBT include homework, diary keeping, role play and practice of skills such as self-soothing.	Linehan, M.M. (2014) *DBT Skills Training Manual,* 2nd edition. New York: Guilford Press. Heard, H.L. and Swales, M.A. (2015) *Changing Behaviour in DBT: Problem Solving in Action.* New York: Guilford Press.

In summary, the family of cognitive and behavioural therapies share core beliefs centred on the way an individual thinks (cognitive) and the way the person behaves (behavioural). This group of therapies believes that it is possible to change the way we think about problems to overcome problems in our lives.

PERSON-CENTRED COUNSELLING

The person-centred view of what goes wrong is that the increasing tension between a person's organismic self and their self-concept – which has been formed from the conditions of worth imposed by others – leads to ever-increasing internal disharmony. Rogers called this tension and split between the organismic self and the self-concept 'being in a state of *incongruence*': in other words, not in harmony. The person becomes increasingly unable to trust and rely on their own internal valuing process and unable to fulfil their potential or self-actualise. Although a person-centred counsellor would not use mental health terminology like 'depression' and 'anxiety', preferring instead to use the client's own language for describing what 'ails' them, these are the kinds of problems that clients present with.

 So, how does a person-centred counsellor help clients to change?

 Rogers was not really interested in change for its own sake or in focusing on 'problems' alone, because he saw people as being much more than the sum of their problems and full of potential. He was interested in creating an environment where a client could realise their potential and grow as a whole person. Alongside this holistic view, Rogers firmly believed that the client was the expert on their own life, and as such rejected the use of techniques that put the therapist in the role of an expert on the client's life.

 Hold on a minute: if person-centred counsellors do not use techniques and are not the expert, what do they do?

 In its simplest form, Rogers believed that the relationship between client and counsellor was the key factor in how therapy works. If you remember the theory, he believed that people become distressed or 'dis-eased' because they have lost touch with their organismic self, as a result of the conditions of worth imposed on them by family and society. Rogers saw the therapist's role as offering the opposite – in other words, a relationship that was not conditional in any way. He did not want the counsellor to be yet another significant person in that client's life influencing how they should act, behave, think or be.

So what you are saying is that the counsellor should in some way be neutral?

'Neutral' is not really the right word because it sounds too detached. The person-centred relationship is more like 'unconditional love'. Rogers believed that the counsellor's role is to provide a particular kind of relationship which acts as a counterbalance to 'what went wrong', and this in turn becomes a catalyst for change. His radical proposition was that six conditions were all that were 'necessary' and 'sufficient' for change to occur, with the most important being the three *core* conditions.

So, first, we have *conditions* of worth and now we have core *conditions* – is that a coincidence?

Absolutely not. Instead of conditions being put on the client that require them to be different from who they truly are, the counsellor offers the right conditions or climate for the client to be who they truly are. Let's look at each condition and see how this works.

1. Empathy

The first core condition is empathy, which we looked at in Part I of the book. Empathy is central to person-centred counselling; the counsellor needs to be able to put themselves so much inside the private world of the client that they can clarify thoughts and feelings or hidden and denied parts of the client that they themselves are barely aware of. Another way of putting it is that the counsellor is able to feel and sense the client's world so accurately and sensitively that they can then translate that experience back to the client. As the client experiences being understood, they are able to understand themselves and get back in touch with their organismic self. The question counsellors need to ask themselves is:

> Can I let myself enter the world of his feelings and personal meanings and see these as he does? Can I step into his private world so completely that I lose all desire to evaluate or judge it? (Rogers, 1990: 121)

2. Congruence

The second core condition is congruence. Rogers also used the words *genuineness* or *realness* to describe congruence. What this means is that the counsellor commits to being real in the relationship; both words are important here – 'being' and 'real'.

Rather than 'doing' something as an expert, like a doctor or a teacher, the person-centred counsellor will offer themselves as they are, not in a professional role. You could call this 'being' rather than 'doing'.

 That feels confusing. What do you mean by 'being' and 'doing'?

 Rather than 'doing' something with, or to, your client, such as imparting knowledge or using techniques, the person-centred counsellor meets the client as their own self. They are not putting on a façade but 'being' with the client. The client is meeting the real person.

 But how is that different from meeting a friend?

 It's different because in a friendship both people make demands on each other and want something from the relationship, whereas in a person-centred relationship the counsellor is real and available – but for the client, not for themselves.

 I'm not sure I understand what being real might mean in the counselling relationship.

 Well, let's suppose you were listening to a client and beginning to feel bored or irritated. You wouldn't just say, 'I'm feeling bored'. Instead, you listen to your feelings and notice you are feeling bored and try to find out what it might mean.

So what would you actually say to a client if you were feeling bored?

Let's imagine that the client has been going over the same ground week after week, talking about how disillusioned they are at work, and you begin to feel a sense of boredom. You would be congruent with your feeling by saying something like:

> You have been talking about your disillusionment with work and I am wondering whether this feeling of boredom that I am picking up is perhaps what you are feeling too?

 Oh, I see. So you kind of put the boredom into the room, so to speak.

 Yes, you will notice that I used the skill of immediacy in this example, which we looked at in Part I of the book. This is the challenge of congruence – being real but for the benefit of someone else.

 Why is congruence so important?

Because it is the direct opposite of the state in which clients come to counselling, i.e. in a state of incongruence. If the counsellor is congruent, it helps the client to be real too. It is a powerful message which says it's OK to be yourself and be real.

3. Unconditional positive regard

The third core condition is unconditional positive regard. The counsellor needs to display unconditionality towards the client to counteract the conditions of worth that the client has grown up with. Unconditional positive regard means fully accepting the client and their individual experience of the world.

 But what if I don't agree with what the client has done or what they represent?

 I think it is important to recognise that this is difficult. We don't have to approve of the behaviour, but we do need to have unconditional respect for the person and how they see the world. This is where congruence is important. To pretend to approve of something that the client stands for would be incongruent, but at the same time it is not helpful to judge the client. For example, if the client expresses racist views, we might not approve of these views but we need to explore what this means to the client. The counsellor might say something like:

> I find it difficult to understand where your racism comes from and wonder what you have experienced that leads you to see things this way.

 I think I understand. I have to be open to understanding where the client is coming from, even if I don't share their values.

 Exactly, although this is often difficult for the counsellor. It's a bit like the kind of unconditional love you might give your children. You might not always approve of what they do or say, but you let them know this while also loving them.

As with the other main approaches, person-centred counselling has broadened and developed to include other ways of working, but the central principles remain the same.

REFLECTION

How do you feel about the person-centred way of working?

One of the criticisms of the person-centred way of working is that the core conditions are 'necessary' but not 'sufficient'. Do you think the core conditions of the therapeutic relationship would be enough to help you change?

TABLE 13.3 Humanistic family of therapies

Therapy	Who	Overview	What goes wrong	Goals of therapy	Therapeutic relationship	Further reading
Focusing-Orientated Psychotherapy	Developed by Eugene Gendlin, an Austrian-American philosopher and psychotherapist who worked closely with Carl Rogers at the University of Chicago in the 1950s.	The research undertaken at the University of Chicago focused on three questions centred on why therapy does not work: 1. Why does therapy not work successfully more often? 2. Why does it not make a significant difference in a person's life more often? 3. When therapy is successful what are the client and counsellor doing? What came out of the research was that the theoretical model itself was not important but the process the client underwent was. Successful clients had the ability to access and focus on their 'felt sense': to pay attention to what was happening bodily inside them beneath the thoughts and emotions associated with the issue.	Instead of paying attention to our inner bodily experiencing of a situation and trusting that we hold the answer within us, we externalise events in our lives through narrative, analysis or reliving old emotions and behaviours. By not paying attention and being in touch with our immediate felt experiencing or experiencing of the whole situation, we remove ourselves from sensing ourselves inwardly.	The goal of therapy is to get in touch with the 'felt sense' and facilitate a 'felt shift' in how the 'felt sense' is experienced in an emotional, mental and bodily way. The counsellor also teaches the client to develop focusing skills. Through focusing, the client learns to take charge of themselves and recognise distinct felt body shifts, or change towards a resolution of their problems.	Although focusing can be done alone as a taught self-help process, the therapeutic relationship is empathic, where the therapist listens to the client, is with the client and, crucially, does not block the client's own process. The counsellor guides the client through the six steps of focusing: 1. Clearing a space. 2. Locating a felt sense. 3. Getting a handle on the quality of the felt sense. 4. Resonating between the felt sense and language to find a match. 5. Asking what the felt sense needs. 6. Receiving changes in the felt sense as they come. The counsellor helps the client to develop focusing skills as an ongoing process for paying attention to what is going on inside.	Purton, C. (2008) *The Focusing-Orientated Counselling Primer*. Ross-on-Wye: PCCS Books. Gendlin, E.T. (2003) *Focusing*, revised edition. London: Rider.

(Continued)

TABLE 13.3 (Continued)

Therapy	Who	Overview	What goes wrong	Goals of therapy	Therapeutic relationship	Further reading
Existential Therapy	Towards the mid-20th century, clinicians such as Karl Jaspers, Otto Rank, Ludwig Binswanger and Medard Boss were some of the first to apply existential principles to therapeutic practice. Later advocates include R.D. Lang, Irvin Yalom, Rollo May and Viktor Frankl.	Based in the roots of psychodynamic therapy, existential philosophy draws on the philosophical ideas of Heidegger, Dostoevsky, Kierkegaard, Nietzsche, Sartre, Husserl, and others. In the view of the existential school, the individual is able to choose between living inauthentically or authentically. The prime focus is on what it is like to be human, faced with the 'givens' of existence. These include: • mortality • freedom and responsibility • isolation • meaninglessness. Existentialists also focus on how we relate to the four realms of existence: • physical realm • social realm • personal realm • spiritual realm.	Opinions of what may go wrong differ within this philosophical approach. One school of thought suggests that disturbance comes from a refusal or inability to confront existential life 'givens'. Common to this approach is the individual's experience and how they relate to the world.	The principle aim is to enable the individual to face their anxieties and identify blocks to freedom and authenticity, and to challenge themselves to become more self-determining and take responsibility for their own life.	The therapeutic relationship places an emphasis on an authentic encounter between two unique individuals, through which the client can discover their own uniqueness and meaning.	van Deurzen, E. (2012) *Existential Counselling & Psychotherapy in Practice*. London: Sage.

Therapy	Who	Overview	What goes wrong	Goals of therapy	Therapeutic relationship	Further reading
Gestalt Therapy	Developed by Fritz and Laura Perls in the late 1940s	Gestalt theory has its roots in the principles of relational theory that each person is a whole system made up of the mind, body, emotions and soul. Gestalt adopts a holistic philosophy whereby meaning comes from understanding the interrelatedness of the whole system rather than breaking it into individual parts.	The individual becomes distressed because the system has become fragmented. The individual has suppressed or unacknowledged their feelings and needs. Gestalt theory also considers the concept of 'unfinished business', whereby individuals have feelings associated with distinct memories of past events, such as anxiety, hatred or grief, that have not been expressed. These issues are brought to the surface and worked on in therapy using Gestalt techniques.	Gestalt therapy will typically explore the client's thoughts, feelings, beliefs, values and behaviours so that they can understand who they are and how they respond to their environment and events in the here and now. Therapy offers the client the space to explore choices, patterns, behaviours and obstacles that are preventing them from fulfilling their full potential. Gestalt therapy will also encourage the client to explore their 'self-dialogue' between different parts of the self which they may not be aware of and are in conflict with, such as the internal parent versus the internal child, or the good side versus the bad side. The individual learns to live with and accept these different aspects of self.	The relationship is based on existential dialogue whereby the therapist experiences the individual for who they are rather than imposing goals on the client. The therapy will usually include a range of creative and expressive techniques, including: role play, 'empty chair' technique, exploration of dreams, focus on body language and dialogue. These techniques provide a root to help the individual to explore the issue and make contact with deeper feelings. It can be experienced as very challenging and very immediate.	Perls, F.S. (1994) *Gestalt Therapy: Excitement and Growth in the Human Personality.* London: Souvenir Press. Clarkson, P. (2013) *Gestalt Counselling in Action.* London: Sage.

(Continued)

TABLE 13.3 (Continued)

Therapy	Who	Overview	What goes wrong	Goals of therapy	Therapeutic relationship	Further reading
Transactional Analysis (TA)	Developed by Eric Berne in the late 1950s	Berne defined personal social contact with another as transactions; hence Transactional Analysis (TA) is a means of studying interactions between people. TA postulates three ego states that make up an individual's personality. Each of the ego states correlates to a system of thought, feeling and behaviour which impacts on how individuals present/define themselves and interact with others. These ego states are: • **Parent (P)** ego state, which can be nurturing in a positive or spoiling way, or controlling in a structured or critical manner. • **Adult (A)** ego state, which is balanced and draws on aspects of both the adult and child in a rational way. • **Child (C)** ego state, which can be adapted by being cooperative or resistant, and free by being either spontaneous or immature/rebellious. TA holds the belief that effective communication between two people is ideally balanced (Adult to Adult) but different ego states can be effective in different situations, e.g. having a temper tantrum in a Child to Adult interaction or being nurturing in a Parent to Child interaction.	The individual develops 'unconscious scripts' which manifest in repetitive behaviours, thoughts and feelings associated with the Child ego state. These scripts overshadow the other ego states. TA also refers to 'strokes'. If individuals receive positive strokes as a child they feel accepted, but if they do not experience positive strokes the individual will develop a dysfunctional pattern of living and relating.	The goal of TA is for the individual to develop autonomy, which is the ability to be spontaneous, have self-awareness and develop intimacy with others. The individual learns about how the three ego states work, how these affect their current behaviour and how they learned these 'life scripts' as children.	The counsellor works with the client to establish specific goals. In TA it is not unusual for a written contract to be used which defines specific goals and how these will be met, e.g. demonstrating assertive behaviour at work. The therapist will help the client become more aware of their patterns of relating and help them look at other ways of responding.	Berne, E. (1961) *Transactional Analysis in Psychotherapy*. New York: Grove Press. Harris, T.A. (1967) *I'm OK – You're OK*. New York: Harper Collins.

Therapy	Who	Overview	What goes wrong	Goals of therapy	Therapeutic relationship	Further reading
Emotion-Focused Therapy (EFT)	Key figures within this approach include Robert Elliot, Leslie Greenberg, Rhonda Goldman, Laura Rice and Jeanne Watson.	EFT emerged from the Person-Centred Process Experiential model in the late 1980s. Central to this approach is that for psychological change to be effective the primary focus for change is centred on our emotions. Our emotions have a profound influence on our behaviour and thoughts on an implicit level. As a consequence we need to accept the emotions that are within us rather than pushing emotions away.	EFT believes that an individual's emotions are the primary mode of processing the impact on their thoughts, behaviours and experience. This approach is based on the premise that our primary emotional responses have somehow gone awry and cannot be trusted or relied upon and are therefore not working for us. It suggests that we have become trapped within variations of the same script. People get stuck or cut off from their emotions. We also have secondary reactive emotions which are a response to the primary emotion. An example might be an emotional response of feeling hurt that manifests itself as anger – in order to cover up or defend against the hurt.	The aim of EFT is to enable the client to experience and become aware of their emotions. The therapy supports the client to express, tolerate, manage and regulate their emotions. Essentially the client is learning the value of emotional awareness and management by bringing back into awareness those experiences that have been pushed away as painful memories. The client is supported in transforming their emotions by expressing, accepting, regulating and making sense of their emotions.	The therapist fosters an emotional contact with the client, building an empathic relationship so that the client can get in touch with their feelings, thoughts, memories and physical senses of the whole that has been pushed away. The client is encouraged to set goals for the therapy. EFT has a set of tasks that are followed in therapy which explore how goals set by the client will be achieved using integrative experiential methods that include psychodrama, working with chairs, focusing, self-soothing and narrative to access deeper emotions in order to find out what the emotions need.	Elliot, R., Watson, J.C., Goldman, R.N. and Greenberg, L.S. (2004) *Learning Emotion Focused Therapy: A Process-Experiential Approach to Change.* Washington, DC: American Psychological Society Press.

Person-centred counselling can be successfully used with a wide range of presenting concerns and its principles have been adopted and used in other areas such as teaching. Rogers himself worked successfully with clients with schizophrenia. Dave Mearns (1997), an eminent person-centred theorist, successfully worked with clients experiencing post-traumatic stress after active service in war.

In summary, person-centred counselling and therapy belongs to the humanistic family of therapies which share a core focus on the individual's ability to self-develop, grow and take responsibility. There is a shared belief that the counsellor is able to facilitate the client to recognise and understand their own self and their strengths, abilities and choices in the 'here and now'.

SUMMARY OF KEY POINTS

A psychodynamic counsellor:

- works with the client to bring unconscious processes into conscious awareness
- takes a neutral stance in the client–counsellor relationship to encourage transference
- works with transference and counter-transference to give the client insight which enables them to change.

A CBT counsellor:

- works with the client to challenge irrational beliefs and to establish beliefs that are based on reality
- establishes a relationship that is like that of teacher and pupil
- uses techniques and homework to facilitate change towards identified goals.

A person-centred counsellor:

- works with the client to recognise the conditions of worth that have affected their self-concept
- builds a therapeutic relationship based on the core conditions which counteract the conditions of worth
- trusts the client to find their own answers in the process of change.

I think I get it. Each approach helps the counsellor to understand what has 'gone wrong' in the client's life so that they can then support the client to cope with life's challenges and problems and work towards change. Change might be something inside themselves, in their relationships or in how they understand and respond to their past history.

Yes, each approach has a different way of looking at the person and this informs how the counsellor works with the client to support them towards change.

This template for understanding different counselling theories can be used to look at any theory. Different theories may emphasise different elements but each theory is an attempt to establish principles which offer a framework to help the counsellor understand and reflect on what they are doing and why.

SOME OTHER DIRECTIONS IN THEORY

Integrative counselling

Many counsellors describe themselves as 'integrative'. This means that they use a model of counselling which is made up of understanding and skills from more than one approach. What is important though is that integrative counselling is not a 'pick and mix' affair but the combination of different elements to form a new whole.

> Think of the integrative process as being like making a cake. All the separate ingredients go into the bowl to make the cake mix but however delicious the uncooked mixture is, it is not the finished product. When the mixture is baked, it becomes the cake and that is the new whole. Different combinations of ingredients and cooking methods result in different kinds of cakes – or different integrative models.

tip

 I might need actual examples to make better sense of this.

 The important thing is to be clear what you are integrating and for what purpose. Some training courses are based on integrative models of counselling which combine two – or occasionally three – different approaches. Other integrative models have developed a specific model of integration, such as Petrūska Clarkson's five-relationship model (Clarkson, 2003).

Finally, most counsellors develop a style of working that, over time, includes new ideas and techniques that were not part of their original training. As such, they develop an integrative model which is unique to them. Sometimes this is a conscious decision but often it is organic. This seems to be a natural process which happens as the counsellor matures and deepens their understanding of their own practice.

Pluralistic counselling

Pluralistic counselling is a fairly recent research-based approach which has been developed at the University of Strathclyde. It is based on the idea that people are different and therefore require different types of therapeutic intervention to help them cope with life's challenges and work towards change. The values for this approach come from the person-centred tradition but its aim is to bring all therapeutic traditions into a harmonious body of therapy.

 That sounds like another way of saying the approach is integrative?

 The main difference is that pluralistic counselling sees all types of counselling as helpful and no one form as more effective than any other. As such, many different types of intervention are potentially useful to the client and it is incumbent on the counsellor to work with the client to find those interventions that will be most useful to them.

 Does this mean that the counsellor needs to be an expert in every approach?

 The therapist has to be open and knowledgeable about different approaches and decide which interventions are best suited to a particular client. This will be determined both by the counsellor's initial assessment of the client's difficulties and by what the client wants from counselling and which activities they are willing to engage in.

 Let me see if I have understood this: the counsellor may think that a client would benefit from a more psychodynamic approach to resolve past trauma, but the client may actually be saying they just want to be heard, to reflect on what they are experiencing and that they want a more traditional, non-directive type of counselling. In other words, it is a more collaborative way of working, with the client taking the lead on what is best for them.

 That's right, and if the counsellor is unable to offer what the client wants, then it is in the client's best interests to be referred to another counsellor. So, rather than being a 'pick and mix' approach or an integration, it is about developing harmonious ways of working.

The time line in Figure 13.1 gives you a rough idea of when key theories were developed and who the key contributors are.

FIGURE 13.1   Time line of key theorists

Cognitive-behavioural	Psychodynamic	Humanistic
Ivan Pavlov (1849–1936) Russian physiologist, Developed theory of *classical conditioning*		
	Sigmund Freud (1856–1939) Austrian neurologist Founder of *psychoanalysis*	
	Alfred Adler (1870–1937) Austrian doctor & psychotherapist Founder of *individual psychology*	
	Carl Jung (1876–1961) Swiss psychiatrist & psychotherapist Founder of *analytical psychology*	
John Watson (1878–1958) American psychologist Founder of psychological school of *behaviourism*		
	Melanie Klein (1882–1960) Austrian-British psychoanalyst 'Mother' of *object relations* theory	
	Karen Horney (1885–1953) German Psychoanalyst Pioneered *feminist psychology*	
	Ronald Fairbairn (1889–1964) Scottish psychiatrist Key figure in *object relations* theory	
		Fritz Perls (1893–1970) German-born psychiatrist & psychotherapist Founder of *Gestalt* therapy with wife Laura Perls

(Continued)

FIGURE 13.1   (Continued)

Cognitive-behavioural	Psychodynamic	Humanistic
	Anna Freud (1895–1982) Austrian-British psychoanalyst Founder of *child psychoanalysis*	
	Michael Balint (1896–1970) Hungarian psychoanalyst Key figure in *object relations* theory	
	Donald Winnicott (1896–1971) English paediatrician & psychoanalyst Key figure in *object relations* theory	
	Erich Fromm (1900–1980) German-born American social psychologist, psychoanalyst Challenged the theories of Freud and associated with the Frankfurt school of critical theory	
		Carl Rogers (1902–1987) American psychologist Founder of the *person-centred* approach
Burrhus Frederic Skinner (1904–1990) American psychologist Developed theory of *operant conditioning*		
George Kelly (1905–1967) American psychologist Considered father of *cognitive clinical psychology*		
		Victor Frankl (1905–1997) Austrian neurologist & psychiatrist Founder of *logotherapy*

Cognitive-behavioural	Psychodynamic	Humanistic
	John Bowlby (1907–1990) British psychologist & psychoanalyst Pioneered *attachment theory*	
		Abraham Maslow (1908–1970) American psychologist Father of *humanistic psychology*
		Rollo May (1909–1994) American psychologist Key figure in *existential psychotherapy*
		Eric Berne (1910–1970) Canadian-born psychiatrist Created *Transactional Analysis (TA)*
Albert Ellis (1913–2007) American psychologist Founded *rational emotive behaviour therapy (REBT)*		
Aaron Beck (1921–) American psychiatrist Considered the 'father' of *cognitive therapy*		
Albert Bandura (1925–) Canadian-born psychologist Key behaviourist figure who developed *social learning theory*		
		William Glasser (1925–2013) American psychiatrist Developed *reality and choice therapy*
		Eugene Gendlin (1926–) American philosopher & psychotherapist Developed *focusing-orientated psychotherapy*

(Continued)

FIGURE 13.1   (Continued)

Cognitive-behavioural	Psychodynamic	Humanistic
		Irvin Yalom (1931–) American psychiatrist Key *existential* therapist
Arnold Lazarus (1932–2013) South African-born clinical psychologist Developed *multimodal* *therapy*		
		Brian Thorne (1937–) English counsellor & psychotherapist Leading theorist & researcher in *person-centred* therapy
		Dave Mearns (?–) Scottish psychologist & psychotherapist Leading theorist & researcher in *person-centred* therapy
		Robert Elliott (?–) American psychologist Expert in *person-centred* *experiential psychotherapy* and one of the founders of *emotion-* *focused therapy*
Windy Dryden (1950–) English psychotherapist Leading *rational-emotive* *cognitive behaviour* therapist		
		John McLeod (1951–) Psychologist Co-developed *pluralistic* approach to counselling
		Mick Cooper (?–) Chartered counselling psychologist Co-developed *pluralistic* approach to counselling

SUMMARY

- Different theories help the client in different ways.
- Different theories call for different kinds of therapeutic relationship.
- Different theories use different understanding and skills to support the client to manage life's challenges and difficulties and work towards change.

14
Using Supervision to Support Counselling

In this chapter, we will look at the role of supervision and how it supports counselling work. Supervision is partly concerned with reflection and feedback but it also has roots in working ethically and safely – so, in a way, we have come full circle from where we began.

> Supervision can also provide a key process to help a living profession or organization breathe and learn. (Hawkins and Shohet, 2012: 237)

Let's begin by looking at what the word 'supervise' means:

> observe and direct the execution of; observe and direct the work of; keep watch over (someone). (*Oxford English Dictionary*)

It is also interesting to reflect on the origin of the term, which comes from the Latin *super-* ('over') + *videre* ('to see'). In other words, it means to *oversee*. In counselling, supervision is just that. All counsellors are required to have their therapeutic work supervised. The counsellor arranges a session for a fixed length of time to discuss their client work with a supervisor who 'oversees' their work in order to ensure their practice is safe and ethical. Sometimes 'clinical supervision' is used to distinguish it from other kinds of supervision in other contexts.

A supervisor is a more experienced practitioner who will probably have a qualification and training in supervision. The person going for supervision is known as the 'supervisee'. The supervisor and supervisee usually agree and sign a supervision agreement which is similar to the counselling contract agreed between the counsellor and client prior to beginning counselling work. This supervision agreement is intended to encompass all areas of the supervision work and would normally include:

- names and contact details of supervisor and supervisee
- length and regularity of sessions
- cost and payment arrangements
- emergency contact arrangements
- confidentiality and its limits
- boundaries
- which clients are being supervised and how many.

ACTIVITY

There are many other things that could be included in the supervision agreement. What else would you want to see included?

Supervision has many functions which we will explore throughout this chapter. A supervisor never actually meets the supervisee's clients, which means they can remain objective, and this can help to provide fresh insights into the counselling work. An extra pair of eyes will, of course, see more than one pair. Some people find the metaphor of a helicopter useful in picturing the role of the supervisor. If you are in a helicopter, you can see the whole landscape, zoom in to look at something more closely, choose a different angle or even land in a particular spot and get out for a thorough search of the area.

 So, I would need to see a supervisor while training to become a counsellor and they would help me with my client work?

 A supervisor would work with you to reflect on and discuss your client work. You would certainly see a supervisor while training, but supervision doesn't stop when a counsellor is qualified. All counsellors require supervision, no matter how many qualifications they have and no matter how many years they have been working as a counsellor. This makes it very different from the kind of oversight where supervision is part of learning and training but not part of qualified practice. Supervision is always part of ethical practice in counselling and will be a requirement for membership of your professional body. The amount of supervision that a counsellor needs depends on their client load and level of experience but professional bodies offer guidelines on minimum requirements.

The BACP recommends, for example:

- For qualified counsellors the minimum recommendation for supervision is 1.5 hours per month, and this is to be increased as necessary. (Can you take all your client hours to supervision within the time frame? If not, then the 1.5 hours would need to be increased as the counsellor sees fit.)
- Guidelines for trainee counsellors: 1.5 hours per month as a minimum. The guidelines recommend a ratio of eight hours counselling to one hour supervision per month, with the trainee to see the supervisor fortnightly.
- Group supervision: with four or less in the group, each counsellor can claim up to 50% of the time together. With five or more the time needs to be divided by the number of counsellors in the group. (BACP, 2016; n.d.b)

As you can see, supervision can also be in groups and not just in one-to-one relationships. Group supervision is popular in many agencies because it is less expensive, but it also offers the benefit that trainees can learn from each other and get a wider breadth of experience. Supervisors need particular skills to facilitate group supervision to ensure that the time is allocated equally and that all the different needs of the supervisees (and by implication their clients) are met.

The supervisory relationship has many similarities to the counselling relationship. It is vital that you, as a counsellor, feel safe with your supervisor and able to talk openly and frankly. Supervision is a place to talk about what you are doing well but also about mistakes you have made, your doubts and fears, perhaps some negativity you are feeling around a client and other difficulties and problems. These challenges cannot be brought into the open if you feel judged or criticised by your supervisor. In addition, your supervisor is not there to tell you what to do or say. As in counselling, you will work together to explore, understand and apply the subsequent insights and findings to your client work.

 Could my tutor be my supervisor or my line manager at work?

 No, that would be a 'dual role'. It is best practice for your supervisor to have no relationship with you other than that of supervisor. This is because it could be difficult for a counsellor to honestly bring their doubts and mistakes to someone who is in a managerial role. However, if you work in an agency you may also have a line manager who will oversee your work from a procedural and employment point of view but not from a clinical perspective. The agency manager may or may not be a trained counsellor, but all supervisors have to be therapeutically trained to the right level with sufficient post-qualifying experience.

The BACP again states:

> Trainee supervision will require the supervisor to ensure that the work satisfies professional standards. (Clause 56, BACP Ethical Framework, 2016)

 So, in a way, supervision would be a support for the counsellor and the client; almost like an external check. When I worked in retail, we had to perform quality checks. Supervision sounds a bit like that.

 That's a very interesting point of view and in some ways supervision could be likened to quality control, if we think of quality control in terms of certain procedures intended to ensure that a service meets the needs of the client or customer. However, I think that definition misses out on the relational, human aspect of the supervisory relationship. It lacks the warmth and humanness that is part of all therapeutic work.

 What would happen if I made a mistake or overstepped a boundary? Also, what about confidentiality? I thought my counselling work would be confidential apart from certain limits but, if I tell a supervisor, won't I be breaching confidentiality? Also, you just mentioned talking about my thoughts and feelings in supervision but I thought I was there to focus on my clients and the counselling work.

That's a lot of questions. Let's look at them one at a time.

First, the role of supervision can change over time. For a trainee counsellor or a newly qualified counsellor, the focus is more likely to be on safety, information, skills development and support. More experienced counsellors would tend to use supervision to focus on the process and dynamics of the session.

Regarding confidentiality, in supervision you do not disclose details about your client; their name and personal information remain confidential. You are there to focus on your work together and the private details are not relevant. Therefore, the client's confidentiality is protected. However, your supervisor can help you and support you to make decisions around the limits to confidentiality. If there are times when you feel there is a serious risk to your client or others, your supervisor can help you decide whether or not confidentiality needs to be breached and, if so, what steps you need to take. In certain agencies, the confidentiality policy may not be that clear-cut. Some agencies operate their own confidentiality policy and the counsellor would need to work within that.

For the other questions, let's look more closely at the purpose of supervision. Hawkins and Shohet (2012) list ten different primary foci:

1. To provide a regular space for supervisees to reflect on the *content and process* of their work
2. To develop understanding and skills within the work

3. To receive information and another perspective concerning one's work
4. To receive both content and process feedback
5. To be validated and supported both as a person and as a worker
6. To ensure that as a person and as a worker one is not left to carry alone difficulties, problems and projections
7. To have space to explore and express personal distress, restimulation, transference or counter transference that may be brought up by the work
8. To plan and utilise their personal and professional resources better
9. To be proactive rather than reactive
10. To ensure quality of work. (Hawkins and Shohet, 2012: 64)

In this book, we have explored and discussed the seven processes involved in working therapeutically, these being:

1. working ethically and safely
2. working with the counselling relationship
3. working with difference and diversity
4. working with a user-centred approach
5. working with self-awareness
6. working within a coherent framework of skills, theory and techniques
7. working self-reflectively.

It might be useful to reflect on how supervision supports each of these seven processes in counselling work.

WORKING ETHICALLY AND SAFELY

As covered in previous chapters, counsellors are obliged to work safely, ethically and legally. Supervision is a great support and a keystone for ethical practice. Your supervisor is like a 'third eye' overseeing your work and may well pick up on some of the ethical issues that may not be immediately obvious.

BACP again states:

> We will use our supervision and any other professional resources to support and challenge how we respond to such situations. We will give careful consideration to the best approaches to ethical problem solving. (Clause 77, BACP Ethical Framework, 2016)

Some possible issues you might take to supervision are:

• child protection issues
• ethical dilemmas

- confidentiality and its limits
- risk of suicide or serious harm
- how to refer a client
- issues around the counsellor's support and self-care
- limits of proficiency.

Supervision can be extremely helpful in working together to decide on the nature of risk and how to work with it, and no matter how many issues you cover in your training there will always be new challenges and situations which you have not met before.

I was worried about how I would know if the risk was enough for me to have to take action and then to be sure about what I needed to do.

ACTIVITY

Imagine you have a client who often talks about how they hate their life. They talk about how their life is not worth living, how they are sick and tired of everything, how there is no hope for the future and they can't see the point in living.

In this instance, a trainee or new counsellor could feel very frightened listening to a client who seems so hopeless.

- If you were this client's counsellor, how would you feel?
- How would you use supervision to help you understand and manage this situation?

Another key role for the supervisor is to help the counsellor monitor their own health, well-being and fitness to practise. Counselling is very demanding work and there are times when the counsellor may not be in a good enough place in their personal life to see clients or to carry a particular workload. The supervisor has a responsibility to keep an eye on this aspect and raise concerns with the supervisee. Ideally, this will be discussed and strategies for coping agreed. This might mean temporarily stopping client work.

WORKING WITH THE COUNSELLING RELATIONSHIP

Supervision will also ensure that you are working within your role as a counsellor and that the relationship is established and contained. Additionally, it will help you reflect on all aspects of the therapeutic relationship.

Some possible issues you might take to supervision are:

- your role as a counsellor within a particular setting or agency
- any aspects of your relationship with your clients
- where you are in the counselling work: beginning, middle or end
- boundaries of the relationship
- dealing with 'stuckness'
- managing endings.

ACTIVITY

Rachel has been coming to counselling for four weeks. Annie is concerned that Rachel keeps asking her for advice and is feeling frustrated that Annie just does not seem to understand what counselling is about. Annie is finding it harder and harder to avoid just giving advice, although she knows this is not what her role is. She is feeling de-skilled and useless.

- If you were this client's counsellor, how would you feel?
- How would you use supervision to help you understand and manage this situation?

WORKING WITH DIFFERENCE AND DIVERSITY

Another area we have looked at is developing an empathic understanding when working with difference and diversity. Supervision is a crucial element for helping you to work with the wide range of client issues and diverse range of individuals you will encounter in the counselling room. Some possible issues to take to supervision are:

- your own prejudices and stereotypes
- your blocks to empathy
- a personal lack of understanding and ignorance
- identifying personal learning needs.

ACTIVITY

You have been working with a client for several months and have built a strong, trusting relationship. You feel very warm towards him and feel you have worked well together to look at how his feelings of low self-worth impact on his life. In your last

> session, he suddenly discloses that he visits prostitutes and is in debt because of internet pornography. This is a very great surprise to you.
>
> - If you were his counsellor, how would you feel?
> - How would you use supervision to help you understand and manage this situation?

Supervision is particularly useful in helping the counsellor identify 'blind spots' – issues which are out of the counsellor's awareness. This is often about exploring reactions which are getting in the way of fully empathising with the client. The supervisor is skilled in picking up on unspoken thoughts and feelings which can then be brought into the room and explored to develop greater insight.

WORKING WITH A USER-CENTRED APPROACH

Crucial to the work that we examined in Chapter 4 was establishing the focus for the counselling work and remaining focused on the client's issue. Supervision, as a place where you present your client work, will facilitate an exploration of whose needs you are focusing on in the counselling work.

Some possible issues to take to supervision are:

- how to identify what your client's needs are
- how to respond to the client's changing needs
- keeping focused on the client
- exploring whose agenda is uppermost.

> **ACTIVITY**
>
> You have worked with a client for several sessions. In the second session, your client spoke about how she had been abused by a family member when she was very young. Since that session, she has only talked about day-to-day issues relating to her job and her home. You have made reference to her disclosure but she changes the subject. You feel very strongly that this is her core issue and it needs to be worked on.
>
> - If you were her counsellor, how would you feel?
> - How would you use supervision to help you understand and manage this situation?

WORKING WITH SELF-AWARENESS

Self-awareness is a key element for the counsellor, as we explored in Chapter 12. Part of the role of supervision will be for your supervisor to pick up on any personal issues that may be affecting the counselling process or blocking your ability to work effectively with your client.

Does that mean I can talk about my own problems and issues in supervision?

Up to a point but not exactly! Although self-awareness issues may be explored in supervision, these need to be directly relevant to your counselling work. The place for working on personal issues is in your own personal therapy, but the supervisor has an important role in helping you identify these issues and in flagging them up for further personal work. Working on your own issues in therapy will in turn support you and your development, which will have a positive impact on your client work. Some possible issues to take to supervision include:

* exploring 'triggers'
* identifying issues to take to personal therapy
* bringing issues into supervisee's awareness
* identifying themes in supervisee's responses.

ACTIVITY

This is your first session with a client. You find yourself really struggling to listen, and find it very difficult not to let your mind wander. Your client is an elderly woman who is very lonely and seldom hears from her family. You are aware of feeling 'sorry for her', which makes your inability to listen well even more surprising. Your own mother was a widow for many years and although you visited as often as you could, you were aware of her loneliness. You really want to support this client but your inability to focus and listen continues.

* If you were her counsellor, how would you feel?
* How would you use supervision to help you understand and manage this situation?

RELATING THEORY AND SKILLS TO CLIENT WORK

Ideally, supervision will be with a supervisor from within your theoretical model. As we saw in Chapter 13, different theories work in different ways. Supervision is a place where your supervisor will be able not only to explore with you how your theory helps you to understand your client's personality, history and patterns of relating, but also ensure that you are working from within a coherent framework of theory and skills.

Some possible issues to take to supervision are:

- how to understand the client's issues within a theoretical framework
- exploring skills and interventions to facilitate change within a theoretical framework
- learning about mental health issues.

ACTIVITY

You are a psychodynamic counsellor and have been working with your client for several months, and the work has been going well. You recently had a holiday which was planned and discussed in the sessions leading up to it. In the sessions since then, your client has been late for every session and you are aware that your relationship has changed. Your client seems impatient with you and has said on a couple of occasions that you don't understand. Your client recounts a dream where she is in an empty house and can't find the door to some of the rooms. Your client was brought up by her father following her mother's death when she was five years old.

- If you were her counsellor, how would you feel?
- How would you use supervision to help you understand and manage this situation?

As we have seen, supervision provides a space to explore all aspects of the counselling process that you have to work with. Of course, the seven processes do not work in isolation and generally what you take to supervision will be a combination of some or all of them.

As a supervisee, it is important to fully utilise the time you have in supervision. It is helpful to prepare and prioritise what you want to take to supervision, and also to reflect on and consider why you have chosen certain things to discuss and what you want to achieve by doing so.

 So I could write a list of what I want to talk about in supervision. Actually, just doing that would help me get my thoughts and feelings in order. Of course, any safety issues or emergencies would be top of the list.

 Absolutely. It is then very important to always ask yourself why you are prioritising certain things. It could be that some clients are easier to talk about than others. You might enjoy talking about clients who are doing well and participating in sessions and reaping the benefits. It could be that you don't want to talk about the clients you find challenging, where you might feel incompetent, unsure or lost, but it is actually those clients who need to be taken to supervision. By doing so, you will probably experience some uncomfortable and even painful feelings of your own, which is probably why you were resistant to wanting to talk about them. This experience, though, will actually provide a greater understanding of why clients may be resistant or reluctant to talk about certain things.

In Part I, we looked at Interpersonal Process Recall (IPR) in relation to a helper reflecting on their work. IPR can also be very useful in supervision for structured reflection on counselling work. In some settings, the supervisor may listen to actual recorded sessions of the supervisee's work with a client. This is only possible where the client's consent has been obtained both for the recording and for its use in supervision.

ACTIVITY

Jeff is a 47-year-old man who has worked for the same company since leaving school. He was made redundant just over a year ago and since then his marriage has broken down and he has had to move from the family home to a much smaller flat. He now drinks quite heavily and when drunk can be quite aggressive. He cannot believe his life has come to this and feels very angry and bitter. He has no family and feels very isolated and alone. Most of his friends were made through work and he has little contact with them now as the reunions feel awkward and strained. He feels he will never work again and has no motivation to look for a job after being turned down for the first few interviews he attended.

If you were Jeff's counsellor and took him to supervision, your supervisor may use IPR to support you to think more reflectively about your client and your work together.

How would you respond to the following IPR questions in a supervisee role?

- Does the client remind you of anyone in your life?
- What do you think Jeff wants from you?
- How do you want Jeff to perceive you at this point?
- Are you aware of any personal feelings?
- Do those feelings have any special meaning for you?
- Are those feelings located physically in some part of your body?
- What did you want Jeff to tell you?
- How do you know what Jeff's level of need is? (service level)
- How do you feel now about the session?
- On reflection, would you do anything different?

As with counselling, supervision has different models and approaches which offer a framework for looking at the supervision relationship and the supervision process. One of the simplest and best known is the Inskipp and Proctor

(1993, 1995) model of supervision. It is known as a functional model because it sets out the three functions of supervision. These are:

- restorative
- normative
- formative.

The *restorative* stage explores the counsellor's well-being, thoughts and feelings. It allows the counsellor to look at how they are affected by their clients' pain, distress and difficulties and how they impact on them. It provides a space for the counsellor's self-care. The *normative* stage is where the focus is on ethical issues and considerations. This might be around boundary issues or other ethical dilemmas. In the *formative* stage, the focus is on the counsellor's learning and development. It might be here that topics for professional development are identified, and the skills and techniques used to work with the client can be honed and developed.

ACTIVITY

From the following example, decide what could be discussed in each stage of Inskipp and Proctor's (1993, 1995) model – restorative, normative and formative.

Gill has been working with Beryl for several months in a bereavement agency. Beryl is quite an elderly woman whose husband of 35 years died suddenly of a heart attack. Beryl is understandably devastated and talks regularly of not wanting to live anymore. She says she is beginning to feel more and more agoraphobic and doesn't want to even leave the house to go to the shops. Gill has never worked with anyone with agoraphobia but remembers feeling a similar way after the birth of her second child. Beryl asks Gill if they can have the sessions in her home, where she feels safe and comfortable. She says she gets a lot out of the sessions but the journey is too much for her.

How could supervision help support both the client and the counsellor?

 But what would happen if I didn't have supervision? I mean, I might not have the time or the money to meet with a supervisor on a regular basis. I can see that it would help me work with my clients, but is it really that important?

 I think this is a useful question and maybe we should try to look at it from another point of view. Let us consider what the risks are of a counsellor working without clinical supervision:

- The counsellor does not have the opportunity to reflect on and learn from their practice.
- There is no one monitoring the counsellor's standard of practice.
- Ethical concerns are not monitored or explored.
- Boundary issues that may arise in client work are not challenged.

- The counsellor is not supported in their work.
- The counsellor's limits of proficiency are not challenged.
- Continued Professional Development issues are not appraised or addressed.
- The counsellor would not be working within the guidelines of their professional body.
- Professional wisdom is not shared or passed on.

EXAMPLE

Bob is a newly qualified counsellor in his early 30s. Bob has been working with Elaine, a 25-year-old woman who has experienced a string of abusive relationships. Elaine has come to counselling to work through her relationship patterns, personal boundaries, feelings of isolation and trust issues. Elaine has clearly said that she would do anything to be loved.

During the last few sessions, Elaine has been pushing the boundaries by continuing to talk over the appointed time. She has also developed the habit of 'hugging' Bob at the end of the session. In the last session, Elaine confessed that Bob was the only person who really listens and understands her, and she wants to take Bob out for dinner as a special thank-you.

Bob has not been having supervision while working with this client, as the agency supervisor has been signed off with stress. Bob really likes Elaine and feels there would be no harm in just going out for a meal as their work is now finished. Bob also feels flattered by the invitation as he has been feeling lonely since he broke up with his partner several months ago.

Bob is not having supervision. How might this be putting Bob and Elaine at risk?

Although you will need to continue in supervision throughout your professional counselling life, the idea is that as the counsellor gains experience they also develop an 'internal supervisor'. While this does not replace professional supervision, it enables the counsellor to contain and work through issues that arise in client work by themselves. This not only reduces the anxiety and urgency which prompts trainee counsellors to call on their supervisor, but also enables counsellors to carry a greater caseload of clients.

SUMMARY

- Supervision is an ethical requirement for all counsellors.
- A supervisor oversees the counselling work.
- Supervision supports both the client and the counsellor.
- Supervision covers all aspects of the counselling work.
- Not having supervision is risky.

15
Motivation and Blocks to Learning

This chapter is about exploring what can get in the way and prevent learning and achievement. It will also look at the different types of motivation and how to overcome blocks and obstacles to learning.

 I think I know what 'motivation' means but I don't understand what motivation has to do with blocks to learning.

 OK. Let's take this one step at a time. What do you think 'motivation' means?

 It's hard to put into words but I think it means having the energy to do something, or the desire.

 That's a good start, and to build on that, let us look at some definitions for 'motivation':

> Reason or reasons for acting or behaving in a particular way; desire or willingness to do something; enthusiasm. (*Oxford English Dictionary*)

 Yes, all that makes sense but where does this fit with blocks to learning?

 Let's look at the definitions: '*reason or reasons for acting or behaving in a particular way; desire or willingness to do something; enthusiasm*'. It could be that we need to complete a piece of course work, which would be a reason, BUT we might not really want or be willing to do the course work, which would be a block. We would need to explore and work out exactly why we didn't want to do the course work in order to challenge and move past the block.

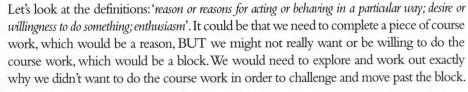

 I see. So the fact that I want to pass the course and achieve the qualification is a motivation to do the work. A block to actually doing the work could be a lack of confidence or ability. I didn't do very well at school and get deeply anxious when it comes to doing any written work. Would that be one of my blocks to learning?

Exactly; your past experiences in a learning environment are influencing your current studies. Let's break this down a little more and look at an example.

There's something you need to do that you can't motivate yourself to do – like an essay to write that you can't get started on. So what do you do? You might have a very good idea of what you *need* to do. You know you need to decide on your essay title and begin to draft a plan outline, and so on. However, something seems to get in the way and, rather than sit down to write your essay, you become very interested in very uninteresting things: you clean out the kitchen cupboards, watch a very boring documentary, take a bath, mow the lawn, bake a cake, vacuum the carpet, feed the cat, play games on your phone, go to sleep. In fact, you do anything rather than write the essay. This is called 'displacement activity', by the way! Nevertheless, the essay plays on your mind and you feel uncomfortable not writing it. So, although you really want to get the essay done, you simply don't do it.

I've done that dozens of times. I even have a little conversation with myself. My thoughts go along the lines of …

> It's not worth starting the essay right now. I know! I will write it at the weekend. I will start first thing Saturday morning and just keep writing till it's finished.

You will probably feel much better at this point, and be able to enjoy the rest of the week without guilt and feel very pleased with yourself for thinking of a solution.

Then Saturday morning arrives and do you sit and write your essay? Or do you clean out the kitchen cupboards, watch a very boring documentary, take a bath, mow the lawn, bake a cake, vacuum the carpet, feed the cat, play games on your phone, go to sleep.

You know me so well: I would almost always do the latter and the dialogue with myself would go something like …

> It's ages until I have to complete this essay. I need to be kind to myself and take this weekend off to de-stress. I will ask for a tutorial next week and then write the essay.

If I was feeling really fed up with it, I might also think …

> I'm sick of this course, and this bloody essay is sending me mad. I don't want to be a counsellor anyway. Plus, the tutor is really annoying.

So actually, whatever the dialogue is, the essay does not get written! It is clear to see that there are very definite problems around motivation and achievement. There are blocks to learning.

If we go back to the definition and apply it to the essay-writing scenario, we can see that there are simply not enough internal and/or external factors to stimulate the desire and energy to write the essay. Therefore, it becomes clear that motivation and learning go hand in hand and that a lack of motivation prevents learning, which in turn hinders motivation and the whole thing becomes a vicious cycle.

I can really relate to that but what can I do about it?

Let's look more closely at motivation. There are two types of motivation – *intrinsic* motivation and *extrinsic* motivation.

> **Intrinsic** motivation drives people to complete something because they want to do it for pleasure or enjoyment. It's about doing something almost for its own sake, without an external reward.

> **Extrinsic** motivation drives people to complete something in order to gain something or avoid punishment. The reward comes from outside yourself, e.g. getting a good mark for an essay from your tutor.

It is important for you to consider which type of motivation is in place for:

- completing your course
- completing an essay.

The type of motivation involved will certainly affect how you think and behave and what choices you make.

If I take the essay-writing example, it is almost certainly extrinsic motivation that is the driver. If I don't complete the essay, I will fail the course, and I don't want to fail the course because I won't get my certificate and achieve the qualification. So, if I'm really honest, I have absolutely no personal interest or enjoyment around completing the essay. Rather, the reward will be when the course is completed, achieved and the certificate is awarded.

Yes, so we can see two opposing forces at work: the need to complete the essay and the part of you that doesn't want to – in other words, the motivation versus the block. This creates ambivalence and it is very easy to be stuck in ambivalence for a long time: one part of you wants to; one part of you doesn't.

Hang on; what exactly does 'ambivalence' mean?

It means 'the state of having mixed feelings or contradictory ideas about something or someone' (*Oxford English Dictionary*). Remember the famous phrase from Shakespeare's *Hamlet*? 'To be, or not to be, that is the question' captures the vagaries of being in a state of ambivalence.

I can clearly see what some of my blocks to learning are but I feel quite worried because I have no idea what to do about them. I tend to procrastinate a lot, and the more I procrastinate the more stressed I get and the more stressed I get the more I procrastinate and ….

OK, I get the picture. So let's explore some possible solutions. A useful way of accomplishing a task is to break it down into smaller pieces which can then be easily tackled. Often, ambivalence in the mind can feel like a fog or a chaotic jumble of thoughts and ideas all swirling together. What is needed is a mental spring clean in order to see what's going on more clearly. As Mary Poppins would say, 'Spit spot!'

Often, how we have achieved something in the past can tell us how we can achieve something in the present and future. What worked then will generally work now.

1. What have you achieved in the past?
2. How did you motivate yourself to achieve?
3. What skills and qualities helped you achieve?
4. What strengths did you bring to bear on the situation?
5. How did the achievement feel?
6. Why do you want to do this particular qualification?
7. What will you gain by achieving the qualification?
8. Who or what inspires you?
9. What motivates you to continue?
10. How will you feel if you don't complete the qualification?
11. How could you reward yourself when you do complete the qualification?
12. What distracts you from achieving?
13. How can you overcome those distractions?
14. Where would you like to be in one year's and in five years' time?
15. How can you use the skills, qualities and strengths that helped you achieve in the past?

I do feel more motivated now; I just hope I can remember everything.

It's an ongoing process. Reminders and prompts are needed to maintain motivation. The next step is to address and overcome the blocks to learning and barriers to achievement. It is worthwhile compiling a toolkit of techniques, strategies and ideas to motivate us when we are feeling stuck and to boost our confidence when we feel inadequate or not good enough. Below is a selection of tools you may wish to employ. Add your own and dip into your toolbox when you feel unable to move forward.

REMINDERS

Write on Post-it notes or postcards your reasons for doing the course and your hopes and dreams for the future, and leave them in prominent places around your house and car. You can also write out personal affirmations to build your confidence if it is flagging. An affirmation is a short positive statement outlining your intention.

I can think of quite a few affirmations or positive statements. I will write them out and stick some onto my computer screen. I often sit down to work and somehow end up surfing the net instead. Hopefully I will see the affirmations and they will help motivate me to do the work I need to do.

*   Whatever I conceive and believe, I can achieve.
*   There are no obstacles on my path, only road-bumps that I easily and swiftly leap over.

- I can overcome any obstacles to achieve my dreams.
- I am worthy and capable of achieving.
- I possess the wisdom, the power and the motivation to make my dreams come true.

ACTIVITY

Think of three affirmations that are meaningful and relevant to you:

1.
2.
3.

 It can also be helpful to set goals.

SET GOALS

Use the SMART goal-setting technique that we explored in Chapter 4 to help you break the task down into manageable and achievable chunks. That way you will have a sense of achievement which will increase your motivation.

 So setting smaller goals would help me to achieve the main goal, which would be completing my essay. Some smaller goals could include: *On Tuesday morning I will write 200 words … or decide on the essay title … or read the first 15 pages of the first chapter.*

 In the examples you gave, the smaller goals are SMART, that is they are: Specific, Measurable, Achievable, Realistic and Time-boundaried. You are much more likely to achieve those goals than having a task that is left open and vague.

Another thing to consider that can have an impact on motivation is the *learning environment.*

 Do you mean the classroom or college?

 Or where you study at home.

 At home I usually just sit on the sofa with my laptop or at the computer in my bedroom because it can be a bit noisy downstairs. Saying that, I do like to be downstairs with everyone else because I'm closer to the kitchen and can have lots of tea and snack breaks. Or maybe that's just another block to learning. I do like to have music on; is that OK?

Where you actually study needs to be a calm and comfortable setting – somewhere you want to be. If possible it needs to be tidy and uncluttered, and contain all your necessities (e.g. computer, paper, stationery, chocolate! and so on). Ensure interruptions and/or distractions are kept to a minimum. If you have children, it might be better if you can study when they are at school or asleep. Other distractions can include internet websites and phone apps such as social networking sites, chat rooms and the like. Many a good essay has been sidelined in favour of a Facebook affair. Therefore, it's best to shut down all extraneous sites and pages not relevant to what you are studying.

There's a lot more to this than I thought.

Which is why you need lots of *encouragement* … from yourself!

Be your own life coach. Write down each accomplishment and remind yourself about them when you feel disheartened. Find ways of challenging your negative thoughts and fears. Use positive language and self-talk, such as 'I will get a good mark in my essay', rather than 'I don't want to fail my essay'. Keep reminding yourself of why you are studying and how you will feel once you have achieved your goals or, alternatively, remind yourself how awful you will feel if you don't achieve them. Before you start, identify how you will reward yourself when you have achieved each element of the task; it could be with chocolate, five minutes on your phone or one episode of your favourite TV series.

Is there anything else that can get in the way of my learning?

That's a very good question. It is important to acknowledge that we are all different and will probably have different blocks to learning. This can be due to many things: our histories, personalities, lifestyle, etc. Therefore, *self-awareness* is very important in order to discover who you are and how you function and learn. What type of learner are you? Do you learn visually by looking, aurally by listening or kinaesthetically by doing? Adapt your study plan to meet your learning style. Know your strengths and weaknesses. You can work on your weaknesses and harness your strengths. Be aware of your needs and take care of yourself. Never let yourself get too hungry, too angry, too lonely, too tired or too stressed. If you do – 'HALT!' It may help to think of this acronym:

H – Hungry

A – Angry

L – Lonely

T – Tired

S – Stressed

So, it's about looking after myself in a way and being gentle and encouraging towards myself. That will be a big change for me. I usually give myself a really hard time when I feel I'm not doing enough.

 That leads us into another area that can really get in the way of achievement – self-sabotage. Sometimes we carry with us messages from the past that powerfully affect how we behave now. These messages become internalised to such an extent that they become a way of defeating ourselves or sabotaging ourselves over and over again. You said earlier that school could be difficult for you. Perhaps there are messages from back then that are affecting how you learn today.

 I hated school. This might sound like a lame excuse but I found it harder because I couldn't see the blackboard. Back then everything would be written on the blackboard and I'd try to copy things down but I'd often get them wrong and would then go away and do the wrong homework. In those days teachers could be very harsh and I'd be singled out in class. Once, my teacher read out what I'd written and everyone laughed. I can still remember how that felt, standing there trying not to cry. It was horrible.

 First, that doesn't sound like a lame excuse. You tried your very best but even after doing the work, you were singled out and humiliated for what you'd written. Could there be a link between back then and your procrastination now?

 Maybe. Well, if I don't do the work, it can't be laughed at, can it? I'd rather have got in trouble for doing nothing at all than my hard work causing that horrible experience. I can't change the past though, so what can I do?

 That's a very powerful realisation and your awareness will help you overcome the block. Let's look at another example.

EXAMPLE

Sean has a twin sister who was always quicker and brighter than him. She moved very quickly into a class above him in primary school and continued one year ahead of him until the end of school at age 18. Sean developed at his own pace and did very well. He went on to read physics at university where he got a good degree, but inside him a powerful message remained that he was 'slow and thick'. This message was particularly powerful when he was faced with a challenge he wanted to avoid.

- Do you sabotage yourself when you are close to achievement?
- Does your negative thinking trick you into believing you aren't competent or able to achieve what you want to do?

As I stated, one way of reducing the likelihood of sabotaging yourself – and this is a useful skill to use with clients and helpees too – is to raise your awareness of what your own patterns of shooting yourself in the foot are!

ACTIVITY

In Table 15.2 are two columns. The column on the left contains a list of negative thoughts that might block your learning. In the right column is the challenge to that 'wounding' thought. There are several spaces at the end of the table where you can add examples of your own.

TABLE 15.2 Thoughts that wound

Thoughts that wound	Challenge
I can't do this.	I am capable and willing to do this.
I fail at everything; I'm just too stupid.	There are many examples from the past where I have overcome obstacles and succeeded. If I need help, I can ask for it.
I will never understand this.	The learning process can be difficult and painful. I will be gentle with myself as it unfolds.
Nobody on the course likes me.	This is an old message from the past and there is absolutely no evidence to back it up. If someone is a little short with me, it is probably because they are having a bad day and nothing to do with me at all.
I failed at school.	What happened back then does not have to happen now.

One way of fighting these negative thoughts is to tell others who you trust what your self-defeating patterns are. Ask them to help you identify when a pattern might be being activated and ask for their support to help you find ways to overcome it. Another simple task is to write yourself a message rejecting the old message.

This is what Sean wrote on a Post-it note on his bathroom mirror:

'I am not slow and thick – this is an old message and I reject it.'

REFLECTION

Fear of failure is a powerful disincentive for not completing difficult challenges. Received wisdom is that it is better to have 'tried and failed' than never to have tried at all. Is this your experience of failure?

Failure is not falling down, but refusing to get up. (Chinese proverb)

So you're saying that I should ask for help. I'm not very good at that. I tend to feel I am burdening other people or being a nuisance.

More old messages maybe, but there are ways of receiving help from others without feeling that way.

STUDY GROUPS AND BUDDIES

Sometimes studying together can be beneficial, as long as the group members are able to focus on the task in hand and not distract each other. It can also be helpful to team up with one other person as a 'study buddy' and work together to motivate each other and share ideas and thoughts. Having other people to bounce ideas off usually stimulates ideas and brings a rich energy to the learning process. Asking for and getting help is an enviable attribute and quality. Aim to ask for help and offer help and support to others.

On a very practical note, I simply can't find the time to actually do the work. If I try to fit it in, I rush and what I do really isn't good enough. On a few occasions I've started to write, then had to stop because I realised I needed to be elsewhere, and later I couldn't find what I'd written. That was really frustrating.

Practicalities are also important and perhaps what you are talking about.

MANAGING TIME

Spread your study out over time rather than trying to do everything at once. Decide whether you are an 'owl' or a 'lark'. If you have more energy early in the morning, plan your study for that time of the day. If you feel more invigorated later in the day, amend your timetable accordingly.

Allow time for breaks at regular intervals and make sure you reward yourself with something you enjoy. If for any reason you fall behind with the plan, don't give up – that is the most common pitfall of all. Just start the next study period with renewed resolve.

 There is a lot around planning, isn't there? I thought I just had to get on with it.

 You can actually save a lot of time by doing some planning and preparation before starting. I don't want to keep you any longer: you have an essay to write! But before we end the chapter, here are some things that might help you further.

MOTIVATIONAL TIPS

Start with the easiest task or the one you are most likely to enjoy. Keep positive and keep company with positive people. There is an old saying that goes: 'Show me who your friends are and I'll show you who you are'. Therefore 'Stick with the winners!'

tip

VISUALISATION

It sometimes helps to visualise the moment after the dreaded task has finally been accomplished. Imagine that you have overcome your habitual blocks and completed your essay one week early.

- What will you be doing afterwards?
- How will you be feeling?

This can be a powerful motivation for getting on with something rather than avoiding it.

Most importantly … just do it! The hardest word to write is the first one. Just write it. The hardest page to read is the first one. Just read it.

Start

Start

Start

Do it now!

16
Essay Writing Skills

This chapter focuses on the skills and qualities needed to write an essay. It will cover content, structure and presentation.

 Essay writing can be a daunting prospect. An essay is generally a requirement on most types of course and is often the main piece of written work. Essay writing is a skill which can be learned. The aim here is to make the process as simple and straightforward as possible.

 Overcoming blocks is one thing, but actually knowing how to go about writing an essay is a very different matter. That could be a very big block for me.

 First, it can be helpful to be clear about what an essay is and what it requires. What are your thoughts on this?

 The last essay I wrote was back in school when we would write on a topic, but I think that was very different from what I need to do now.

 You are right, there are many types of essay. An essay is generally written for someone, usually your tutor, as a way of assessing your learning. Therefore, it is essential to be able to evidence what you have learned in your essay.

 tip

> Another meaning of 'essay' is *to attempt or try*, which originated from the late 15th century as a verb which meant 'to test the quality of' (from the French word *essayer*). It is also linked to the Old French word *essai*, meaning 'trial' (*Oxford English Dictionary*). So, in a way, you could think of an essay as your tutor testing the quality of your learning or putting it 'on trial'!

Once you are clear about the task and what is required, you can go about collecting what you need to complete the task.

I am still not clear what the actual task is. What is it I have to produce?

A simple way of looking at it is that you will be given a title and you then need to write about that title. Sometimes the title can be in the form of a question which you go on to answer. We will look at this later in the chapter but first let's look at the very beginning of the process.

The key to writing a successful essay is good preparation. It can be compared to decorating a room, where it would be foolhardy to just pick up a tin of paint and start painting. Before doing this, the room needs to be prepared. You will need to know how much paint you need and what size brushes. You will need to decide what colours you wish to use and what type of paint is suitable for the surfaces you want to paint. You may decide to use wallpaper instead, in which case you will need to measure the room to estimate how much wallpaper you need to buy. You will need to clear some or all of the furniture out of the way so that there are as few obstacles as possible. You will need a range of tools which need to be on hand before starting work. Of course, you will also need to know what you want the room to look like at the end, and therefore it would be helpful to know what the room is going to be used for and by whom.

I understand that; so what tools will I need to write an essay? I don't think a paint roller will help me very much.

True, but there are similarities. With an essay, you need to make solid preparations. You will need to know what 'tools' you need to write it – the tools could take the form of books, reference material, a computer, tutorial notes and a study group. You will need to know the scope of the essay and how long it needs to be so that you can draw up a timetable. You will also need to move all obstacles out of the way before you start.

The better the preparation, the better the essay! The seven Ps are a good way to remember this:

Prior

Planning and

Preparation

Prevent

P★★s

Poor

Performance.

The seven Ps are thought to be an old army saying given to recruits. OK, let's revisit what it is you are actually going to do. From the information so far, what do you understand an essay to be?

An essay is a piece of writing that meets a set task or brief. It needs to be structured and laid out in a certain way. Generally, there is a set title and the whole of the essay is related to the title. The language used in an essay is more formal than the kind of language I would use in a conversation or in my journal. Is that right?

Exactly. It is also very important to be clear about what you are going to do.

PLANNING TO WRITE

Now is the time to begin collecting the information you need to write your essay; this is the decorator's equivalent of visiting B&Q!

You can get information from a wide range of sources – books, the internet, articles in professional journals, reports, your course notes, television programmes, newspapers, interviews, and so on. But it is not wise to collect so much information that you get snowed under, overwhelmed and confused.

How will I know what I need to collect? I don't want to get lots of information that I can't use. It would take forever to sift through it all.

Therefore, be selective. Ask yourself:

- Is this piece of information relevant?
- Do I need it?
- Have I already got information that covers this point?
- How will I use the information to support my argument?
- Is it from a credible or trustworthy source?

It will also be useful for you to plan a timetable for completing your essay. This may seem a bit basic and obvious but it will help you to structure and organise a task which can be especially challenging when the rest of your life is busy and there are competing demands on your time and attention. The example timetable offered in Table 16.1 has been partially completed to give you an overview.

So far all I've done is collect material to write my essay. I have never written anything like this and it's the biggest piece of work on my course. I just don't know how I will put it all together.

It can be daunting, so let's move on to actually writing it.

TABLE 16.1 Planning your essay

Task	What do I need?	When will I study?	How long will it take?
Agree essay title	Group discussion, tutor input	In class	1–2 hours
Decide content and collect information	Books, notes, internet research, handouts	Tuesday evenings, 7pm to 9pm, and Saturday mornings, 9.30am to 11.30am	1–2 weeks
Structure essay and assign approx. word count to each section	Tutor feedback	Tuesday evenings, 7pm to 9pm	1 week
Draft essay	Books, notes, internet research, handouts		
Get feedback	Tutor, peers		
Complete essay			
Reference essay			

EXECUTION

This does not mean what you would like to do to your tutor when you hear your essay title, but rather how you actually go about structuring and writing your essay. This is where you plan how you will structure your work. The basic structure of any essay could look like this:

Title (Your essay should relate to this title throughout.)

Introduction: Explain what you will cover in your essay and how you will respond to the essay title.

Main body of essay: Once you are clear about what points you want to make and what order you want to make them in, decide how many paragraphs to include and what each one will contain before you start writing. The first paragraph normally refers back to the first thing you mentioned in your introduction. The first sentence of every paragraph should be an introduction to what that paragraph will cover. Each paragraph should provide a link to the following paragraph.

You will have a word count for your essay and it is important to plan roughly how many words you want in each section. It is a classic mistake to write expansively in the first part and then cram lots of arguments into a few sentences towards the end because you have run out of words. You want to aim for balance throughout.

Summary: The conclusion of the essay should take the form of a summary of what has been covered in the essay. The summary should be clearly linked to the title of the essay.

That really helps. It separates it out into manageable chunks.

And now …

PLANNING THE CONTENT OF YOUR ESSAY

If you don't know where to start, a creative way of beginning is to use a mind map or a spidergram. These diagrams enable you to think freely while also beginning to look for a possible structure for your ideas. This can be a helpful way of capturing a number of ideas that don't sit easily under structured headings or bullet points. There may be numerous things you wish to include in your essay that aren't easy to prioritise.

 So, once I've completed the diagram, it will be easier to see what to include in my essay and what to discard, rather than it all being a big jumble in my head.

 Yes, and you will begin your spidergram or mind map by putting your question (or key word) in the middle of the page – the larger the piece of paper the better. Use lines around the title to put all your ideas relating to the title. Each of your ideas can then have its own group of lines branching off, like the map in Figure 16.1.

 And then I just get on with writing it. So, it's one step at a time and if that feels too much, one paragraph at a time, even one sentence at a time.

 There is one final thing.

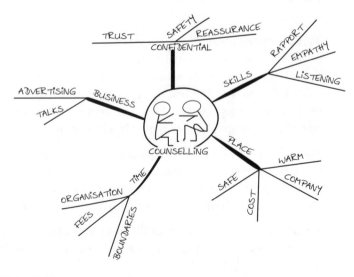

FIGURE 16.1   Spidergram example

REFERENCING

Referring to the work of others not only strengthens the validity of your essay, but also being able to reference work properly is a professional skill which you need to develop. You can use references to support an argument, illustrate a point, highlight or emphasise relevant issues and generally demonstrate the breadth of your reading and understanding of the subject you are writing about.

If you do refer to published work by someone else, you need to acknowledge this fact in your essay. If you do not state the source of ideas that you rely on, or if you give the impression that what you are saying is your own idea or your own words, this is called 'plagiarism' which is defined as:

> the practice of taking someone else's work or ideas and passing them off as one's own. (*Oxford English Dictionary*)

Plagiarism is a serious offence which has serious consequences. It is regarded in the same way as cheating and could result in your work being discounted or, in extreme cases, you being asked to leave the course. This is not very likely at this level of learning but it is important to get into the habit of properly referencing other people's work.

 If I read relevant things in books and articles, can I still use them in my essay?

 Yes you can, but you need to reference what book or article and who wrote it.

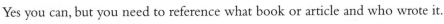 I think I would need to be very organised and write my references as I went along, rather than getting to the end of my essay and then having to trawl all through the books and articles again to find quotes or information. Do I have to write it word for word as it appears?

Yes, if it is a direct quote. When referencing, you need to state clearly where you found the information and who wrote it. You need to write the reference in such a way that someone reading your essay could use your reference to find the actual work you were referring to. Therefore, the more information you include, the better. The Harvard referencing system is most commonly used, but check what style and format you are advised to follow to meet your course requirements.

Although formats will differ, the essential information required is the same:

- the author's name
- the title of the book
- the year of publication
- the page number(s) – if a specific quotation is used
- the place of publication and the publisher.

The normal convention is to include a shortened version of the reference in brackets in the body of the text, while the full details are listed in the References section at the end of your essay.

EXAMPLE

If the original piece of information you wanted to refer to was:

'I rejoice at the privilege of being a midwife to a new personality' (Carl Rogers, *On Becoming a Person*, new edition, March 2004, page 5)

... your essay might say:

Carl Rogers saw his way of working as like 'being a midwife to a new personality' (Rogers, 2004: 5).

Then in your reference list at the end, you would have:

Rogers, C. (2004) *On Becoming a Person* (new edn). London: Constable and Robinson (original work published 1961).

Those examples refer to books. Can I use the same pattern when I reference articles and journals?

Yes. However, in addition to the author and the title, you need to include the name of the journal, the volume and/or issue number and the page numbers of the article you are referring to. For example:

Itch, I. (2012) Studies in counselling fleas. *Weird Journal*, 12, 78–93.

If the book has multiple authors, they should be listed in alphabetical order in the reference list or bibliography at the end of your essay and be referred to in the body of your text with only the first author's surname and then 'et al.' (Latin for 'and the rest'), like this: (Bonkers et al., 2012: 17).

If you use an internet source, you must quote the http address in full and include the date you accessed the web page.

This sounds very complicated.

You will become more adept with practice. When you begin your studies, you may only use one or two references, but as your essays become more academic when you progress to higher levels of study, you will become more accomplished and able.

FINISHING TOUCHES

You could write a very good essay that has been well thought out and planned, but if it is not appropriately presented its quality can be diminished. Even a super-model looks less than salubrious in rags! So when thinking about presentation, consider the following:

- Ensure your name is on all the pages and that the pages are numbered.
- Check whether you are expected to type your essay or whether you can write it by hand. It is very frustrating for tutors trying to read an essay that has been written in illegible handwriting.
- If you are typing your essay, use a font and size that is easy to read.
- Add a front cover with your name and the essay title.
- Ensure the margins are appropriate and that the line spacing allows the script to be read easily.

The finishing touches include:

- a spell-check and final read-through (ask a peer to double-check your spelling and grammar)
- a list of references
- the final word count.

When I've finished I think I'll deserve a cup of coffee and a slice of cake.

And also a pat on the back for a job well done.

17
Journal Writing Skills

This chapter focuses on writing a journal that will support and enhance your learning and personal development.

 I should be fine with this. I kept a diary when I was younger and a journal is the same as a diary, isn't it?

 Yes … and no!

 There seems to be a lot of 'yes and no' in counselling.

 Well, it depends on what sort of diary you used to write, its contents and also the reasons you were writing it.

 I just wrote about what was happening, really. I think I wrote it because I was given a diary for Christmas.

 OK, well this journal writing is a little different and has a different purpose. This is called a reflective learning journal and the purpose of a reflective journal is exactly what it says – to enable you to reflect on your learning experience. In counselling training, it is good practice to keep a weekly learning journal. This is also a useful and rewarding habit to cultivate in everyday life. The purpose is not simply to write about what happened in the lesson or the day, but to record how you experienced what happened, to reflect on your experience and to apply the learning from your reflection to your life and helping or counselling work.

 In my diary when I was younger I would write about what happened when I was on holiday, but in the journal writing you are talking about, I'd write how I thought and felt about the holidays and what I got up to. Is that right?

Exactly. The activity below will help you see more clearly the differences between the two types.

ACTIVITY

Read the following two examples of journal entries on a counselling skills course and answer the questions at the end.

Journal entry 1

I arrived at college tonight at 6pm, just in time for the lesson to start. I noticed that B and D were not in class.

The topic today was asking questions. There are two types of questions: open questions and closed questions. Closed questions are those that generally require a 'yes' or 'no' answer or a factual response, for example 'What is your name?' or 'Do you like beans?' Closed questions gather information. Open questions require a longer answer, for instance 'What do you plan to do on holiday?'

We had a break for 20 minutes and I read the feedback my tutor gave me on my essay.

In the second half of the session, we did skills practice. This is where we get into groups of three. One person plays the role of counsellor or helper, one person plays the role of client/helpee and the third person plays the role of observer. The observer gives feedback to the counsellor/helper on the session. I played the role of client/helpee, and in a second skills practice session I played the role of observer and gave feedback.

I give feedback in a sandwich format. This means I give an area for growth sandwiched between two things that went well. Therefore, I give the counsellor/helper a positive comment, followed by an area to work on or something they could have done differently, and then I end with something else positive.

At the end of the evening, we did a closing circle. This is where we go round the circle and say how we feel. We also start each class with an opening circle where we talk about our feelings.

Journal entry 2

When I arrived at college this evening, I felt quite uncomfortable that B and D were not in class. During check-in, I said how I felt and wondered if there was a link to the previous week when D and B had some conflict around something D had said that B found offensive. Part of me was secretly quite glad they weren't in class because I find conflict very difficult to manage. Last week D spoke to me about the situation and I felt I was being manipulated into agreeing with him. I felt I really let myself

(Continued)

(Continued)

down because I nodded and agreed, which was very dishonest because I didn't agree at all. This is a very old pattern for me. I find it so hard to have a different opinion or viewpoint from someone else and often agree with what they are saying, or say I like the things they do, when actually I don't. I think this links to my need to be approved of and I'm frightened that people won't like me or will get angry with me if I disagree. My mother was a very angry woman and would shout a lot if I ever disagreed with her. She would say I was being cheeky and disrespectful and so I just agreed with her, and this seemed to make her happy.

We covered the topic of 'questions' today. We looked at the difference between open and closed questions. I realised I ask a lot of closed questions because I am quite a nosey person. That is something I definitely need to work on in skills practice and also in my everyday life.

During break, everyone was talking about the conflict that happened last week. Part of me wanted to join in and feel a part of things. It felt quite dramatic and I wanted to talk about how D had spoken to me and what he said about his side of the story. It sounds like I'm making a big deal about nothing but I started to feel really uncomfortable and awkward and I wanted to just leave and go home. I did go and talk to my tutor and she said that it sounded like the situation might have triggered something in me from my own life. I think she's right but I'm not quite sure what is going on. I know how I felt – uncomfortable and almost guilty – but I am not sure why I felt that way. This is something for me to explore and reflect on in personal therapy.

In skills practice, I played the role of helper/counsellor. I still get really nervous, especially when my tutor sits in. We were given some rules for the session. As counsellor/helper, I was not allowed to ask any questions or give any advice or make suggestions. I found this really difficult and there were some very long silences which were excruciating. I felt really bad for the helpee/client when we just sat there and it looked like they didn't know what to say. I wanted to jump in with a question or comment. I felt really silly just sitting there saying nothing. My tutor asked us afterwards what was in the silence and we brainstormed our answers. All I said was 'not good enough' is in the silence. I am not quite sure why I said this. I certainly have a lot of work to do on myself!

During the closing circle, I struggled to put words to what I was feeling and just said I felt exhausted. I still can't believe that such a little thing affected me so much.

1. What is the difference between the two versions of the journal entry?
2. If you were the student's tutor, what feedback would you give on both versions?
3. How can expressing personal feelings, thoughts and opinions support you as a helper/counsellor in training?
4. What are the benefits of regular journal writing?

I've never really thought about the benefits of journal writing. For this type of journal, I would be doing it for the course. But it occurs to me that there might be other benefits too, such as helping me focus and think more deeply about issues. If I was also reflecting on how I felt about things, that would help me learn more about myself. So it would be good for my self-development and to raise my self-awareness.

 Absolutely. As you say, you would be 'reflecting', and being able to reflect on your practice and experience is a skill well worth developing. There are some models of reflective practice that will support your journal writing, especially in relation to your helping/counselling work.

GIBBS' MODEL

Gibbs' (1988) model of reflection, shown in Figure 17.1, offers a template for your journal work. It has six stages which prompt and encourage you to learn as much as possible by reflecting on each stage. This model supports self-development and fosters insight and self-awareness. You can use it to write your journal and also to reflect on a helping/counselling skills session. The learning from both will enhance and develop your helping/counselling work.

Stage 1: Description

What happened? It can be useful to include here who was involved, exactly what happened, what was said, and so on. This section needs to be brief and factual.

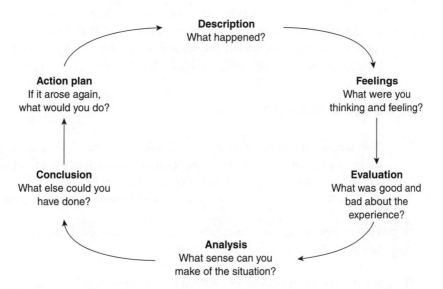

FIGURE 17.1   Gibbs' model of reflection

Stage 2: Feelings

What were you thinking and feeling? Here, you can focus on your thoughts and feelings at the time and also on whether those thoughts and feelings changed over time. You can begin to ask yourself too what effects your thoughts and feelings had on your actions and behaviour, and how those in turn impacted on the helping/counselling work.

Stage 3: Evaluation

In this section, give yourself feedback. What was good and bad about the experience? What caused you to make those judgements? What feedback did you get from others – your peers and your tutor?

Stage 4: Analysis

In this stage, break down the experience even further and consider what helped or hindered. What sense can you make of the situation? Analyse the skills session in relation to the skills and theory you have learnt. How can you apply your insights and findings to your future work as a helper/counsellor?

Stage 5: Conclusion

Here is the place to consider what else you could have done and why you didn't do it. Could you have done anything differently? If the session was not effective, what could you improve? If the session went well, what will you take from it to inform future sessions?

Stage 6: Action plan

The action plan sums up what you will take from the experience. What would you do in a similar situation? Would you do the same thing or something different? What areas of your knowledge and understanding do you need to improve? How will you do this? What goals can you set yourself and how can you meet those goals?

 That makes things very clear; I can follow each step and apply this to my studies and also my actual life events too.

 What would you get out of going through these steps?

I was thinking about something that happened in class this week. I thought someone had been very rude and disrespectful towards something I'd said. All I could see was what she'd done and that she was wrong. By applying Gibbs' model, I can now see my part and how I responded and reacted. I am now able to identify some things that I could do differently.

 So, reflection brings clarity and also the space to see things differently. You rightly state that Gibbs' model is very useful when applied to skills practice, but it can also be used to reflect on what happens in a variety of other course settings, such as group work, lessons and so on, and also in your personal life.

 I can see why journal writing is not just about what happened during class.

It is important to approach journal writing in a holistic way and to draw on experiences in other parts of your life. You can reflect on experiences at home, in social situations, at college or at work. You might want to include books you have read or films/TV programmes you have seen. The important thing is to record your thoughts, feelings, opinions and behaviour. You can focus on your learning in terms of skills, techniques and theories. You can include just about anything in your journal if it allows you to reflect and grow.

REFLECTION

- In what ways is a reflective learning journal different from a diary?
- Would you want your tutor to read your diary?
- Do you think your tutor would want to read your diary?
- What would you leave out and why?

Remember that a learning journal is usually regarded as part of your portfolio of assessable work. It may be seen by others involved in your teaching and learning, such as moderators, verifiers, or other internal quality assurance staff. It is important to check out exactly who will see your journal before you start.

 So some questions that would be useful to me when writing could include:

- What did I feel?
- What did I think?
- What did I do?
- What was happening in the group?
- How did I feel in relation to my peers?
- How did I feel in relation to the topic(s) covered?

Your journal is about you and your learning experience. You communicate who you are through it. Honesty, open-mindedness and a willingness to learn and grow are the main components.

BENEFITS OF JOURNAL WRITING

As you have identified, there are many benefits to this discipline. To recap, there are the obvious benefits around learning and development, and also personal development and self-awareness. You will be able to go back through your journals and see how much you have achieved and grown.

EXAMPLE

Sam's journal – term 1, week 1 (extract)

Today in class we watched a DVD of Carl Rogers working with a client, Gloria, using the person-centred approach. I didn't really understand the bit where he was explaining what he was going to do, and actually he didn't really seem to do anything! I found the pace extraordinarily painful and slow. I kept wishing he would just get on with it and was rather surprised that so many of the others seemed to be gasping in awe. I just don't get it. Give me Fritz Perls any day; at least he seemed to give Gloria her money's worth.

Sam's journal – term 3, week 7 (extract)

Our tutor put on the Gloria video again today. I was amazed at how different it seems to me now. All I could see first time round was a guy doing not very much and my journal entry shows that I was not impressed! This time I actually understood what he was saying at the beginning. I had a real appreciation of just how hard it was for him to stay in her frame of reference, to stay with her language and her pace, to allow her to struggle until she found a way forward herself (internal locus of evaluation) rather than expect him to tell her what to do (external locus of evaluation). It made me think how very hard it is to do this well and how demanding it is of the therapist.

Journal writing ...

- charts personal growth and development
- helps to identify patterns and trends in behaviour and lifestyle
- encourages self-reflection

- builds insight and self-awareness
- processes events
- crystallises thoughts
- can bring about clarity
- facilitates understanding
- helps to identify, notice and connect with feelings
- creates inner space
- helps to make sense of life
- records and bears witness to significant events
- improves writing ability and style
- makes a commitment to goals and tasks
- is a written commitment to self
- is even reported to have many physical health benefits
- can reduce stress by releasing thoughts and feelings
- can also be a treasure for the future.

 I never thought there was so much to it. Will my tutor read it all? I'm a bit nervous about what they will think of me, my thoughts and feelings.

 Actually, your tutor reading it has an additional benefit. You will form a relationship with your tutor through your journal. Your tutor will assess your work and give you feedback. There will be a dialogue between you and your tutor that will last for the duration of your training.

 I've never let anyone read about my personal thoughts and feelings, though.

 I can understand how challenging that might be. You don't have to worry about being judged. Your thoughts and feelings are personal to you and will be accepted and respected by your tutor.

EXAMPLE: THE ROLE OF TUTOR ASSESSMENT AND FEEDBACK

Excerpt from student journal

The topic today was Karpman's (1968) triangle. It explains that we play different roles in our relationships. The main three roles are Victim, Rescuer and Persecutor. I reflected on my patterns of relating in relation to Karpman's triangle. I am definitely a Rescuer in lots of ways and I certainly can take on the Rescuer role in my helping/counselling work.

(Continued)

(Continued)

I cannot relate to the Persecutor role but maybe that's because I don't want to. I can certainly slip into the Victim role. I am a mum with two children, three actually if I count my husband. I very often feel put upon and slip into a martyr role, where I am doing everything for everybody and putting myself last and then feeling resentful and full of self-pity. I am learning to change that pattern thanks to this training.

Possible tutor feedback

You identify the three roles from Karpman's (1968) triangle and are beginning to consider what roles you adopt in your relationships. I would like to hear more about how you adopt the role of Rescuer. Why do you think you do this? In a helping/counselling session, what feelings make you want to rescue your client? I wonder how you would feel if you didn't rescue. Who are you really helping?

I was very interested to read your final sentence where you write that you are learning to change the pattern of falling into the Victim role in your family. What's behind this change, I wonder?

You are developing a reflective and honest dialogue in your journal. Well done!

Next excerpt from student journal

I have been doing a lot of work on why I tend to rescue in my helping/counselling work. I rescue because when my client/helpee appears uncomfortable or in pain, I want them to feel better. I am learning that counselling/helping is about healing, not fixing. I am learning slowly to allow a space for feelings and hurt. The feedback on my last journal entry really shocked me. I realised I rescue to make myself feel better. Well, I must do, mustn't I? I have learnt that it is healing for people to be able to sit with their feelings and just let them be; to be able to cry if needed, and that is healthy. Therefore, I am trying to stop 'rescuing' – as it is actually for my benefit, not the helpee's. I think it comes back to me not feeling good enough and also trying to avoid my own feelings. Something for personal therapy, I think!

The above example shows how the dialogue between tutor and student supports self-awareness and, in turn, better practice.

 You were wondering about putting your thoughts and feelings on paper and we can also wonder if it is always appropriate to put all thoughts and feelings into your journal? Sometimes there may be things that occur during your class which involve your tutor in ways that make it difficult to write freely about them in your journal.

 Exactly. So what is OK and not OK?

CRITICAL THINKING

Example 1

Two candidates in your group had an argument which ended up in a physical scuffle. Your tutor's decision was to ask both candidates to leave the class permanently. You think this was unfair as one candidate provoked the other.

Example 2

Your tutor has just announced that she is leaving the training centre before your course finishes. You know she has been struggling with personal problems and feel sorry for her. At the same time, you are angry because this will disrupt your learning. She is also really behind with marking your work.

Example 3

You think your tutor is picking on you and your friends agree with you. Your tutor says it is down to your personal issues which you need to work on if you want to pass the course. You are feeling unsafe and lacking in trust.

- What would you write in your journal?
- Would you want to take any other course of action?
- Is there a conflict between the tutor's role as assessor and facilitator?

A final word: journal writing is a very ancient tradition. Journals have been found dating back to 10th-century Japan!

18
Self-care

The aim of this chapter is to define the meaning of self-care and to explore why it is a crucial part of working ethically and safely as a helper or counsellor. We will also look at how to monitor your well-being and take care of yourself.

 I understand that we all need to take care of ourselves but I don't see why this has anything to do with working ethically and safely.

 We'll come on to that in a minute. But what is the first thing that comes to mind when I say the word 'self-care'?

 Oh, I suppose I think it means looking after myself and not getting too stressed out. But counselling and helping work is about looking after others and not thinking about ourselves, isn't it?

 Hmm, you are asking an important question here. Focusing on oneself can be seen as selfishness in our society, but self-care is an important part of being able to care for others. Let's start with definitions.

DEFINITIONS

Definition of 'self':

> A person's essential being that distinguishes them from others. (*Oxford English Dictionary*)

Definition of 'one's self':

> One's particular nature or personality; the qualities that make one individual or unique. (*Oxford English Dictionary*)

This definition makes it clear that everybody is different and unique so when we think about self-care it might mean different things depending on who you are.

Definition of 'care':

> The provision of what is necessary for the health, welfare, maintenance, and protection of someone or something; serious attention or consideration applied to doing something correctly or to avoid damage or risk. (*Oxford English Dictionary*)

I get the importance of 'health and welfare' as part of taking care, but it's a bit scary to see words like 'damage and risk'. Does that mean damage and risk to me or damage and risk to the client?

Well, actually it could be both. And this takes us back to your question about why self-care is part of working ethically and safely. The BACP Ethical Framework for the Counselling Professions (2016) mentions 'care of self' specifically and makes it quite clear that self-care is an ethical requirement.

REFLECTION

Extract from the BACP Ethical Framework for the Counselling Professions (July 2016):

Care of self as a practitioner

75. We will take responsibility for our own wellbeing as essential to sustaining good practice by:

(a) taking precautions to protect our own physical safety.

(b) monitoring our own psychological and physical health.

(c) seeking professional support and services as the need arises.

(d) keeping a healthy balance between our work and other aspects of life.

(BACP Ethical Framework, 2016: 15)

Take a few minutes to reflect on each of these points and consider:

- Why might self-care be important for a counsellor/helper in their professional life?
- Why might self-care be important for a counsellor/helper in their personal life?
- Why might your well-being as a counsellor/helper be important for the client/helpee?

Let's take a moment to look at the different elements of the extract from the BACP Ethical Framework in turn to help you answer these questions.

PHYSICAL SAFETY

This one seems a bit obvious really. You can only really pay attention to the needs of someone else if you are in a safe and secure place yourself. This might mean quite practical things like being in a safe building with appropriate access and with no hazardous obstacles. It might mean ensuring that outside lighting is adequate after dark or being able to walk to your car without fear of being attacked. But lack of physical safety could come in other forms too.

> **REFLECTION**
>
> Consider the following scenarios and how they might affect your sense of physical safety.
>
> - You are a care worker in a residential home listening to a young man who tells you that he has been in trouble for carrying a knife.
> - You are a counsellor/helper whose client/helpee turns up drunk and abusive for a session.
> - A young person you have been supporting at the youth club starts sending you threatening messages.
> - A woman you have been seeing for counselling texts you to say she is feeling suicidal and can't wait until the next session.
> - You work in the evenings as a volunteer counsellor in an agency where other staff go home at 6pm.
> - Your counselling appointments are spaced so closely that there is no time to go to the toilet between sessions.
> - You are working with a client who has expressed romantic feelings for you and you have seen them in the street near where you live.
> - The police turn up at an agency asking to interview a client you are working with.

Woah! I thought it was just the health and safety-type stuff that you hear so much about on the news! Now I can see that it is much wider than that. Anything that leaves me feeling unsafe is likely to mean I can't focus on another person and might even mean that I am putting myself in danger.

Yes. This next area is both straightforward and complicated.

PSYCHOLOGICAL AND PHYSICAL HEALTH

In terms of physical health, it is obviously not a good idea to be working with anybody if you have an infectious tropical disease or are likely to give them a nasty bout of flu! But often decisions about when you are well enough to work are much more complicated and there is the added dilemma of what to tell the client/helpee if you are unable to keep an appointment.

 I suppose I would know if I wasn't well enough to work and would have to let the other person know somehow. That might be difficult in itself.

 Do you think you always recognise when you are not well enough to work? I think that is sometimes really hard. Quite apart from common ailments like colds and flu, supposing you were dealing with a long-term health issue. If you were coping with cancer or adjusting to being a diabetic or suffering from chronic fatigue, would that mean you wouldn't work at all during that whole period? Would you always know whether you were going to be well enough to work?

 Good point. Sometimes I think I am well enough to work and then go rapidly downhill before the day is out. Also, I have just realised that once you start thinking about psychological health it is even more complicated because we all have good days and bad days; some days I feel so bad myself I am not sure I would be any use to another human being.

REFLECTION

Consider the following scenarios and reflect on whether these individuals are fit to work.

- Janine had another mega-row with her partner the night before and they have finally decided to separate. She realises that she is tired but decides that she is OK to see the clients. She works as a bereavement volunteer.
- Support worker Jai's 12-year-old son was rushed into hospital again last night with an asthma attack. They came home late and tired, but her son has gone to school and Jai went to work.
- Pauli has suffered from periods of mild depression and anxiety throughout his life. He manages this with support from his GP and regular medication. He works as a counsellor in the NHS.
- Meg has discovered a lump in her breast and can't get an appointment with her GP for a week.

(Continued)

> *(Continued)*
>
> It might help to think about who is at risk of harm or damage in each case. Now consider the following questions about the scenarios above:
>
> - Would it make a difference if Janine was working with people suffering from social anxiety or agoraphobia rather than bereavement?
> - Would it make a difference if this was the first time Jai had seen her son rushed to hospital with an asthma attack?
> - Would it make a difference if Pauli's bouts of depression were more unpredictable and/or more severe?
> - Would it make a difference if Meg's mother had died of breast cancer?

Resilience

 Another thing to consider is how resilient a person you are in the first place. The more resilient you are the better you cope with stress and difficult experiences.

 I am not sure what you mean by 'resilient'. I thought the word applied to materials.

 It does, but I am talking here about psychological resilience. Let's look at some definitions:

> The capacity to recover quickly from difficulties; toughness; the ability of a substance or object to spring back into shape. (*Oxford English Dictionary*)

The first two definitions refer to people and the last to materials and objects. But actually being able to spring back into shape is also a pretty good description of what we mean by resilience when talking about people.

 So if I can recover from something and 'spring back into shape', this shows I am pretty resilient – that I am tough under pressure.

 Exactly. It's not that bad things don't happen to resilient people; it's just that some people seem to be able to recover from difficulties or cope with stress more easily than others. They seem to be able to bounce back and deal with stress in their personal or work lives better. Resilient people seem to be able to balance the positive with the negative more effectively. There is plenty of research on resilience, especially with children, because the seeds of resilience are developed in early childhood. But the good news is that resilience can be learned and developed – it isn't simply a fixed personality trait. It also helps to have good support, which is what we will look at next.

PROFESSIONAL SUPPORT AND SERVICES

 I know that supervision is important for supporting your work as a counsellor. Is that what you mean by professional support here?

 Well, supervision is an important part of professional support and we have already looked at the role supervision can play in supporting counselling work. But although counsellors are ethically required to have clinical supervision, many people who use counselling skills in other roles might not have any supervision at all, or they might not have the kind of supervision that offers space for reflection and personal support.

EXAMPLE

Peggi is an experienced health visitor with a particular remit for working with troubled families. She frequently goes into people's homes and experiences very distressing situations. She does her best to provide support using counselling skills as well as offering advice and support as a health visitor. She has a heavy caseload. Peggi has weekly 'supervision' with her line manager in a small group but the sessions are focused on case management, that is, practical issues like balancing workload, getting advice from experienced colleagues, and ensuring that all the right steps have been taken and all actions recorded.

At the end of the day Peggi frequently arrives home exhausted and finds the distress of what she has witnessed still with her. Sometimes she finds herself in tears and desperate to talk to someone about her day.

- How might supervision help Peggi?
- How might supervision help her clients?
- What are the risks of lack of support to both Peggi and her clients?

 So if supervision is only one kind of support and some people might not get supervision at all, what do you mean by professional services and support?

 Well, it might help to list the different kinds of support we may need at different times (see Table 18.1). Personal therapy is an important one on the list. Working with other people's distress can trigger all kinds of difficult feelings in us – it is an occupational hazard of this kind of work. While this can sometimes be managed by self-nurture or support from family and friends, this may not be enough. This is the moment to consider therapy for yourself, even if it is not a requirement of the training course.

TABLE 18.1   Different kinds of support

Kind of support	Examples
Practical support	Child care, a day off, help with transport
Emotional support	Personal therapy
Problem-solving	Rational focus on sorting priorities, identifying solutions
Specialist support	IT skills, legal advice
Medical support	Physical/mental health and well-being
Practice support	Supervision, consultancy, coaching

 Well, that is a sobering thought. Of course you are quite right but I would not necessarily have thought of this straight away … which is interesting in itself.

 It is very important to know when professional help is needed and when it is enough to rely on friends, family or simply a group of people with whom you can have a laugh, go out with, or simply let your hair down with from time to time.

ACTIVITY

Create a diagram showing all your own sources of support, thinking about the different areas identified in Table 18.1 as well as other less formal sources of support. For example:

FIGURE 18.1   Sources of support

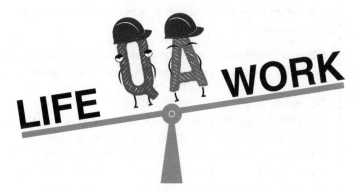

FIGURE 18.2   Work–life balance

 I have to admit that I kind of switch off when I hear the dreaded words 'work–life balance' because it seems to me impossible to achieve this happy state in the real world. Of course I would like to have more time for things I enjoy and less time juggling everything just to keep the show on the road. But this just does not seem possible.

 I expect you are not alone in feeling like that. It is true that some things are beyond our individual control but sometimes we can make changes. Taking the time to look at our own work–life balance can be very illuminating as often we are not fully aware of what is missing in our lives because we are so busy just trying to live! Although this doesn't mean that you can suddenly have extra holidays or copious amounts of money to indulge in a spa day, it can mean that you can make small changes which tip the scales slightly towards a better balance. One way of analysing your work–life balance is to use a template which is offered freely on the internet called the Wheel of Life and then you can decide for yourself.

ACTIVITY

Wheel of Life instructions

The eight sections in the Wheel of Life represent balance.

1.   Change, split or rename any category so that overall categories make sense to you.
2.   If the centre of the wheel is 0 and the outer edge is 10, draw a line across the segment showing how satisfied you are in each area of your life.
3.   The new edge of the circle following the lines you have drawn represents your 'Wheel of Life'.
4.   Reflect on how 'bumpy' your life is.

(Continued)

(Continued)

If possible, work with another person and take it in turns to ask each other the following questions. If you don't have a partner you can ask yourself:

(a) Are there any surprises for you?

(b) How do you feel about your life as you look at your Wheel?

(c) How do you currently spend time in these areas?

(d) How would you like to spend time in these areas?

(e) Which of these elements would you most like to change?

(f)   How could you make this happen?

(g) Can you make the changes on your own?

(h) What help and cooperation from others might you need?

(i)   What would make that a score of ten?

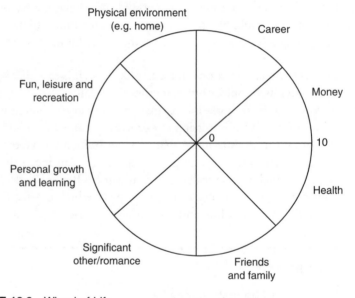

FIGURE 18.3   Wheel of Life

Asking for support

Asking for support means being able to ask for what you need.

Well, that sounds easy but sometimes I don't know what I need. I just know I need something.

You might want to revisit Maslow's *hierarchy of needs* in Chapter 4 which describes different kinds of needs that humans have. Or it can be more helpful to look out for warning signs that suggest you might need some help. Look at this list of warning signs and see if any are familiar:

- low energy
- lack of sense of humour
- world feels unsafe
- mild feeling of resentment towards certain clients/helpees
- feelings of being burdened
- lacking in empathy
- emotionally detached/distracted
- sick/ill
- not available to family/children
- short fuse
- isolation.

 Hang on a minute – that sounds just like me on a bad day!

 I am sure you are not alone! It can be hard to tune in and listen to yourself and what you need. In fact there is a view that 'care-givers' are particularly bad at identifying their own needs and asking for help, because they are more used to helping others than asking for help. This puts counsellors and helpers at high risk of not recognising and finding ways to meet their own needs.

The following activity might help you identify your needs in terms of self-care.

ACTIVITY: EXERCISE IN PAIRS

Work with a partner and try to fill in the gaps in the following statements:

When I am feeling .... I need ....

When I am feeling .... I need ....

Share with your partner:

five things that energise, uplift, restore you

five things that sap energy, lower your spirits.

Now write yourself a personal self-care prescription which is:

unique to yourself and your circumstances

unique to this moment.

So, what were you saying about counsellors/helpers finding it hard to ask for help? I'd like to explore that a bit more. It's a bit rich asking for help when your job is supposed to be helping others.

 You have named the dilemma exactly. Not only might you think you ought to manage without asking for help, but also there is sometimes a kind of shame about seeking support, especially as a counsellor/helper, because there is a fantasy that a person in this kind of role is 'sorted'. This adds a special kind of extra 'guilt' which goes something like: *How can I help my clients/helpees when I can't help myself? I feel a bit of a fraud.* Do you recognise that feeling?

 Oh yes. I think if only my clients/helpees knew what a mess my own life is in, they would be out of the door in a flash. It is an uncomfortable place to be and fills me with self-doubt.

 Hmm, it is interesting that you should say that, because there has been some relevant and surprising research on self-doubt. Have a think about this:

CRITICAL THINKING

A recent Norwegian study (Nissen-Lie et al., 2015) has found evidence that clients do better when their therapist has professional self-doubts. Furthermore, there is a link between therapists' self-doubt and self-compassion. The most successful client outcomes were seen for therapists who admitted to a combination of professional self-doubt and greater self-compassion.

Think critically about why it might be important for a therapist to question themselves and be compassionate towards themselves.

- What kind of support might help a counsellor or helper explore their self-doubt?
- What kind of support might help you become more self-compassionate?

EXAMPLE

Throughout Dana's life her achievements and successes were always 'topped' by her younger sister Tina. The girls were close and had a lot in common but the reality was that Tina did better in exams, was better at college and was better at music and sport. Tina was also petite and pretty. Dana always hated how she felt and denied it was anything other than healthy sibling rivalry.

One morning she woke from a vivid dream in which she recognised her feelings towards Tina as jealousy. Her inner self immediately tried to banish these unacceptable feelings but instead, for the first time, she allowed herself to stay with the difficult feelings and felt for the first time a deep and boundless compassion towards the hurt child within and all the pain this relationship had caused her. She wept for herself.

After this moment of profound compassion towards herself, Dana found that she was much more able to listen to her clients when they explored 'unacceptable' parts of self.

 I see what you mean and how important it is to really listen and accept myself … but that does mean shutting off the big loud voice in my head that tells me the opposite.

 You are so right.

 And even if I learn to turn off the internal voice and become self-aware and self-accepting, is that going to be enough?

 No. Insight and self-awareness are not an inoculation against burnout or compassion fatigue, which are the inevitable consequences of not taking care of yourself. But exercising the discipline of constantly paying attention to how you are and how you are doing makes a big difference.

You might find it helpful to place yourself on the continuum of wellness in Figure 18.4.

well …….. stressed …….. distressed …….. impaired

FIGURE 18.4 Continuum of wellness

 The continuum of wellness might be a tool you could use with clients/helpees as well. You will be surprised how often a person does not realise how stressed they are until they start to talk about it. Quite a lot of the tools and exercises in this chapter could be useful in helping and counselling work. But knowing all this stuff is not the same as putting it into practice, and part of knowing yourself is knowing what prevents you from taking care of yourself when you really need to.

REFLECTION

A client/colleague asks for an appointment when you are already very busy. You find yourself fitting them into your diary even though you haven't really got time and are putting extra pressure on yourself.

Consider what is driving this behaviour and score this out of 5, where 0 is 'not at all' and 5 is 'quite a lot':

Fear of letting the other person down	0 1 2 3 4 5
Inability to say 'no'	0 1 2 3 4 5
Secret pride that your help is being sought	0 1 2 3 4 5
Belief that you might be the best person to help	0 1 2 3 4 5
Superhuman fantasy – I can handle anything	0 1 2 3 4 5
Not considering your own needs	0 1 2 3 4 5

What have you learned about yourself and what might need to change?

Sometimes counsellors/helpers don't put their own needs first because the hassle of rearranging appointments with clients/helpees is more problematic than struggling through the sessions when feeling unwell. This is a slippery slope which must be avoided!

Sometimes it helps to have a ritual for leaving stresses behind. You will find your own way of doing this but here are a few ideas:

- Change your clothes after work.
- Light a candle at the end of the day.
- Cross a threshold as part of a conscious decision to change roles.
- Name your clients/helpees individually and mentally 'lay them down' before you leave the room.

The thing about all counselling and helping work is that you, the person, ARE the instrument or tool of your trade. You don't have anything else to fall back on and you must keep yourself in good shape. The analogy of a workman's tools reminds me of this quotation from the American Psychological Association (APA) website:

Universality of Vulnerability: Just as everyone in a construction site must wear a hardhat, everyone working in a mental health setting needs to attend to issues of occupational vulnerability and self-care. (APA, n.d.)

FIGURE 18.5   Protecting yourself

19
Critical Thinking

This chapter clarifies and explains the nature and purpose of critical thinking in relation to counselling and helping work.

 Throughout this book, you have been applying the skills of critical thinking to the ideas being presented.

 I don't agree. I have tried really hard not to be critical but instead to be open-minded and willing to learn.

 The type of critical thinking I'm referring to does not mean to be negatively judgemental, which is what you seem to be thinking.

 That is what critical means, isn't it? To find fault with something and point out what is wrong with someone.

 Yes and no.

 More 'yes and no's. Is there ever a straight answer?

 Yes and no! Seriously, in this chapter we need to look at two questions:

- What is critical thinking?
- Why is critical thinking important in counselling and helping work?

Let's begin with these.

WHAT IS CRITICAL THINKING?

Let's start with the word 'critical', which is immediately problematic because of all the negative associations it has for many people. There are more than five definitions of 'critical' on the Oxford Dictionaries website (including specific meanings relating to nuclear processes and mathematics), but the first one that comes up is:

> expressing adverse or disapproving comments or judgements.
> (*Oxford English Dictionary*)

 Yes that's exactly what I thought it meant, but you are saying it means something else. This is very confusing. I thought we worked towards being non-judgemental helpers and counsellors, not the other way round.

You are right about both things. The idea of being critical is often linked with the idea of being judgemental of others. As we have seen, being judgemental of others is unacceptable in counselling and helping work (see Chapter 3) and is the very opposite of what counsellors and helpers actively try to be, which is accepting, non-judgemental and empathic. However, the word 'critical' has other meanings too:

- involving the objective analysis and evaluation of an issue in order to form a judgement
- having a decisive or crucial importance in the success, failure or existence of something.

 I find those definitions very difficult to understand. Does it mean to step back and try to work out what's going on in order to understand something? I have no idea what the second definition means.

 It can be quite difficult to grasp as it is a new concept, but the two meanings above are the ones that are important in helping and counselling work. The definitions show that being 'critical' is not about 'criticising', with all the negative connotations of being critical of others, but about being able to weigh things up carefully before reaching a conclusion. It is also about recognising that this process is, in itself, crucially important.

 You talk about weighing things up carefully and that makes sense. So, does it mean taking all aspects of something into consideration before arriving at an opinion or judgement?

 Let's look at an example.

Joe was very bright at school. His school reports often made reference to his ability to critically appraise information and arrive at judgements very rapidly. At the same time, teachers noted that he needed to be more patient with those less able than him. Joe grew up believing that being able to exercise critical faculties was a fault which he needed to suppress. At work, he would often withhold his opinion when it was likely to involve criticising ideas presented by colleagues. This was both frustrating and unproductive. In therapy, his counsellor challenged him to explore this pattern. Joe realised that his capacity for critical thinking was not automatically a fault but a skill and an asset which was valuable to his employer. He came to see that while it was still important to be sensitive to others in the way his views were expressed, the skills themselves were critical to the success of the business and his own career progression. He ended up as a senior manager in the company.

 Therefore, critical thinking does involve making a judgement, but it does not mean being judgemental.

 tip

Try using the word 'discernment' instead of 'judgement'. 'Discernment' implies an ability to make a 'judgement' but it does not carry the negative meaning.

 So critical thinking means going through a particular kind of cognitive process.

 Yes, and it is one which requires open-mindedness, integrity, fairness, logic and reason, while taking into account the particular features, credibility and context of each situation. This is especially important where the answer or conclusion you are trying to arrive at is not clear-cut and where there may be no right answer.

THE JUDGEMENT OF KING SOLOMON

King Solomon was an Old Testament king in the Christian Bible renowned for his wisdom and discernment. People would come to him from all over the kingdom to seek his help in solving disputes. Two women who lived in the same house both had baby sons of the same age. During the night, one of the babies died in his sleep and both women claimed that the living child was theirs. The women came to King Solomon to seek his judgement. The first woman said that the second woman had accidently smothered her own son while sleeping and then exchanged the dead baby for her own. The other woman denied it. Solomon listened to their arguments and then called for a sword to be brought. He declared that the only fair solution was to cut the living child in two and give half to each mother. The lying mother did not try to stop him, but the true mother cried out that she would relinquish her claim and give up the child to her rival. Solomon declared this woman to be the true mother and gave her the baby. (1 Kings 3 v. 16–28)

So how can I learn to be a critical thinker?

SKILLS FOR CRITICAL THINKING

Edward Glaser (1985) proposed that the ability to think critically involves three elements:

1. An attitude of being disposed to consider in a thoughtful way the problems and subjects that come within the range of one's experiences.
2. Knowledge of the methods of logical enquiry and reasoning.
3. Some skill in applying those methods.

To be honest, that doesn't really help me. I understand what critical thinking is now but I'm still not sure how to do it, and also how it would help me in my studies and in my future work as a counsellor.

Let's break things down a little. The skills that you need to think critically are:

- **observation** – what did you see, understand or perceive?
- **awareness of gaps** – what did you not see or perhaps were unaware of?
- **interpretation** – what knowledge do you have which helps you make sense of what you saw?
- **self-challenge** – what aspects of yourself (thoughts, feelings, sensations, personal history, values) might be influencing the way you interpret what you observed?
- **analysis** – what are all the different elements/factors of the situation and how do they interrelate?
- **evaluation** – how are you weighing up all the different aspects and where does this leave your thinking?
- **conclusion/judgement** – what judgement have you reached after going through the process above?

I like a step-by-step approach. I could apply this to many different things to formulate an opinion and bring clarity. You are right that it would be hard to be judgemental in a negative way because I would be looking at all aspects of a situation and on balance nothing is ever all right or all wrong.

John Dewey (1910) believed that if individuals could develop the skills of critical thinking this would not only be useful to the individual but also to the wider community, and to the process of democracy as a whole. His view was that critical thinking is an essential part of learning, which has two stages:

1.   The learner builds their own internal picture of the ideas, principles and theories of what is being studied.
2.   The learner then applies these ideas, principles and theories as they become relevant.

This is why it is important to foster these skills, even at the beginning stage of learning.

Critical thinking skills are necessary when studying and preparing for any professional role, but they are particularly important in helping and counselling work. These are some of the reasons:

- Everything to do with human beings and human interactions is complex. Nothing in counselling or helping work is clear or straightforward because each client is unique, each counsellor or helper is unique and the relationship which they create is unique. Learning when and how to use the right skills is a complicated process and the motivation and context of the work are variable. In fact, there are so many variables at any given moment that it is a wonder that any consensus can be reached at all about how to work with clients!
- Critical thinking is thinking that questions assumptions. Challenging assumptions is particularly important for challenging ourselves and our own thinking and for challenging any assumptions we make about clients. There may be many reasons why you need to do this. For example, you might not have all the relevant information; you might not have the underpinning knowledge; you might not appreciate the significance of something you have observed; your thinking might be illogical or biased in ways you are not fully aware of; or your feelings might be affecting your judgement. Rather than allowing our blocks, prejudices and blind spots to affect our judgement, we need to have a heightened awareness of these to avoid making judgements which are distorted. This is of course an ideal!
- Training as a counsellor or helper involves both stages identified by Dewey (1910). First, the trainee takes in all the ideas, principles and theories from others and then, over time, develops a style and way of working which is a synthesis of all these but also unique and personal. For this reason, we need to be able to think critically about our own work.
- People who are drawn to counselling and helping work often have strong skills in working with feelings and emotions and have enhanced emotional awareness and emotional intelligence. These are skills which are important in the process of reflection and reflective practice. However, there are times when feelings can get in the way of reason and logic, so it is useful to be able to separate out the two and to have skills for focusing on the cognitive process.

How will I ever be able to do all that? Wouldn't I be too busy thinking about everything to actually listen to a client or helpee?

Like all the other skills, critical thinking is something that happens over time. There will come a time when it will be almost second nature and you will do it without actually having to think too hard. It's a little bit like driving a car: at first every move and turn requires conscious thought and action but after a while your arms and legs just know what to do; indicating, braking, steering … you become a competent driver and you will become competent at critical thinking.

EXAMPLE

Donna worked as a Samaritans volunteer at her local branch, supporting callers on the telephone. Part of Samaritans policy is that if a client arrives on the doorstep during the day and a volunteer is free, the client can talk to the volunteer face to face. A client, Lea, walked through the door. She had no shoes on, despite it being winter time and the weather cold and wet. Lea was low and her life was in chaos. Donna showed Lea into the client room and worked with her using her counselling skills. Throughout the session, she was distracted by the thought that she had a pair of flip-flops in her bag and was wondering whether she should offer them to Lea. When the session came to an end, she offered the sandals to Lea who accepted them gratefully.

- Did Donna do the right thing?
- Would you have given your flip-flops to Lea?
- Think critically about whether Donna did the right thing, taking into account the possible consequences of her actions for Donna, her centre and the Samaritans as an organisation.

Do you have a natural tendency to act on your feelings or your thoughts?

Much of the process of reflecting on and thinking about counselling and helping work involves exploring all the variables, spoken and unspoken processes and possible interventions. This is central to the process of supervision and to all reflective processes (see Chapter 7). Critical thinking is a core element of all these activities. It is also useful in order to understand the past, present and future: what has happened, what is happening and what might be important in the future.

A bit like learning from mistakes in some instances.

You previously asked how to apply and use the skills of critical thinking; the activity below will help with this.

ACTIVITY

Dom was working with his client Kye. He had only qualified as a counsellor recently and still found it a struggle to keep within the time boundaries and end sessions on time, especially when the client lost track of time and was deeply into their emotions. This was Kye's third session. She was quite distressed at the end. Dom was aware that they were coming to the end of the session but found himself unable to remind her that their time was nearly up and consequently overran the session by 10 minutes. The ending was messy and rushed and he was 15 minutes late for his next client.

- Make a judgement about Dom's course of action and consider what issues might be raised by his supervisor. Use critical thinking skills to go through a logical process of reaching a judgement. Be aware of your own reactions to what Dom did.

Additional information: Dom's family were not good at expressing emotions at home, and throughout his training course Dom had to work hard to stay with client feelings, especially feelings of sadness and distress, which he often avoided.

- Go through the process above again with this new information in mind. Does this change your judgement of Dom's course of action?

Additional information: Kye's history is that her mother left the family when the children were very young. She walked out one day, leaving Kye and her sister in the bath, aged two and three, but she took their baby brother with her. The girls never saw her again and were lucky to be found unharmed. Kye has struggled throughout her life with the feeling that she is never 'put first'. This issue is causing problems in her relationship with her current partner.

- Go through the process again with this new information in mind. Does this change your judgement of Dom's course of action?

Additional information: Kye returned for counselling the following week. She seemed stronger, brighter and more confident. Dom invited her to reflect on the ending of last week's session. Kye said that she did not realise until she left and looked at her watch that Dom had given her 10 minutes' extra time. She found this very moving as she knew he had other clients waiting. She said she experienced this as being 'put first' for the first time in her life. This had been a powerful and healing experience.

- Does this change your judgement of Dom's course of action?
- Does it make a difference whether Dom was, or was not, aware of the impact of what he did?

In counselling and helping work I'm worried that I might not have all the information or be fully aware of all the elements which have a bearing on a particular moment.

 The answers being sought are rarely clear-cut. This adds endless potential for creativity and transformation in the therapeutic process, but it also highlights the need for thinking critically.

20
Experiential Learning

This chapter focuses on the nature and benefits of experiential learning and how it can be used in counselling and helping roles.

 What does experiential learning mean? Is it to do with experimenting and if so what has that got to do with counselling?

 Experiential learning isn't only to do with counselling: it is relevant to all learning. It isn't really to do with experimenting. Let's begin by looking at a definition of the word.

EXPERIENTIAL

Experiential: based on or involving experience; experiential knowledge; experiential learning methods. (*Oxford English Dictionary*)

 So, is it a way of learning something? I do know that we all have different ways of learning.

LEARNING STYLES

Some of us learn better by looking at something, reading maybe. Some of us learn better by listening, to lectures for example. Is experiential learning just another learning style?

 It is a type of learning. Experiential learning simply means learning from your own experience. This is very different from formal learning or academic learning. All human beings learn from experience right from the start, and you can see this in the way that a baby tries to put every object into his mouth. The baby trusts his own senses and knows that his mouth will tell him if it is something nice or something nasty; something to hold on to or something to drop; something to swallow or something to spit out. Nobody has told the baby that a lemon is sour or that the nipple tastes good. The baby finds out for himself. This is experiential learning.

 So it means I would learn from actually doing. Could that apply to things like counselling skills practice?

 It could. Already we can see that academic learning or formal learning is very different. This is about learning from other people's collective knowledge, insight and experience. You could think of it as the collected wisdom not of just one individual, like an author or a teacher, but of thousands of individuals whose collective knowledge and wisdom have been handed down from generation to generation. This knowledge widens our understanding of our world and everything in it.

 OK: you are describing two types of learning – academic and experiential. Which is more important? I know which one I enjoy more. I find academic learning quite dry sometimes, but I really like learning from my own experience and that seems to be the one I remember longer. It's as if the experience itself stays with me.

 But both kinds of learning are necessary and important. There is a tendency to privilege academic knowledge over experiential knowledge once a certain level of academic study and maturity has been reached. In the world of counselling and helping work, this hierarchy of learning is not necessarily helpful because experiential learning is critical for developing attitudes and qualities that are sometimes referred to as 'soft' skills. The evidence shows that the attitudes and qualities of the individual practitioner play an important part in the outcome of the helping or counselling work.

 What does that actually mean?

 In terms of counselling, it means that you as a person are a very important part of the work. Earlier in the book we saw how important the relationship is between counsellor and client, and part of building this relationship includes personal qualities and traits that you simply couldn't learn from a book but only from your personal experience.

 If experiential learning involves a completely different set of skills and a different hierarchy of knowledge from academic learning, how do I know what parts of my experience and what parts of myself I should call upon to use?

 It may come as a surprise to you to find out that some aspects of yourself which have not previously been valued or prized in a learning situation are suddenly likely to be important assets in this kind of training. I am talking about the following kinds of gifts and qualities:

- intuition
- sensitivity to others
- reading body language
- common sense
- spontaneity
- being yourself
- being willing to try things out to see what happens
- not being afraid to look a fool
- thinking 'too much'.

EXAMPLE

Gareth's mother always told him that he was over-sensitive and over-emotional. 'The trouble with you is that you think too much', she would say. Then when his face crumpled in an effort not to cry, she would say, 'There you go again … see what I mean? … you are just over-sensitive'. Gareth was ashamed of these weaknesses and learned to toughen up. It was a key turning point in Gareth's own training as a counsellor when he realised that in the world of counselling and helping work the traits that he had come to despise in himself were strengths, not failings.

I see. They are almost like transferable skills, but these are transferable personal qualities and relational skills.

That is a very creative way of looking at it. It can be quite mind-blowing to reframe weaknesses as strengths. Use the suggestions in Table 20.1 to make your own list of all the things you have been criticised for or that you dislike about yourself and see if you can reframe them as strengths.

The idea of 'reframing' weaknesses as strengths is a useful tool to use when working with clients and helpees because often childhood messages about what we are 'good' at and what we are 'bad' at become firmly fixed in our minds at an early age. Furthermore, this often has more to do with where we fitted into the family order than any real truth about our strengths and weaknesses. So, shaking up these fixed messages can be a catalyst for change which is empowering for the

TABLE 20.1   Reframing weaknesses as strengths

Weakness	Strength
Thinking too much	Thinking deeply
Fussing about every little thing	Having an eye for detail
Being messy and disorganised	Being open to being flexible and creative
Being nosey about other people	Being interested in other people

client or helpee. Of course, it also means that the opposite is true – that strengths can also be reframed as weaknesses. This can be quite challenging too! You might want to have a go and repeat the previous exercise the other way round.

 Straight away I thought of an example. I was always told as a child to keep my feelings to myself and not talk to anyone about my feelings. I was told not to do this because people couldn't be trusted and would betray me. I think my mother had been very badly let down and she passed her beliefs on to me. I grew up telling everyone I was fine, regardless of how I felt. Since beginning my counselling training, I am slowly opening up and letting people know who I am and how I feel, and this has helped me so much. I feel accepted now. It's a relief.

 That's a good example. If we look back into our childhood, we can learn a lot about ourselves, our assets and other parts of ourselves that we may have outgrown or that could be self-defeating or unhelpful to our present life. The following activity is helpful for building self-awareness and moving past and letting go of things that are no longer helpful.

REFLECTION

- What were you told you were 'good' or 'bad' at when you were a child?
- If you had siblings, what were they 'good' or 'bad' at?
- Do these messages still affect your view of yourself today?
- Is it time to shake these ideas up?

 I feel quite relieved. I never did too well at school and was really worried that my lack of academic ability would stop me being a counsellor.

 As I said, both are important but the key point here is that training in counselling and helping work requires life skills and soft skills which are as important as academic ability, and if you were not 'good' at academic learning previously, you may find that you are good at learning experientially and good at this kind of work. Furthermore, if you were 'good' at academic learning previously, then you may find the experiential way of learning very challenging.

EXAMPLE

Gemma was the 'brainy' one in the family. She got a first-class degree in psychology at a good university. She then decided to train as a counsellor and was surprised to find out that she had to start at the bottom with a level 2 counselling skills qualification. She

(Continued)

(Continued)

felt irritated because she was not being given credit for her knowledge of psychological processes and human development and her understanding of the psychological theories which underpin counselling practice – all of which she had studied in some detail. She reluctantly enrolled on a level 2 counselling skills course where her sense of being 'way ahead' of the others was reinforced by her perception that others in the learning group had a much lower level of academic ability than she did.

Extract from Gemma's learning journal

Another frustrating day at college, looking at open and closed questions. Yawn! I hardly dare admit it but I got the gist of the difference straight away and started to feel quite frustrated by the slow pace. It is so different from uni, which seems like another life. At the end of half an hour, some people did not seem to have grasped that closed questions are not simply questions which elicit the answer 'yes' or 'no' but also questions which provide specific information which at times can be quite useful, like 'When did the problem first start?' In other words, not all closed questions are 'bad' and not all open questions are 'good', although obviously open questions do help people to open up and talk about their problems more effectively than closed ones.

We went on to practise the skills of using appropriate questions in a role play. I was the 'helper' and the feedback I got was that I had clearly got the hang of when to use which type of question. I also learned how open questions are important in making sure that the helper or counsellor stays with the helpee/client's agenda rather than leading the way. B said she wanted to give me written feedback next week as well as what she said today. She said she wanted more time to think about what she wants to say. This seemed a bit strange.

Written feedback sandwich from B (in the role of observer) given to Gemma the following week

I thought you did really well in demonstrating how different questions are useful for different reasons. When you said to X, 'Would you like to tell me more about the difficulties you are having at home?', the helpee suddenly opened up to say that she is having problems with her partner as well as problems with her daughter. This was useful because it opened up a new avenue of exploration and showed that the problem was not all about the daughter.

I am not sure how to say this but I did find your manner quite off-putting. I am sure you did not mean it but you came across as very scary … sort of unapproachable. I wonder if this is because you are very confident and 'together'. If I had been the helpee, I would not have found it easy to disclose weakness or failings. I wondered afterwards whether this is why you did not really go into any detail about her feelings or exactly what was troubling her. It all stayed rather on the surface. I did not have the courage to say this to your face in verbal feedback – sorry. You seem more at home with facts than feelings.

I think you are very quick on the uptake and understand things straight away, and watching you using the occasional closed question helped me to see that, for example, asking 'How old is your daughter?' was actually relevant and helpful.

Extract from Gemma's journal

Pretty shattering day at college. B gave me her written feedback on my role play last week and I was really shocked by it … actually not just shocked but, well … devastated. I had no idea that my manner makes it hard for some people to approach me – pretty hopeless if I want to be a counsellor. I did not realise that I was giving off a confident vibe. What's worse is that I now realise that I was making huge judgements about my fellow students – thinking that I knew stuff or was somehow better than them. But when it comes to it, knowing stuff is not the key to being able to be with people and enter into their world and their pain. In fact, I now see that B, who said much less than me and really focused in on the helpee, was much more effective at getting through to the underlying feelings. This is hard for me. I have always been 'good' at work and suddenly I feel like I am in territory that I don't understand and don't know how to 'work' at. I know this is important though and I feel, well, quite humbled.

 It is important to remember that people who come for help as clients or helpees come in varying states of vulnerability from every walk of life and have a wide range of experiences that no one person can ever understand or know about. The ability to build a relationship that enables trust and opening-up to occur is more important than being a grade-A student in academic work. Professional and academic skills are important, especially for understanding theory and process, but so are relational soft skills.

 It is encouraging to know that having a breadth of life experience and that coping and surviving my own troubles and difficulties are definitely assets in this kind of work.

REFLECTION

The more diverse your learning group is (including diverse in terms of academic experience and ability), the more opportunity you have as a trainee to learn from, and practise your skills with, a wide range of people.

One of the criticisms of 'talking therapies' is that they are more geared to, and therefore more helpful to, clients who are good at expressing themselves in words.

(Continued)

(Continued)

There has been a growing interest in types of therapy which use other forms of expression as an integral part of the therapy, such as art and drama therapy, body work therapy, music therapy and a whole range of creative approaches.

If you could not use words, what kind of therapy would appeal to you as a vehicle for self-exploration?

FEEDBACK AND EXPERIENTIAL LEARNING

All practitioner courses put emphasis on 'feedback' as a way of maximising experiential learning. The learning group provides a unique opportunity for others – with your explicit permission – to help you learn from your own experience. This includes both tutor and peer feedback.

I find feedback very difficult, both giving and receiving.

It can be very difficult but reflecting on your experience, especially on feedback from others, is a crucial way of challenging yourself and learning how to work more effectively. You may want to dip into Chapter 17 on journal writing as an element of reflective practice.

David A. Kolb (with Roger Fry in 1975) developed a model (set out in Figure 20.1) which describes the process of experiential learning (Kolb, 1984). This is often referred to as the 'Learning Cycle'.

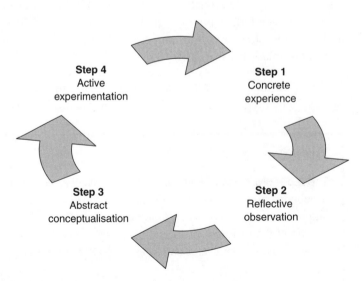

FIGURE 20.1 Kolb's Learning Cycle

As you can see, the model has four stages but it is important to realise that the cycle can begin at any one of the four points and would in fact be better described as a continuous circle rather than four stages.

 I can understand it better if I begin the cycle by doing something, skills practice for example. After skills practice I would get feedback from my peers and my tutor, and I would have to think about or reflect on what I thought was happening in the session and things I felt I did well, alongside things I wanted to improve on. Hopefully I could use all this information to make me a better helper or counsellor in my next skills practice session, and continuously develop and improve as the cycle continues.

That is a very good example of experiential learning in action and it easily fits into Kolb's Learning Cycle. As you rightly say, learning often begins after *doing* something or *experiencing* something (step 1) and then reflecting on the effect of this, either by oneself or by receiving feedback from others (step 2). After reflecting on the effects in the particular circumstances in which they took place, it may be possible to see whether any general understanding or learning can be gained which would be useful in a similar context (step 3). Finally, there are new opportunities to test what has been learned by experimenting with it in new situations or by changing something about the original experience (step 4). Eventually, the learner will be able to integrate new learning and thereby anticipate possible outcomes in a way which improves their overall practice. This is the theory anyway!

 I think we both said the same thing in different ways.

 You can never get enough of a good thing.

To summarise, the two important aspects of this process are: (1) the use of concrete 'here-and-now' experience to test ideas; and (2) the use of feedback as the catalyst for reflecting on practice and theory. This is quite different from a cognitive learning process.

EXAMPLE

John was a very good student on a counselling skills course. He was intelligent and hard-working. In his former life, he was a successful senior manager for a UK blue-chip company. John's decision to retrain as a counsellor and begin a counselling skills course was life-changing and heartfelt, but to his frustration he was not getting good feedback from peers on the course. One day, he again took on the role of helper during a skills practice session. The observer noted that he did a perfect

(Continued)

(Continued)

opening, explaining all the boundaries of the session and the limits of confidentiality. The observer said that he explored the helpee's issues well using open questions and showed his understanding of the helpee's problems by using reflecting and paraphrasing skills. At the end, he did an excellent summary covering both meaning and feeling. Once again, however, the helpee's feedback was disheartening. She said, 'You did everything right, John, but I just didn't feel that you cared about me or my problems – I didn't feel that you were really there for me or that you understood my feelings even though you reflected them accurately.' The tutor observed part of this session and promised to give him written feedback the following week.

John's journal reflected his frustration and annoyance: 'I really don't understand what I am doing wrong. Perhaps they just don't like me,' he mused. 'I know that I can come across as powerful and knowledgeable, and some people, especially women, find this intimidating – I am sure it does not help that I am so physically tall. I have always had this problem, even in the playground at school. In a way, you could call it a kind of prejudice against me. I think I need to challenge the group's attitude towards me. How can I be me if being me is not acceptable? I think this is clear prejudice against me.' *The following week, he received this feedback from his tutor:*

I have struggled to find the words to help you reflect on your helping session. I know you were frustrated and bewildered by the feedback from your helpee, even though you seemed to do everything right. You have a great aptitude for learning, you use all the skills perfectly and your body language is open and welcoming. The only way I can think to put it is that you seem to listen with your head and your brain rather than with your heart. Next time when you are sitting with your helpee imagine that your heart is opened up – like a flower – to the person. I think you will find that it makes a difference. You may also like to reflect on your own experience or lack of experience of being listened to by someone whose heart is open to you.

This feedback affected John deeply. His journal reflected first his bafflement and then his gradual realisation that he had never really been listened to with an open heart by his own parents. He then began to make connections with the emotional sterility of his marriage. He found this painful but enlightening, and something in him shifted.

At the next session, when John took the role of helper, he sounded different and seemed different even though his words were not very different. The positive feedback from the helpee confirmed this change. John's learning was not about knowledge or skills but about reflecting on his experience, listening to and assimilating the feedback, and reflecting on its meaning, which ultimately changed something inside him. This is experiential learning.

21
Research in Counselling and Helping Work

The aim of this chapter is to introduce the meaning and purpose of research, and understand the role of research in counselling and helping work.

 I don't see what research has to do with counselling. Isn't it what scientists do?

 Yes, it is something scientists do but it's relevant in many other areas, including counselling.

 Wouldn't it be unethical to research clients?

 Well, it depends what you mean by that ... but you are right that any research on clients gives rise to many ethical issues. Yet it would certainly be useful to research what would help clients.

Anyway, let's take a step back and think about what we need to understand about research. We will:

- look at what we mean by research
- look at why research is important in the field of counselling and helping work
- explore some of the challenges of research
- encourage you to identify yourself as a 'researcher'
- provide a basic framework for understanding research findings.

DEFINITION

 I would be interested to know what you think research means.

 Is it about finding out about things? SEARCH is in the word and RE. So I just look at the two parts of the word and come up with: research is to do with looking for things.

 Interesting; now let's look at the dictionary definition.

> Research: the systematic investigation into and study of materials and sources in order to establish facts and reach new conclusions. (*Oxford English Dictionary*)

 When did research start informing counselling? Is it a recent thing?

 Research in counselling is not new. Early research into the effectiveness of psychoanalysis was carried out in the 1930s and 1940s, and in the 1940s Carl Rogers engaged in research on the process of change in the development of the person-centred approach. However, it has been an uphill struggle to embed a consistent culture of research in the training and ongoing practice of counselling today. This may be because, although some counselling training takes place in institutions with a culture of research (i.e. the university sector), much of it takes place in private training organisations and Further Education colleges where the culture of research is not so well established.

 We've never talked about it on my course.

 It is probably something you will encounter as you continue with your studies.

 I don't know if I want to!

 I understand. Research can be difficult to access, both physically in terms of resources (books, articles, journals and online material) and linguistically, in that the language used by researchers can be off-putting and difficult to make sense of by those not engaged in research themselves.

 I agree. I am much more comfortable when things are written simply. When big words are used I feel inadequate and stupid.

 So it really is challenging for you and you aren't alone. Research generally can be seen as an activity carried out by 'experts' well versed in numbers, statistics, outcomes and overall effect.

tip

> The term *effect size* is a statistical measure which helps you understand how important something is.
>
> A large *effect size* means that the two things are strongly linked, e.g. 'People who received counselling improved more than those who did not'.
>
> A small *effect size* means that the two things are not strongly linked, e.g. 'People who received counselling fared no better than those who did not'.

This perception of research was reinforced by the fact that the preferred and most commonly adopted research methods in the recent past were quantitative rather than qualitative and fitted better with those therapies, notably CBT, which lend themselves most readily to the measurement of goals, outcomes and degrees of change.

Practitioners in the humanistic approaches reacted particularly negatively to the predominance of quantitative research methods, especially randomised controlled trials (RCTs), which seemed unsuited to capturing therapeutic change or client experience.

 From that it looks as if there are two different types of research.

 Yes, *quantitative* and *qualitative*. Basically, quantitative research is about measurement and qualitative research is about the meaning of experience.

 I don't understand; what does 'the meaning of experience' mean?

 Let's look at the types of research more closely.

- **Quantitative research**: This is to do with measuring and quantifying, which usually means numbers, graphs and statistics. The researcher is very much on the outside looking in and not part of the research. The intention is often focused on measuring outcomes and effectiveness.

> A popular quantitative research method is the randomised controlled trial (RCT). In an RCT, the people involved in the research project are randomly assigned to two groups:
>
> 1. The group taking part in whatever is being tested.
> 2. A 'control' group which is similar but not part of the experiment.
>
> *(Continued)*

(Continued)

This method of study is often used to compare the effectiveness of different interventions. A straightforward example might be a study to find out whether CBT is an effective therapy for treating clients with depression. The first group might receive six sessions of CBT therapy, while the other group would not receive any therapy at all. Client outcomes in both groups would be measured – using a numbered scale – before and after the therapy to evaluate if there was any improvement.

- **Qualitative research**: This is to do with understanding experience by describing, observing and explaining things which cannot be easily measured. The researcher is often involved in the research in some way and the focus is more likely to be on what factors contributed to change rather than on the final outcome.

In essence, quantitative research is about measurement and qualitative research is about the meaning of experience.

A popular qualitative method of research is case study research. In case study research, the details of a particular case or cases are looked at in terms of what can be learned by investigating the experience of an individual client or a small group of clients in several cases. There are systematic tools for analysing case studies but the data are usually descriptive rather than numerical. This method might be used to find out, for example, which particular interventions during counselling were most helpful to the client and why.

 This sounds a lot more complicated and less straightforward.

 The predominance and popularity of quantitative research methods have shifted in the last decade, and counselling and psychotherapy research now can be a mixture of both methods. Knowing a little about different types of research and having some familiarity with the most common research techniques are useful, even if you are not going to carry out research yourself, because they give you some tools for evaluating research done by others. But that's getting ahead of ourselves. Let's first look at why research is important in this field.

WHY IS RESEARCH IMPORTANT IN COUNSELLING?

 Research is important because it can provide evidence that certain things are happening or not happening. This word *evidence* is crucial because of the increasing demand across a wide range of sectors for evidence of what works for whom and why.

That makes sense. I use the work I do on my course as evidence to show that I have understood and can apply the things I have been learning.

 Exactly. Practitioners, policy makers and funding agencies all have a common interest in trying to find out what is most effective when it comes to providing services to clients. More importantly, perhaps, 'evidence-based practice' is now a common way for policy makers to determine how much money to spend on different types of counselling for different kinds of clients. This move towards looking at the evidence base for certain interventions started in the medical field with 'evidence-based medicine' and then spread more widely into the fields of nursing, social care, education and psychology, including counselling and helping work.

The American Psychological Association (APA) definition of evidence-based practice is: 'the integration of the best available research with clinical expertise in the context of patient characteristics, culture and preferences' (APA, 2006: 273).

So there are three elements to evidence-based practice: the evidence from research, the expertise of the practitioner and the particular characteristics of individual clients. A simple way of setting out this relationship is given in Figure 21.1.

 I see, so all these factors are taken into consideration to provide evidence of what is best for the client.

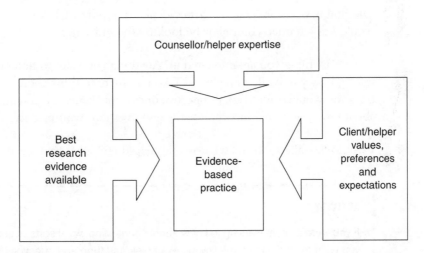

FIGURE 21.1   Evidence-based practice

EXAMPLE: NICE GUIDELINES ARE BASED ON EVIDENCE

You may have heard of the NICE guidelines which are used by health and care professionals to make choices about what kinds of treatment to offer patients. The National Institute for Health and Care Excellence (NICE) publishes recommendations, for example, for which 'talking therapies' should be offered for the treatment of common mental health problems such as anxiety and depression (NICE, 2011). Their general website information states clearly that their guidelines 'are based on the best available evidence' with the stated aim 'to improve the quality of healthcare'. Their guidance is:

- Designed to promote good health and prevent ill health
- Produced by the people affected by our work, including health and social care professionals, patients and the public
- **Based on the best evidence**
- Transparent in its development, consistent, reliable and based on a rigorous development process
- Good value for money, weighing up the cost and benefits of treatments
- Internationally recognised for its excellence. (www.nice.org.uk)

NICE has been criticised for recommending too narrow a range of talking therapies which are biased in favour of CBT approaches, with few other alternatives. The challenge from critics is that these approaches are more likely to fulfil the requirement to be evidence-based because there is MORE evidence for such approaches, not because the evidence itself is more convincing.

 OK, you have convinced me that evidence is important, but what sort of evidence would I as a trainee counsellor be looking for and why?

 Is there anything you are interested in? Anything you want to find out which would inform how you work with clients? Take a moment to think about the kinds of questions you would want to ask prospective or current clients. It is also important to think about how you would incorporate the responses into your practice.

 I would just like to know what would help them, what they need from me.

ACTIVITY

If you were a client wanting to know about counselling, what sorts of questions would you want to ask? Use the following examples and then add questions of your own:

- Does counselling work?
- How do I choose what kind of counsellor to see for my particular problem?
- How many sessions will I need?

If you were an NHS practice manager purchasing mental health services for patients in your area:

- Which type of counselling is most cost-effective?
- What is the optimum number of sessions for each client?
- Why do some clients drop out of counselling?

If you were a GP trying to decide whether to refer a patient for counselling:

- Is counselling as effective as or more effective than prescribing medication?
- Is it a good idea for patients to see a counsellor while on medication?
- Which kinds of clients benefit most from counselling?

If you were a potential trainee trying to choose a counselling course:

- Which theoretical approach is most effective?
- What kind of training is likely to lead to paid employment?
- What should I look for in a training course?

If you were a counsellor or helper:

- Am I better or worse than other therapists at what I do?
- Why did client A do better in therapy than client B?
- Why does X seem to happen when …?

 As you can see, all these questions could be the starting point for trying to design a research project. In each case, the motives may be different but a systematic search for answers is both necessary and possible with the right kind of research.

 What about past research? How can I use that? You said there has been research for decades, so it sounds like an ongoing process. It feels very important to keep up to date with what's happening in the field of counselling.

 I agree. So, let's take a moment to look at some of the answers which have already been provided by research. These findings have already had an impact on how counselling and helping work are viewed, on what practitioners do with their clients, on which therapies are supported, on the number of sessions offered and on where the funding is allocated, to give just a few examples.

Here are some facts we have learned from research. These examples are taken from Mick Cooper's book, *Essential Research Findings in Counselling and Psychotherapy: The Facts are Friendly* (2008). As you will see, the facts are indeed 'friendly' but there are also some surprises. Things we know about therapy:

- Therapy works.
- Most people improve.
- 60% improve to the extent that they no longer have a clinical diagnosis.
- More sessions lead to better outcomes in the early stages.
- 5–10% of people deteriorate as a result of therapy.
- Improvement in therapy mostly lasts, but it is not clear for how long.
- Talking therapies are as effective as taking medication and seem to have a lower relapse and drop-out rate.
- Therapy is relatively cost-effective. (Cooper, 2008: 34)

Wow, it's really good to know that counselling is as effective as medication but I am a bit concerned that some people seem to get worse. I wonder if that's because they might be getting in touch with very painful and traumatic memories that are just too overwhelming.

You could be right but I don't have the evidence to hand to confirm that! Let's move on to what we know about different counselling approaches. Things we know about different counselling approaches:

- Different counselling approaches are equally effective.
- Different clients may do better in different kinds of therapy. (Cooper, 2008: 59)

So it is not 'one size fits all'. I'd like to know more about that and what it is about a particular person that means certain approaches are more helpful than others.

That's a research project in its own right and one you may wish to undertake in the future. And now, what about the things we know about the client?

- Clients themselves play the biggest part in positive outcomes.
- Highly motivated clients do better in therapy. (Cooper, 2008: 78)

- Hope and encouragement are important for client outcomes.
- If client expectations are too high, then outcomes are less good. (Cooper, 2008: 65)

And … Things we know about the therapist:

- Therapist factors are not as important as once thought but the variation in outcomes for different therapists is considerable. (Cooper, 2008: 96)

That really challenges what I thought. I believed that the therapist was the most important person in the work and that really good therapists helped people more.

 Ah, but then we have to look at what you believe makes a good therapist. There are a lot of things to take into consideration.

 Wow, this research stuff could go on and on, couldn't it?

 It certainly could. There are also ... Things we know about the therapeutic relationship:

- The quality of the therapeutic relationship affects the outcomes.
- The therapist's level of empathy affects the outcomes. (Cooper, 2008: 125)

 We have already covered that – that the relationship between counsellor and client is very important and now there is actual evidence to back it up. Finally ... Things we know about outcomes:

- If the therapist gets feedback from clients on how things are going during the therapy process, this can dramatically improve outcomes. (Cooper, 2008: 155)

 This is very obvious. It reminds me of the counselling skills practice at college. The helper or counsellor gets feedback from the tutor and their peers about what they've done well and what they need to improve on, and they use this feedback to improve.

 As you can see, these findings are very important. For example, the last piece of evidence means that therapists are now more likely to use client feedback forms at the end of each counselling session rather than just at the beginning and end of the course of therapy. In this way, therapists can check what is going on for the client and, if necessary, adjust what they are doing in the sessions.

 So it's important for a counsellor to have regular reviews with a client to see if the client's needs and expectations are being met.

 Most therapists understand that research is necessary and important for training practitioners, for improving their own practice and for building professional recognition and credibility. It is also vital for raising the profile of the 'talking therapies' as an effective (and cost-effective) intervention which attracts funding and resources from policy makers. Some counsellors are still ambivalent about research but perhaps the other way of looking at it is that not doing research is hugely risky to the profession, and that the right kind of research can significantly improve our understanding of the process of therapy and the therapeutic outcomes for clients and helpees.

Until now I hadn't understood why research was important and was a bit scared of it, to be honest. It does make more sense now and also feels less intimidating.

BACP, the leading professional body for counsellors, has worked hard to promote research by establishing a research foundation, offering seedcorn funding for research projects, offering awards and bursaries for research and, most importantly, publishing a well-respected research journal which is widely read.

It actually sounds really good.

But there are some challenges.

CHALLENGES OF RESEARCH

The challenges of research in this field are considerable and it is important to spend a moment thinking about why this is the case. One of the main reasons is that human beings are very complex, with each person being unique and every therapeutic relationship being different; the range of possible interventions also keeps growing; each therapist is different and works differently; clients themselves are all different and have different characteristics and expectations; and researchers come with their own bias and perspective.

That must make it very hard for researchers to be objective, especially if they begin with an opinion or want to use research to prove a point.

Yes, and there are, as I said, a huge number of variables to take into consideration. Figure 21.2 gives a very simple representation of all the different factors that impact on the counselling experience.

In addition, most counselling and helping work takes place between the client (or more than one client in the case of couple or family therapy) and the therapist behind closed doors or in complete privacy. This means that it is not easily open to objective scrutiny by others. It also means that there are complicated ethical problems of confidentiality and client consent in any research project. Table 21.1 lists some of the variables likely to impact on the counselling experience and therefore counselling research.

It must be very hard to get reliable information because in actual fact only two people are in the room, the counsellor and the client, and how they view what is happening could be very different.

It also means there are complicated ethical problems of confidentiality and client consent in any research project.

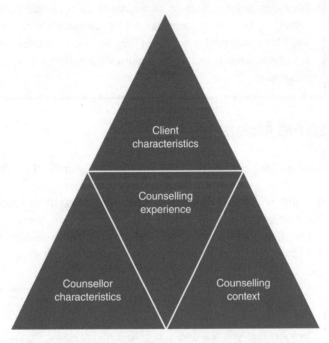

FIGURE 21.2   Factors that contribute to the counselling experience

TABLE 21.1   Counselling variables

Client characteristics	Counsellor characteristics	Counselling context
expectations	training	agency
problem(s)	qualities	private
personal history	personal history	NHS
culture, values & beliefs	culture, values & beliefs	face-to-face
class	class	telephone
gender	gender	Skype
sexuality	sexuality	email
age	age	time-limited
preferences	race	open-ended
race	patterns	length of session
patterns	personality	individual, couple or group
personality	income	specialist or general
income	supervision	
other support		

> Research projects have to be approved by an ethics committee before they are signed off. The ethics committee will be particularly interested in how client consent was obtained, what impact this is likely to have on the research itself and what steps have been taken to protect the client's identity, both in the research and in any future publication.

SELF AS RESEARCHER

Let's say I would like to go and do some research. How do you suggest I start?

It is important not to be intimidated by research and not to see it as something done by others or only by academics in research institutions. All of us have some of the skills needed to engage with research and probably use these skills in every-day life, more often than we realise. Let's start with a simple research task.

ACTIVITY

Imagine that you are about to go out and spend a significant sum of money on a new product, such as a car, a fridge-freezer, a laptop, a mobile phone or a child's buggy. You would need to go through a number of steps to reach a decision about what to buy. It might help to answer the following questions:

- Why would you want to research different products?
- What would you be looking for?
- How would you go about researching the pros and cons of each product?
- How would the research help you make a decision?

Do you recognise that this is the kind of research that you do every day?

You are right; I would never have thought of that as research before now. However, I can see that the principles involved in this kind of research activity are equally applicable to the field of counselling.

Furthermore, questions and issues that arise in your own practice often provide the impetus for finding out about something and then making changes based on any discoveries that you make.

EXAMPLE

Lou started work as a trainee counsellor in a GP surgery. The surgery information sheet informed clients that they could have 'up to six sessions' of counselling and that missed sessions would be made up wherever possible. Lou would normally arrange the next session week by week. Like most counsellors, there were a couple of sessions a week when clients would cancel at short notice or not turn up, which were recorded in the practice records as 'Did Not Arrive' (DNA). This was not helped by the practice manager making snide comments like, 'Another DNA then? Oh dear. That won't do our figures any good.'

Lou would sit in her empty counselling room feeling de-skilled. She also felt guilty because there was a long waiting list of clients waiting to be seen for the first time. The situation was made worse because when clients re-booked the missed sessions, they used up slots that could have been allocated to new clients. Lou also felt that the work with her clients was sometimes fragmented and interrupted by the missed sessions.

When Lou saw Garry for counselling, he asked if they could book all six sessions at the outset as he worked shifts on an oil rig and needed to plan his counselling sessions around his timetable. Garry attended all six sessions and the work was dynamic and helpful. This also happened when she saw Sandra, a nurse who worked an irregular shift pattern. Lou reflected on this and wondered whether the actual method of booking might be having an effect on how clients approached their commitment to counselling. She decided to experiment by changing her approach with all her clients. She made two changes:

1. She changed the information sheet to say, 'You will be offered up to six sessions. It may not be possible to make up any missed sessions as the time may have been allocated to other clients.'
2. She routinely booked in all remaining sessions with each client at the end of the first session.

To Lou's amazement, she found that the number of cancelled and missed sessions more than halved – much to the practice manager's delight.

This simple change had a significant impact on the waiting list, her confidence and the progress of therapy.

 Now here are some questions you can ask yourself.

CRITICAL THINKING

Would you class this as a piece of research? Ask yourself:

- Was it systematic?
- Did it establish facts?
- Did it lead to new conclusions?

Researchers would argue that in order for a piece of research to be accepted in the academic world, it must also be 'communicated to interested others' (McLeod, 2013: 2).

- Was this research communicated to interested others?

 I'm not sure that this is proper research.

 In strict terms, this cannot be defined as a piece of research but it does show how research questions present themselves and how every practitioner is in a position to engage in researching their own practice. There are specific skills which you need to learn to take this kind of personal enquiry to the level of formal research, but the idea is that it is clearly not a completely unfamiliar activity!

 You still haven't answered the question I asked before about how I can make sense of and use research findings to be a better counsellor.

MAKING SENSE OF RESEARCH FINDINGS

At this stage of your training, you are probably not going to engage in formal research yourself. However, it is still important to start being able to make sense of the research that has been carried out by others and to be able to make use of their research findings. This means knowing something about how to read and what to look for in a research article. It also means getting into the habit of taking account of research findings and seeing how these relate to practice. Here are a few useful questions which you can use as tools for making sense of the evidence presented in a research article.

ACTIVITY

Choose a research article that interests you from, for example, the BACP *Counselling and Psychotherapy Research Journal* and consider:

- What was the aim of the research?
- Did the research focus on a particular client group?
- Was the research located within a particular theoretical orientation?
- How was the research undertaken?
- Were the methods used quantitative or qualitative?
- What were the findings of the research?
- What are the implications of the findings for the counsellor?
- What are the implications of the findings for the client?
- Do these research findings have any wider implications, e.g. for funding, government policy, agency policy, and so on?

Then consider:

- Why did you choose this article?
- How will you use your learning from this exercise in your own helping or counselling work?

This is just a very brief and simplified introduction to the process of research and its importance for counselling. There is a danger in presenting such a complex topic in a simple way that it gives a misleading idea of what is involved in research. Don't worry – you will have the opportunity to find out more and perhaps engage in your own mini-research project later on in your training.

References

Allen, J. (2013) *As a Man Thinketh* (new edition). Online: Rise of Douai Publishing (original work published 1903).

American Psychiatric Association (APA) (2006) 'Evidence-based practice in psychology', *American Psychologist*, 61 (4): 271–85.

American Psychiatric Association (APA) (2013) *DSM-5*. Washington, DC: American Psychiatric Association.

American Psychiatric Association (APA) (n.d.) Occupational Vulnerability for Psychologists. Available at www.apapracticecentral.org/ce/self-care/vulnerability.aspx (accessed 07.02.17).

Berne, E. (1961) *Transactional Analysis in Psychotherapy*. New York: Grove Press.

Bond, T. (2002) 'The law of confidentiality: a solution or part of the problem?', in P. Jenkins (ed.), *Legal Issues In Counselling and Psychotherapy*. London: Sage.

Bond, T. (2015) *Standards and Ethics for Counselling in Action*, 4th edition. London: Sage.

British Association for Counselling and Psychotherapy (BACP) (2016) *Ethical Framework for the Counselling Professions*, 2nd edition. Lutterworth: BACP.

British Association for Counselling and Psychotherapy (BACP) (n.d.a) What is Counselling? Available at www.bacp.co.uk/crs/Training/whatiscounselling.php (accessed August 2014).

British Association for Counselling and Psychotherapy (BACP) (n.d.b) Member Briefings. Available at www.bacp.co.uk/policy/Policy%20Publications/member_briefings.php (accessed 07.02.17).

British Association of Counselling and Psychotherapy (BACP) (n.d.c) FAQ's Ethical – BACP Customer Services. Available at: www.bacp.co.uk/crs/Ethics%20in%20Practice/ethicsfaq.php (accessed 15.08.16).

Brookner, A. (1983) *Look at Me*. London: Penguin.

Cambridge English Dictionary (2016) [online] Cambridge University Press, http://dictionary.cambridge.org (accessed December 2016).

Clarkson, P. (2003) *The Therapeutic Relationship*, 2nd edition. London: Whurr.

Clarkson, P. (2013) *Gestalt Counselling in Action*. London: Sage.

Cooper, M. (2008) *Essential Research Findings in Counselling and Psychotherapy: The Facts are Friendly*. London: Sage.

Dewey, J. (1910) *How We Think*. Lexington, MA: D.C. Heath & Co.

Elliot, R., Watson, J.C., Goldman, R.N. and Greenberg, L.S. (2004) *Learning Emotion-Focused Therapy: A Process-Experiential Approach to Change*. Washington, DC: American Psychological Society Press.

Gendlin, E.T. (2003) *Focusing*, revised edition. London: Rider.

Gibbs, G. (1988) *Learning by Doing: A Guide to Teaching and Learning Methods*. Oxford: Further Education Unit, Oxford Polytechnic.

Glaser, E. (1985) 'Critical thinking: educating for responsible citizenship in a democracy', *National Forum: Phi Kappa Phi Journal*, 65 (1): 24–7.

Gray, T. (1771) 'Ode on a Distant Prospect of Eton College', in *Poems by Thomas Gray*. Dublin: Thomas Ewing.

Harris, R. (2009) *Act Made Simple: An Easy-to-Read Primer on Acceptance and Commitment Therapy*. Oakland, CA: New Harbinger.

Harris, T.A. (1967) *I'm OK – You're OK*. New York: Harper Collins.

Hawkins, P. and Shohet, R. (2012) *Supervision in the Helping Professions*, 4th edition. Maidenhead: Open University Press.

Hayes, S.C., Strosahl, K.D. and Wilson, K.G. (2011) *Acceptance and Commitment Therapy: The Process and Practice of Mindful Change*, 2nd edition. New York: Guilford Press.

Heard, H.L. and Swales, M.A. (2015) *Changing Behaviour in DBT: Problem Solving in Action*. New York: Guilford Press.

Hinshelwood, R.D., Robinson, S. and Zarate, O. (2011) *Introducing Melanie Klein: A Graphic Guide*. Cambridge: Icon Books.

Holmes, J. (2014) *John Bowlby and Attachment Theory* (Makers of Modern Psychotherapy). Hove: Routledge.

Inskipp, F. and Proctor, B. (1993) *The Art, Craft and Tasks of Counselling Supervision, Part 1: Making the Most of Supervision*. Twickenham: Cascade Publications.

Inskipp, F. and Proctor, B. (1995) *The Art, Craft and Tasks of Counselling Supervision, Part 2: Becoming a Supervisor*. Twickenham: Cascade Publications.

Jenkins (ed.), *Legal Issues in Counselling and Psychotherapy*. London: Sage. pp. 123–43.

Jung, C. (1973) *Psychological Reflections: A New Anthology of His Writings* (ed. J. Jacobi). Princeton, NJ: Princeton University Press.

Kagan, N. (1975) *Interpersonal Process Recall: A Method of Influencing Human Interaction*. New York: Wiley.

Karpman, S. (1968) 'Fairy tales and script drama analysis', *Transactional Analysis Bulletin*, 7 (26): 39–43.

Kolb, D. (1984) *Experiential Learning: Experience as the Source of Learning and Development*. Englewood Cliffs, NJ: Prentice-Hall.

Lago, C. (2006) *Race, Culture and Counselling: The Ongoing Challenge*. Maidenhead: Open University Press.

Linehan, M.M. (2014) *DBT Skills Training Manual*, 2nd edition. New York: Guilford Press.

Luft, J. and Ingham, H. (1955) *The Johari Window: A Graphic Model for Interpersonal Relations*. Los Angeles, CA: University of California Western Training Lab.

Lundin, R.W. (2015) *Alfred Adler's Basic Concepts and Implications*. New York: Routledge.

Maslow, A. (1954) *Motivation and Personality*. New York: Harper & Bros.

McLeod, J. (2013) *An Introduction to Research in Counselling & Psychotherapy*. London: Sage.

McLeod, J. and McLeod, J. (2011) *Counselling Skills: A Practical Guide for Counsellors and Helping Professionals*, 2nd edition. Maidenhead: Open University Press (Kindle edition).

Mearns, D. (1997) *Person-centred Counselling Training*. London: Sage.

National Institute for Health and Care Excellence (NICE) (2011) Common mental health problems: identification and pathways to care. Clinical guideline [CG123]. Available at http://guidance.nice.org.uk/CG123 (accessed 07.02.17).

NHS (n.d.) Counselling. Available at: www.nhs.uk/conditions/counselling/Pages/Introduction.aspx (accessed 07.02.17).

Nissen-Lie, H., Rønnestad, M., Høglend, P., Havik, O., Solbakken, O., Stiles, T. et al. (2015) 'Love yourself as a person, doubt yourself as a therapist?' [online] *Clinical Psychology & Psychotherapy*, doi: 10.1002/c00.1977.

Norcross, J.C. (ed.) (2011) *Psychotherapy Relationships that Work: Evidence-Based Responsiveness.* New York: Oxford University Press.

Oxford English Dictionary (2016) [online] Oxford University Press, www.oxforddictionaries.com/definition/english/ (accessed February 2016).

Perls, F.S. (1994) *Gestalt Therapy: Excitement and Growth in the Human Personality*. London: Souvenir Press.

Purton, C. (2008) *The Focusing-Orientated Counselling Primer*. Ross-on-Wye: PCCS Books.

Rogers, C. (1942) *Counseling and Psychotherapy: Newer Concepts in Practice*. Boston, MA: Houghton Mifflin.

Rogers, C. (1951) *Client-Centered Therapy: Its Current Practice, Implications, and Theory*. Boston, MA: Houghton Mifflin.

Rogers, C. (1961) *On Becoming a Person: A Therapist's View of Psychotherapy*. Boston, MA: Houghton Mifflin. Also published in 1965 with a new introduction by Peter Kramer.

Rogers, C. (1964) 'Toward a science of the person', in T. Wann (ed.), *Behaviourism and Phenomenology*. Chicago, IL: University of Chicago Press. pp. 109–30.

Rogers, C. (1990) 'The characteristics of a helping relationship', in H. Kirschenbaum and V. Henderson (eds), *The Carl Rogers Reader*. London: Constable. pp. 108–26.

Rogers, C. (2004) *On Becoming a Person* (new edition). London: Constable and Robinson (original work published 1961).

Ryle, A. (1997) *Cognitive Analytic Therapy and Borderline Personality Disorder: The Model and the Method*. Chichester: John Wiley & Sons.

Ryle, A. and Kerr, I.B. (2002) *Introducing Cognitive Analytic Therapy*. Chichester: Wiley-Blackwell.

Stevens, A. (2001) *Jung: A Very Short Introduction*. Oxford: Oxford University Press.

Storr, A. (1986) *Jung*. London: Fontana Press.

van Deurzen, E. (2012) *Existential Counselling & Psychotherapy in Practice*. London: Sage.

Yalom, I. (1989/2012) *Love's Executioner and Other Tales of Psychotherapy*. New York: Basic Books.

WEBSITES

BACP – www.bacp.co.uk

CORE – www.coreims.co.uk

Jane Elliott – www.janeelliott.com

NICE – www.nice.org.uk

CPCAB – www.cpcab.co.uk

NHS – www.nhs.uk

APA – www.apa.org

Index

Figures and Tables are shown by page numbers in bold print.